COST, UNCERTAINTY, AND WELFARE: FRANK KNIGHT'S THEORY OF IMPERFECT COMPETITION

For Liza

Cost, Uncertainty, and Welfare: Frank Knight's Theory of Imperfect Competition

STEPHEN JOHN NASH

Ashgate

Aldershot • Brookfield USA • Singapore • Sydney

Published by
Ashgate Publishing Ltd
Gower House
Croft Road
Aldershot
Hants GU11 3HR
England

Ashgate Publishing Company
Old Post Road
Brookfield
Vermont 05036
USA

British Library Cataloguing in Publication Data
Nash, Stephen John
Cost, uncertainty, and welfare : Frank Knight's theory of imperfect competition
1. Knight, Frank Hyneman - Contributions in welfare economies 2. Welfare economies 3. Competition, Imperfect
I. Title
330.1'556

Library of Congress Catalog Card Number: 98-71967

ISBN 1 84014 585 4

Printed and bound by Athenaeum Press, Ltd.,
Gateshead, Tyne & Wear.

Contents

List of Figures vi
Preface vii
Acknowledgements viii

1 Introduction 1
2 The Knightian Pyramid 8
3 Intellectual Influences 49
4 Comparison of Knight with Chamberlin and Robinson 93
5 Some Policy Implications 126
6 Conclusion 159

Bibliography 166
Index 200

List of Figures

2.1	Knight's Taxonomy of Assumptions Underlying the Standard Notion of Economic Efficiency	23
2.2	The Knightian Pyramid: Knight's Conceptualisation of the 'Social Welfare Function'	32
2.3	Ranking of Economic Policy Mixes within the Conceptual Framework of the Knightian Pyramid	47
4.1	Chamberlin's Long-run Equilibrium Solution	105
5.1	Cost Variations across the Imperfectly Competitive Industry	139
5.2	Normal and Abnormal Profit in Knight's Analysis of Imperfect Competition	144
5.3	The Trade-off between Equity and Efficiency	149

Preface

This work comprises an effort to enrich our understanding of Knight by analysing his work as a whole. While Knight's vision of economics is not always easy to discern, the effort involved in understanding this view is worthwhile. Not only can we come to understand the things which interested Knight, but we are also drawn to consider the broader aspects of the economic landscape which he surveys.

In contrast to the wide open plains of his homeland, Knight sees a rugged and inaccessible economic landscape. Throughout this economic terrain, uncertainty forces Knight to expand the orthodox conception of welfare economics because a lack of perfect knowledge effectively entraps individuals within separate sociological environments; access to both market knowledge and economic opportunity varies widely between each unique environment. In turn, such diverse circumstances shape the range of choice which is open to the individual so that all individuals do not participate in the benefits which economic progress may deliver (Knight 1921a, 233-63; Knight 1943a, 115).

Indeed, Knight's account of how uncertainty segregates individuals shows us that economic freedom is highly diverse. Uncertainty differentiates individuals as well as the economic outcomes which they strive to create. As a result, Knight shows that the orthodox goal of economic efficiency is incapable of incorporating the disparate freedoms and powers of individuals as they exist under conditions of uncertainty. Knight asks economists to supplement the search for allocative efficiency with an examination of both economic freedom and power if they wish to understand why poverty so consistently perpetuates itself (Viner 1958, 134). I hope that both this and the other Knightian problems discussed herein are topics which still concern most economic theorists, because if they do not then we cannot hope to perpetuate the free-market system of exchange.

Acknowledgements

Throughout this project I have been fortunate to receive assistance from many friends and colleagues. I wish to thank my wife Liza Rybak, for her support and encouragement as well as her editorial assistance with this work. In addition, I would like to express my gratitude to Dr Richard Staveley whose inspirational scholarship prompted me to begin this work. Thanks also to the following scholars at the University of Cambridge from whom I received encouragement: Dr Geoff Hodgson, Dr Tony Lawson, Dr Jochen Runde, and Dr Geoff Harcourt. Moreover, I would like to thank Heidi Rybak, whose comments were both pertinent and beneficial. Finally, I thank the editors and publishers of the following works for permission to reproduce here revised versions of material that earlier appeared in their pages.

American Economic Review: Dorfman. J, 1955, The Role of The German Historical School in American Economic Thought, pp. 17-28; Clark, J.M., 1940, 'Toward A Concept of Workable Competition', p. 2; Knight, F.H, 1936, 'Some Issues in The Economics of Stationery States', pp. 393-411; Knight, F.H., 1951, 'The Role of Principles in Economics and Politics'; pp. 1-29; Patinkin, D. 1973, 'Frank Knight as Teacher', pp. 787-807. Economic Inquiry:Barzel, Y., 1986, 'Knight's Moral Hazard Theory of Organisation', pp. 117-20.Blackwell Publishers, Young, A.A., 1928, 'Increasing Returns and Economic Progress', Economic Journal, vol. 38. Harcourt Brace and Company: Taine, H., 1976, *The Ancient Regime*. Harvard University Press: Chamberlin, E.H., 1933, *The Theory of Monopolistic Competition*. John Wiley and Sons, Inc: Bain, J.S., 1967, 'Chamberlin's Impact On Micro-economic Theory', in R.E. Kuenne (ed), *Monopolistic Competition Theory: Studies in Impact*. F. B. Knight: F.H. Knight, 1935, *The Ethics of Competition and Other Essays*. The University of Chicago Press: Knight, F.H., 1921, *Risk, Uncertainty, and Profit;* Knight, F.H. 'Bertrand Russel on Power', *Ethics,* pp. 360-66; Clark, J.M., 1925, *Social Control of Business*; Pangle, T.L., 1973, *Montesquieu's Philosophy of Liberalism: A Commentary on The Spirit of the Laws,* p. 17; Stigler, G.J. (ed), 1957, 'Perfect Competition, Historically Contemplated', in *Essays in History of Economics*; Stone, J, and Mennell, S., 1982, *On Democracy, Revolution, and Society;* Strauss, L., 1952 *Persecution and the Art of Writing*; Schumpeter, J.A., 1934, 'Robinson's Economics of Imperfect Competition', *Journal of Political Economy*; Patinkin, D., 1973, 'Frank Knight as Teacher', *Journal of Political Economy*. Macmillan Press: Stigler, G.J., 1987, *The New Palgrave: A Dictionary of Economics*. Penguin USA: Dorfman, J. 1949, *The Economic Mind in the American Civilisation,* Vol 3-5.Yale University Press: Fisher, I., 1906, *The Nature of Capital and Income*. W.W. Norton and Co: Mansfield, E. 1974, *Microeconomics: Theory and Applications*.

1 Introduction

Economists recognise the theoretical significance of the risk-uncertainty distinction, which Knight delivers in his seminal work *Risk, Uncertainty, and Profit* (1921a). While this distinction is important, we argue that it cannot be properly understood unless we grasp Knight's major contribution to economic theory: the establishment of an alternative theory of welfare economics (Myint 1948, 10). This contribution remains obscure because a broad range of commentators classify it as 'social philosophy', rather than economic theory. For example, non-economists, such as Allan Bloom (1990), support that classification. As Bloom (1990) says, "Philosophy came first, I think, for Frank Knight" (Bloom 1990, 198). Similarly, economists such as Breit and Ransom (1982) portray Knight as a social philosopher, resembling David Hume, rather than as an economic theorist (Breit and Ransom 1982, 197-9). We disagree. In contrast, we argue that the methodology which is used to evaluate Knight, rather than the content of Knight's work, leads to such a conclusion. This methodology has three basic assumptions. First, it assumes that a valid distinction can be drawn between Knight's contribution to economic theory and his contribution to 'social philosophy'. Second, it assumes that Knight's risk-uncertainty distinction is his only major contribution to economic theory. Third, it assumes that the overwhelming majority of Knight's other published work is 'social philosophy', being largely irrelevant to economic theory. We disagree with all three assumptions.

In addressing the first assumption, we argue that the dissection of Knight's work into economic theory and 'social philosophy' is difficult, if not impossible. Indeed, the precise nature of the distinction still represents a source of discordance between eminent economists. For example, Buchanan (1968) argues that Knight's collection of essays, *The Ethics of Competition* (EOC) (1921-1935) is relevant to economic theory (Buchanan 1968, 426). In contrast, Stigler (1987) argues that the EOC is not of particular relevance to economic theory (Stigler 1987, 58). Whereas one eminent economist includes the EOC as being relevant to economic theory, another excludes it as irrelevant. Such disagreement highlights the difficulty of attaining broad agreement on which of Knight's works pertain to economic theory, and which pertain to 'social philosophy'; we argue that a more comprehensive form of assessment is required. Other economists indicate that Knight's work requires such an assessment. For example, Myint (1948) observes that Knight is responsible for, "... a broader welfare economics, ..." (Myint 1948, 10). Myint (1948) argues that this broader welfare economics is not based on a narrow examination of uncertainty. Rather, Knight concentrates on the axiomatic premises of orthodox economic theory, with "... a more self-conscious examination of the methodological difficulties ..." which pertain to these premises (Myint 1948, 10). We concur; it is only by addressing such methodological difficulties, that we can begin to clarify Knight's argument for a broader type of welfare economics.

Recently, some evidence of a more wide-ranging assessment of Knight is emerging in the literature, which supports our questioning of the existing methodology. For example, Le Roy and Singell (1987) argue that previous economists interpret Knight's risk-uncertainty distinction much too narrowly, resulting in a misunderstanding of the distinction (Le Roy and Singell 1987, 394). We agree. By broadening the scope of our analysis we effectively reconstruct the context in which Knight draws the distinction between risk and uncertainty. Similarly, Raines and Jung (1988) extend the scope of their analysis. These authors draw on some of Knight's 'philosophical' writings as a means of grasping his economic theory of monopoly. However, the authors still insist on the separation of Knight's philosophical discourse from his economic argument; they stop short of abandoning the existing methodology which is used to evaluate Knight (Raines and Jung 1988, 139-43). In contrast, we extend this more encompassing approach to Knight by abandoning the existing methodology.

In our examination of the second assumption, we argue that Knight's conception of the social welfare function, which we define as, "... an aggregate measure of national, or social, well being", constitutes a major contribution to economic theory (Mansfield, 1979, 450). Moreover, we cannot properly understand Knight's view on the regulation of imperfect competition unless we see his 'philosophic' discourse as the narration of his concept of the 'social welfare function'.[1] Knight's supposed 'philosophical' discourse includes the definition of economic freedom, economic power and economic efficiency. Each of these comprise a component part of Knight's 'social welfare function';

economic efficiency does not subordinate all other considerations. Orthodox theory, however, considers the achievement of economic efficiency as the most important means of delivering economic welfare.

In our analysis of the third assumption, we argue that it is necessary to accept Knight's 'philosophical discourse' as providing an economic analysis of imperfect competition. Knight's academic career exhibits his primary focus on economic, rather than philosophical, issues. For example, Knight provides a detailed account of economic freedom in 1943, which outlines the difference between economic freedom and political freedom (Knight 1943a). At all times Knight focuses on the economic definition of freedom; he contrasts the notion of political freedom with the notion of economic freedom. To Knight, the two are completely different. Whereas writers of political philosophy, such as John Locke, discuss the right of all to the, "... fundamental political principles of freedom and equality ...", (Tarcov 1984, 1) Knight points out that economic actors do not enjoy the right to equality of economic freedom. Knight argues that orthodox economic theory posits that, under conditions of perfect knowledge, all economic actors enjoy the right of equal economic freedom. While Knight accepts that this right may exist under perfect knowledge, he disagrees in the case of uncertainty. For Knight, uncertainty seriously undermines - even destroys - this right; a large inequality of economic freedom exists in the case of uncertainty. In this way uncertainty creates a host of opportunities for utility maximisation, yet only those economic actors with economic freedom have access to all of these opportunities, according to Knight. Economic freedom, therefore, shapes an economic actor's access to the economic opportunities which uncertainty creates. Knight develops this novel conception of economic freedom in later works, such as *Free Society, its Basic Nature and Problem* (1956a). Here, Knight (1956a) proposes that investment in human capital can help to redress the problems which result from the unequal distribution of economic freedom. Later, Knight (1960a) integrates this more refined notion of economic freedom into his discussion of economic welfare in, *Intelligence and Democratic Action* (1960a). Here, Knight concludes that the recognition of a broader policy objective, which embraces a consideration of both economic freedom and economic power, is vitally needed. Throughout his academic career, therefore, Knight's analytical focus is firmly on economic, rather than philosophical, issues.

Before we can be convinced that Knight presents an economic, rather than philosophical, argument we must question previous evaluations of Knight. We argue that such evaluations confuse, rather than clarify, the appreciation of Knight. An example of such an evaluation is the American Economics Association's valediction to Knight (1973). Here, the American Economics Association presumes that from the beginning of 1930 Knight's, "... main interests began to shift from economic theory to social philosophy" (American Economics Association 1973, 1048; Stigler 1987). We disagree for two principal reasons. First, we demonstrate that all Knight's major published works display his continued involvement in economic theory, rather than 'social philosophy'. Second, Knight's Presidency of the American Economics Association. in 1950, almost one quarter of a century after his supposed departure from economic theory, highlights his continuing involvement in the profession (American Economics Association 1973, 1048). Moreover, even if we disregard these two reasons we argue that neither the American Economics Association nor any other economist, provides a detailed rationale for why one part of Knight's work relates to economic theory while another relates to 'social philosophy'.

Our strong disagreement with the standard assessment of Knight's scholarship leads us to challenge the existing assessment of Knight's policy stance. For example, on the subject of monopoly regulation Raines and Jung (1988) argue that Knight accepts monopoly as, "... a mechanical defect ..." in the free-market system (Raines and Jung 1988, 141-3). Here, the authors argue that Knight perceives monopoly as being responsible for some short-run costs; these costs are outweighed by the long-run efficiency benefits which flow from monopoly (Raines and Jung 1988, 143). Monopoly, therefore, delivers a net efficiency benefit to the free market system, over the long-run. In other words, the authors construe Knight as placing his support behind monopoly because of the efficiency gains which monopoly delivers. However, we argue that Knight's conception of economic welfare forces him to replace the single-minded pursuit of economic efficiency with a broader policy agenda; economic efficiency is only one of several equally important policy goals. Consequently, Knight's policy approach to monopoly is significantly different to that which Raines and Jung (1988) suggest.

Such differences in the assessment of Knight's policy stance are, however, merely indicative of a much more significant contribution: Knight argues that the orthodox notion of profitless equilibrium and the existence of uncertainty are inconsistent. According to orthodox theory, the separate activities of economic actors lead to a situation of stable equilibrium, in the long-run. Such equilibrium is primarily characterised by the absence of abnormal profit. In contrast, Knight, argues that uncertainty creates abnormal (or super-normal) profit in the long-run. Firms compete for this abnormal profit by continually seeking ways to reduce the costs of production, particularly the costs which flow from uncertainty.[2] Knight maintains that firms can alter the level of such costs by changing the scale of production, in turn, uncertainty forces firms to operate in a way which promotes a continuous variation in the level of economic activity, over the long-run. This absence of any long-run equilibrium, combined with the presence of abnormal profit, characterises Knight's perception of the competitive outcome which exists under uncertainty. This leads Knight to conceive of a specific perspective on imperfect competition which focuses on the supply, rather than the demand, side. Knight does not ignore product differentiation. Instead, Knight argues that the competitive differentiation of cost is of more importance to the explanation of the variation in profit margins under conditions of uncertainty. However, this conclusion requires that we grasp Knight's work as an integrated whole.

We commence our examination of Knight by looking at the axiomatic premises which comprise Knight's conception of welfare economics. We then follow with a survey of the main influences on Knight. This survey serves a dual purpose; it supports our examination of Knight's welfare economics while also narrowing the focus of our analysis to Knight's theory of imperfect competition. By comparing and contrasting Knight's analysis of imperfect competition with the work of other eminent economists, we are able to extract the unique characteristics of Knight's analysis. These characteristics, combined with our assessment of Knight's welfare economics, form the basis of the discussion on Knight's policy response to imperfect competition. Given this broad structure of argument, let us now explain each Chapter of this thesis in greater detail.

To best understand Knight's concept of welfare economics, we argue that it is necessary to visualise economic freedom, the balance of economic power, and economic efficiency as representing the three extreme points of an equilateral triangle; every extreme point in the triangle represents an objective of economic policy. In Chapter Two, we argue that economic welfare depends on achieving a balance between each objective, according to Knight. However, the omnipresence of uncertainty makes the accurate identification of such a balance particularly problematic. Despite this difficulty, we argue that as long as these three objectives are kept in a rough balance, economic welfare can be enhanced by progressing in all three fronts *pari passu*. Any attempt to pursue large gains in one direction, at the expense of one of the remaining two, will not only be futile, but will be detrimental to overall welfare. In summary, judicious economic policy must pursue a balanced progress in all three directions; single-minded concentration on any one objective is deleterious to economic welfare.

Knight's conception of welfare economics draws on some of the most influential economic theorists of his time. Indeed, we argue that an understanding of these influences is crucial to our analysis of Knight's linkage of uncertainty with profit (Knight 1921a). Our first task in Chapter Three is, therefore, to define how Knight's influences shape the creation of this linkage. For example, Knight argues that Marshall obscures the analysis of uncertainty by burying the premises of his analysis under a plethora of, "qualification and detail" (Knight 1921a, 15). By explaining profit as the result of intra-firm cost differentiation Knight indicates that profit is yet another example of utility (or profit) maximising behaviour. In addition, Chapter Three seeks a rationale for why Knight develops the linkage between uncertainty and profit. We argue that Knight seeks to develop 'fair' standards of competition; something which J.B. Clark attempts, yet fails, to define. Clark argues that such standards are necessary to prevent the competitive economy from becoming self-destructive. According to Clark, examples of cut-throat competition tend to overshadow the meritorious aspects of free-market; Knight continues to seek ways of preserving the free-market system. In other words, Knight creates the linkage between uncertainty and profit so as to ensure the long-run survival of the free-market system.

Given that Knight provides a new perspective on the economics of imperfect competition, we argue that it is essential to juxtapose this contribution to the acknowledged founders of imperfect (and monopolistic) competition, J. Robinson and E.H. Chamberlin. Chapter Four provides such a juxtaposition. By comparing and contrasting these authors we discern the essential difference in Knight's approach. Both Chamberlin and Robinson disagree with orthodox theory because it fails to incorporate product differentiation into the analysis of competition. However, in expressing their disagreement with orthodox theory they both describe an analysis of monopolistic (and imperfect) competition which centres on the slope of the demand curve. In contrast, Knight argues that orthodox theory fails to incorporate cost differentiation into the analysis of competition. Thus, one view of imperfect competition focuses on the demand side, while Knight focuses on the supply side. Knight argues that larger market share creates better access to market knowledge, when compared to the marginal (small) firm. This, in turn, means that the large firm reduces the impact of uncertainty on the cost of production. As long as the marginal (small) firm exists, product prices are set at a level which allows them to earn a normal level of profit. The large firm, in contrast, earns economic rent because industry price is higher than the average cost of production. In other words, a differentiation of profit exists in the imperfectly competitive market, because uncertainty inflicts higher costs on the marginal (small) firm. Knight argues that this analysis of imperfect competition leads to a distribution problem, along with an efficiency problem.

In Chapter Five, we briefly outline a policy which goes some way to alleviate the distribution problem which exists in Knight's analysis of imperfect competition. We suggest that a lump-sum tax can capture the economic rents which the large firm earns without reducing economic efficiency. Orthodox economic theory is indifferent to such a policy suggestion, because the policy does not change (narrowly defined) economic efficiency. In contrast, the spirit of Knight's discourse is sympathetic to the imposition of such a tax mainly because of his conception of the 'social welfare function'.

Notes

1 We use the term 'social welfare function' to describe Knight's integration of the 'social' aspects of existence with the 'economic'. As we will show in this work, Knight perceives both as being intimately linked.

2 In contrast, John Kay (1993) argues that firms derive economic rent from the creation of a unique set of relationships or contracts, which he describes as "architecture" (Kay 1993, 66-87). Instead of extracting economic rent from the knowledge set of the industry, Kay (1993) argues that each firm creates economic rent from its own knowledge set. Proprietary knowledge, therefore, creates economic rent (Kay 1993). Knight (1921a) argues that a latent pool of potential proprietary knowledge exists in every industry. If firms employ this latent knowledge to reduce the costs which emanate from uncertainty, then this latent knowledge becomes the proprietary knowledge of the firm. As we illustrate in Chapters Four and Five of this work, Knight discovers the way firms extract abnormal profit by transforming latent proprietary knowledge into actual proprietary knowledge (Kay 1993).

2 The Knightian Pyramid

Introduction

> There appears to be a deep-seated conflict between liberty [economic freedom] and equality [economic power balance] on the one hand and efficiency on the other [brackets added] (Knight 1935c, 61).

Frank Knight's economic thought is centred on the integration of three economic objectives. Reduction of the significant tensions between each of these objectives is the goal of Knight's economic thought. Optimal levels of economic freedom, imbalance of economic power and economic efficiency are interrelated into a unified whole by Knight. The aim of this Chapter is to present, with the assistance of an explanatory device which we term the 'Knightian Pyramid', the essence of this significant system of thought.

Knight's interrelation of economic objectives has been identified by other economists. For example, Kern (1987) argues that Knight follows a process of maximising the marginal contributions of each independent objective, so as to maximise the overall well being of the economy (Kern 1987, 642; Hammond 1990). By way of contrast with Kern, we argue that Knight does seek to maximise the marginal contributions of each objective, mainly because each objective is mutually interdependent. Substantial incongruities between each objective cause Knight to abandon the notion that each economic objective can be treated independently. As a result we argue that Knight views each objective as being part of an integrated whole, rather than separate components.

First, we investigate Knight's understanding of economic freedom. Economic freedom is generally subject to two constraints: economic power and sociological conditioning.[1] Knight introduces the concept of economic freedom in a gradual fashion for three reasons: (i) to clarify the debate over which conception of freedom is appropriate in the humanities generally, and more specifically in economics, (ii) to demonstrate that freedom is ambiguous in both the physical sciences and economics, and

(iii) most importantly, to document how the substantive definition of economic freedom exposes distributional issues, which are hidden by orthodox theory. Knight's discussion of economic freedom indicates that an uneven distribution of benefits is derived from improvements to economic efficiency. Knight argues that the distribution is not due to random factors, but systematically biased toward those who posses a high level of economic freedom. Furthermore, sociological conditioning constrains the ability of governments to alter the distribution of substantive economic freedom, in the short-run.

Second, we turn to a discussion of economic power. Knight argues that economic power is not simply a question of defining existing title to property. Rather, Knight supplements the orthodox notion of economic power with the idea that economic power comprises access to the opportunities which uncertainty provides. Knight argues that there are three sources of access to economic power, these are: (i) access to investment in human capital, (ii) access to the opportunities which are presented by uncertainty, and (iii) access to credit. In other words, economic power modifies the degree of access, to the cost benefits derived from economic efficiency, which an economic actor may enjoy. Knight argues that such access is unevenly distributed. Knight then emphasises that uncertainty, combined with differential access to the opportunities presented by uncertainty, generates a distribution problem which is disguised by orthodox theory.

Third, we investigate Knight's analysis of economic efficiency. Here, we illustrate Knight's critique by detailing the assumptions which underpin the notion of efficiency, as it exists in perfect competition (Knight 1921a, 51). These assumptions are defective in two main respects. On the one hand, Knight argues that the assumptions are inequitable because they make the unsubstantiated presumption that the existing distribution of economic power is the best possible (Knight 1921a, 85-6). On the other hand, the assumptions imply a situation of instability, which is inconsistent with the notion of equilibrium. Here, Knight argues that uncertainty amplifies the incentives which lead away from a perfectly stable equilibrium towards a more volatile competitive environment. Moreover, if left unchecked, these incentives would rapidly transform perfect competition into perfect monopoly (Knight 1921a, 193; Knight 1935c).

These reservations culminate in the proposition that achievement of economic efficiency, without consideration of economic freedom or the imbalance of economic power, does not improve social welfare (Knight 1921a, 191-2; Knight 1947a, 14). Consequently, this proposition forces economics to evaluate economic efficiency in the context of achieving two other objectives. These objectives are: (i) increasing the general level of economic freedom, and (ii) decreasing the general imbalance of economic power. Such additional objectives are necessary for the achievement of sustainable improvements in efficiency; all three are part of the 'social welfare function' On this basis, we argue that an exclusion of this pair of objectives will generate social costs, which in turn will eventually reduce economic efficiency over the long-run. Accordingly, some mechanism for evaluating the relative merits of all three economic objectives is required. Unfortunately, only an outline of this mechanism is provided by Knight. We aim to correct this deficiency by proposing a more detailed account of these interrelations, which can broadly be described as Knight's welfare economics. Firstly, we outline each objective, namely economic freedom, power and efficiency. Secondly, a series of two variable relations is outlined. Lastly, we critically analyse the interrelated structure of these goals, highlighting the significant tensions which exist between them.[6]

Economic Freedom

Freedom in the Physical Sciences

Freedom, Knight (1943c) proposes, is a relative notion. Knight argues that in the sphere of the physical sciences, the notion of freedom is relative to some predetermined 'normal' position; just as a falling object is free to fall through the air, it is impossible to say whether the object is still free to fall once it hits the ground, unless we define its normal position. If the normal position is defined as falling, then the object will be free only when it is falling, and unfree when it hits the control. Conversely, if the normal position is defined as resting, then the object will be unfree when it is falling and free when it is resting. The same type of ambiguity exists in economics. On the one hand, we can define economic freedom as the absence of legal restriction on choice. On the other hand, we can define economic freedom in terms of the particular choices which are available. Orthodox theory chooses the former definition, and this can be termed 'formal freedom'.

> Freedom, in its primary [formal] ... meaning, refers negatively to the absence of some more or less abnormal interference with acting in some normal way in which the individual would otherwise be able, would posses the power, to act [brackets added] (Knight 1943c, 64).[2]

Depending on a sufficient level of education, every economic actor enjoys what Knight terms the 'fact' of freedom (Knight 1943c, 93). Freedom as 'fact' refers to the individual's capacity to control his or her thoughts in a rational fashion. However, while the training of the rational faculty enables freedom of thought it does not guarantee freedom of action.

> [The economic actor] is always free to choose, in thought and action, between 'possible' alternatives; possibility is a matter of power, and power is what freedom as a desideratum really means [brackets added] (Knight 1943c, 68).

Knight employs the term 'desideratum' to convey the distinction between formal and substantive economic freedom. Even though no formal impediments are placed in the path of the economic actor, usually a lack of economic power constrains the range of alternative actions which are available to the economic agent. On this basis, we argue that it is possible for an economic agent to entertain the notion of having missed an opportunity to perform an economic act which would result in a net economic benefit. This is a result of a deficiency in the level of economic power to which the economic agent has access. For example, even though an economic agent is capable of a business success, he may not be able to realise his capability because he lacks the requisite economic power, which is required to either start the business, or borrow the funds. In other words, the term 'desideratum', is equivalent to what orthodox theory now terms, a 'barrier to entry'. In this case, the economic agent is not legally restricted from entering an industry, rather he is constrained by a deficiency in economic power.[3]

Freedom in the Humanities

In the broad social context of the humanities, as opposed to the physical sciences, Knight (1943c) demonstrates further ambiguity with the term 'freedom'. Three separate notions of freedom exist. Two of these are extreme notions of freedom, which Knight describes as the 'religious' and the 'romantic' notions of freedom. The third is a more moderate notion, which Knight terms the 'modern' notion of freedom. First, Knight describes a religious conception of freedom which involves the suppression of any desires, so that the contemplative life is encouraged. Knight summarises this type of freedom as 'thinking without acting', because the emphasis is on not acting (Knight 1943c, 90). In contrast, the romantic conception of freedom involves 'acting without thinking' (Knight 1943c, 90). Knight argues that this conception of freedom is 'inveterate', or habitually ingrained. Here, the preference for action tends to override any degree of thoughtful evaluation of the particular activity.

> The natural man is still a romantic, disposed to act without much regard for rational knowledge and thought (Knight 1943c, 93).

Between these two extremes lies Knight's preferred 'modern view' of freedom, which allows the individual the widest range of choice in compromising between the two extremes (Knight 1943c, 90). Here, the romantic preference for action is checked by religious preference for reflection. In other words, the modern view of freedom is where the passionate romantic who fails to think before acting, becomes a reasonable romantic, who enjoys an, "... interesting life ... realised through free constructive activity within the possible limits" (Knight 1943c, 90). However, despite the possibility of most economic actors adopting the modern concept of freedom, Knight remains pessimistic about this possibility becoming a reality. This means that economic actors, "... must be cured of the age-old inveterate romanticism (Knight 1943c, 92-3). Knight argues that educating the popular mind to become less romantic is one of the reforms necessary to sustain free society.

> Otherwise, we must admit in advance that free society is an impossibility, and give up the problem as hopeless (Knight 1943c, 93).

Ideal Freedom - The Isolated Individual

After considering freedom in the broad social context of the humanities, Knight then considers the special case of the isolated economic actor who Knight terms 'Crusoe' (Knight 1943c, 63). As Knight explains, the example of Crusoe allows Knight to speak about the pure economic man in isolation from other economic actors. Here, "... the isolated individual is an 'economic man', or a pragmatist; all of his thinking is instrumental about means and their use in achieving given or found ends ..."(Knight 1943c, 69). Despite Crusoe being an economic man who is free from all the restrictions normally applied to society, the freedom he enjoys is still quite marginal (Knight 1943c, 72). Automatic instincts, which are defined as mechanical responses to environmental stimuli, dominate Crusoe's actions. Over time Crusoe supplements these environmentally conditioned instincts with other automatic responses, which we term habits. Both forms of automatic response then produce an established pattern of response, or character (Knight 1943c, 71-2). Education has the potential to alter bad habits so that they become good habits. For example, the propensity to spend and borrow is replaced with the propensity to save and invest (Knight 1943c, 117-8; Knight 1943c, 70).

Even though Crusoe has a character which is mostly comprised of automatic responses, Knight does not call Crusoe an automaton (Knight 1943c, 71). Although the majority of Crusoe's actions are automatic not all are, and it is this minority of interests which define Crusoe's freedom. These limitations are capable of full realisation in Crusoe's solitary world because he has no other human contact which could interfere with his unique interests. In other words, Crusoe's interests can be fully realised without recourse to any social structure. Crusoe, therefore, represents the closest approximation to the human being with the highest, humanly possible, level of freedom. However, as soon as we introduce another human being we find that Crusoe's freedom is radically transformed. As Knight puts it, both Crusoe and his new companion, will enjoy a totally different type of freedom than they did in isolation (Knight 1943c, 69).

> Men who live in the same world cannot be 'free' in the sense in which Crusoe is free. They become subject to a new and categorically different type of limitation or restriction on their activities, and freedom in society must be defined in entirely different terms (Knight 1943c, 71).

The rationale for this transformation of freedom becomes apparent when we consider the conflict of interest between members of society. Presence of more than one economic actor necessarily involves a conflict of interest. This occurs because of conflict, between economic actors, over scarce resources.[4] Freedom, instead of being ideal freedom, becomes only an ideal aspired to by society; something society reaches out for, but can never fully attain (Knight 1943c, 71).

Economic Freedom - Within a Social Context

Knight focuses his analysis of economic freedom on two opposing forces. On the one hand, Knight examines the conflict of interest which arises in the social context and tends to divide society. On the other hand, Knight examines the benefits from trade which exist in the social context and tends to bind society closer together (Knight 1943c, 71). Despite the benefits from trade which exist in the social context, Knight argues that freedom is not the ideal freedom, which exists in the context of the isolated economic actor. Rather, economic actors can only enjoy what Knight terms economic freedom. Despite the differences which exist between these two forms of freedom some similarities exist. For example, economic actors possess 'characters' in both cases. However, the social context reduces the scope of an individual's freedom, because custom, or established patterns of behaviour within each society, reduce the impact of 'interests' on an individual's actions (Knight 1943c, 73). Here, we can illustrate Knight's argument by allocating Crusoe's actions between those driven by 'character' and those driven by 'interest'. For example, if seventy per cent of Crusoe's actions are driven by 'character' and thirty per cent are driven by 'interest', then Knight argues that the emergence of society reduces the scope of 'interest' to, say, twenty per cent. This result is the effect of custom assuming ten per cent of the driving force behind the individual's actions.

> Custom is still ultimately mechanical. But man as we know him, who is always highly 'civilised' in comparison with any known animals, is characterised not merely by the fact of custom, but by a strong disposition against passive conformity, reflecting the individual and conflicting interest; and human society is characterised by deliberate, organised control (Knight 1943c, 74).

In addition, enforcement of custom further diminishes freedom as the size and complexity of society increases. Enforcement of custom can range from informal social sanctions, to formal coercive enforcement, supported by punitive procedures (Knight 1943c, 73-5).

Apart from reducing the scope of the individual's interest, society also shapes both the character and the interests of the individual. Here, Knight adopts Weber's sociological analysis, which describes the impact of the sociological environment on the individual (Knight 1943c, 72).

Knight argues that the particular sociological environment, within which the individual operates, can shape the overall level of economic well being, which an economic actor enjoys (Knight 1943c, 71-2, 117-8). For example, the economically powerful will tend to be subjected to the sort of sociological conditioning which promotes the propensity to save and invest. In contrast, the economically powerless will be subject to the opposite form of conditioning, so that they will possess the propensity to spend, and to borrow in order to spend. In turn this propensity will constrain economic activity so that they will tend to remain economically powerless.[5]

Economic Freedom - Conclusion

Knight argues that the definition of economic freedom is extremely difficult, because of the "... complex mixture of categories none of which can be clearly defined ..." (Knight 1943c, 75). Despite these difficulties, and by way of summary, a reasonably precise definition of economic freedom can now be attempted along the lines outlined by Knight.

(a) Economic freedom, both formal and substantive, pertains to the minority of an economic actors' activities. The majority of activities are controlled by what Knight describes as 'character', which varies according to the particular sociological environment of the individual (Knight 1943c, 117-8).

(b) As society grows in size and complexity, the scope for economic freedom is reduced by the voluntary observation of custom, in conjunction with the formal enforcement of custom. These restrictions on freedom uniformly define the boundaries of 'formal' freedom.

(c) The remaining set of economic actions (that is all those not governed by either custom or habit), comprise those activities in which the individual can express his or her own interests. In other words, these actions are where we find the individual enjoying substantive economic freedom. This subset of economic actions has three main dimensions:

> (i) ... Choice, based on purely quantitative comparison, among partial or provisional ends for which means are to be used, [namely] the different given 'wants' to be satisfied in consumption, (ii) choice among concrete modes of using means, the technique or technology employed, (iii) decision as to the amount of means to be used in maintaining or increasing the stock of the means itself, [namely] the human and material

> capital of the individual and society [brackets added] (Knight 1943c, 100-1).

The latter two of these categories of choice, or realms of economic activity, mostly relate to production of goods and services. Those who lack substantive economic freedom are therefore not able to participate in these realms of economic activity. Accordingly, it can be concluded that both the degree and the nature of substantive economic freedom varies between economic actors. Variations in sociological conditioning will lead to variations in the character of the economic actor, whereas variations in the economic power will compound these sociologically inspired differences. In the next section, we will show how a disproportionately large command of economic power facilitates the growth of an economic actor's substantive economic freedom.[6]

Economic Power

Introduction: The Static Dimension of Economic Power

Essentially, Knight defines economic power as the productive capacity of an economic actor. Productive capacity includes internal attributes, such as labour power, and external attributes such as the ownership of property (Knight 1943c, 110). For Knight, uncertainty transforms economic power from being an end in itself, to becoming a means of controlling uncertainty over future income streams. In performing this instrumental role, economic power grants economic agents 'access' to the profitable opportunities which uncertainty presents; we illustrate this analysis by discussing the various forms of access to the opportunities presented by uncertainty. First, we discuss access to investment in human capital. Second, we discuss access to the opportunities provided by uncertainty. Lastly, we discuss access to credit.

Dynamic Dimension of Economic Power

> In this long view ... the cumulative tendency [toward an imbalance of economic power] is ... intensified, by the role of uncertainty ... It is a situation which gives rise to a relatively permanent inequality, the so called 'class structure' of society, and at least a tendency to its accentuation, in the absence of preventative measures [brackets added] (Knight 1943c, 115-6).

In order to understand Knight's analysis of the dynamic dimension of economic power it is necessary to define the term 'unit' of study. As Knight says: "From the viewpoint of the long-run transmission of economic power the family is the social 'unit' of study, not the individual as economics generally contends" (Knight 1943c, 115). The reason for Knight's disagreement with economic theory is that the family - not the individual - provides a mechanism for the transmission of economic power over time. Inheritance of economic power, through the institution of the family, is the blunt inter-generational method of economic power transmission.

> In an economic order based on the private family, the ownership of wealth [or economic power] by individuals is not dependent alone on the economic role played by them in the past, but largely on the accident or brute force of inheritance [brackets added] (Knight 1943c, 9).

This broadening of the social unit allows the identification of the factors which force the imbalance of economic power to increase over time (Knight 1943c, 115).[7]

Access to Investment in Human Capital

By investing in human capital, with a view to improving an offspring's understanding of the methods for dealing with uncertainty, economic actors can increase the chance of the social unit's wealth increasing over time. Knight examines these methods throughout his prolific academic career, and they feature in his book, *Risk, Uncertainty, and Profit* (1921a).

The first method analysed is that which Knight terms the 'grouping of activities', which effectively amounts to the gaining of market share. Where individuals group together into firms, and acquire large market share, they are able to increase the quantity of economic data on which estimates of economic variables can be based. This procedure of aggregation can be construed as Knight's novel application of statistical methodology to economic theory.

Another classification of investment in human capital is (economic) cultural training. This instruction generally refers to the economic actor's knowledge and appreciation of his culture. More specifically, it refers to the economic actor's predisposition to spend or save. On the one hand, those who lack economic power will tend to possess the economic 'habits' of a poor man, namely to spend and to borrow in order to spend. This is the long-run importance of economic power; by means of both intellectual and cultural training those economic actors can increase economic power in the long-run. Knight explains this process in, *Free Society: its Basic Nature and Problem* (Knight 1956a).

By linking this effect of economic power to the foregoing analysis of economic freedom, it is possible to demonstrate how one classification of economic action effects the other. Differences in substantive economic freedom tend to generate further differences in economic character, such that the latter tends to add to the former through time. By this we mean that greater freedom tends to lead to greater investment in human capital, which in turn alters economic character in a fashion that predisposes an economic actor to acquire still greater economic power. Accumulation of economic power, therefore, tends to become cumulative and increasingly concentrated over time, according to Knight.

> Those who have more productive capacity at any time are obviously in a better position to save and invest, in themselves (knowledge, training) or in external wealth, and so to accumulate personal or physical capital and to increase their differential advantage over others (Knight 1943c, 115).

Access to Invest in the Opportunities Created by Uncertainty

Another reason for the cumulatively increasing imbalance of economic power is to be found in Knight's (1921a) seminal dissertation on uncertainty. However, to examine the effect of uncertainty, on the cumulative growth of economic power, we must highlight Knight's understanding of uncertainty, being the opportunity whereby the motive to possess economic power can be realised;

> ... social progress on the material side is largely motivated by a desire to posses wealth, and ... the role of uncertainty ... is to make it possible for an individual ... to obtain a large increase in wealth in a short time (Knight 1921a, 333).

Without uncertainty the opportunity 'to increase wealth in a short time' would cease to exist and social progress would lose its driving force. The driving force, being the desire to accumulate economic power by seizing the opportunities that are brought about by uncertainty. Even though capacity to utilise uncertainty differs because of biologically unpredictable factors, Knight contends that a significant proportion of this differential in capacity is the result of investment in human capital. We propose, therefore, that economic actors are differentially equipped to deal with uncertainty. Yet, this proposition presumes that all economic actors have the opportunity to profit from uncertainty. Here, Knight argues that the existing imbalance of economic power tends to restrict a high proportion of economic actors from utilising opportunities presented by uncertainty. Most economic actors, Knight argues are restricted to the purchase of a narrow range of subsistence goods for themselves and their immediate families (Knight 1921a, 315-75).

As the short-term economic power of an economic actor grows, the relative percentage of the budget, which is allocated to necessities, falls. Accumulation of economic power thereby increases the proportion of an economic actor's budget, which is available for either saving or investment (Knight 1933c, 113). According to the economic actor's preference for risk, he will design a portfolio which allocates a proportion of his surplus funds to risk reducing investments or to more uncertain investments. Surplus economic power, therefore, assists the economic actor to realise the benefits of exploiting the opportunities presented by uncertainty. In addition, as the quantity of economic power increases, the opportunity for uncertainty to be converted into risk also increases.[8] In this way, economic power offers a reduction in the relative exposure of 'high' powered economic actors to uncertainty, as compared to 'low' powered economic actors.

> The death of a particular individual, burning of a particular building, loss of a particular ship at sea, etc; is uncertain; but in a group of a hundred thousand similar cases the proportion of losses is very accurately predictable. There are many ways of applying this principle, in addition to the various forms of insurance called by name. A large corporation, by broadening the scale of its operations, distributes and reduces its risk (Knight 1933c, 119; Knight 1921a, 333).

This procedure of converting a part of uncertainty into risk, by spreading investments, also transforms profit (and loss) which is generated by uncertainty, into a normal revenue (or expense) which is incurred from insuring against risk.

> The essential point for profit theory is that so far as it is possible to insure by any method against risk, the cost of carrying it out

is converted into a constant element of expense and it ceases to be a cause of profit and loss (Knight 1933 c, 119-20).

Access to Credit

Another factor, intimately related to this last point, regarding the investment capacity of an economic agent, is access to credit. As an economic agent's economic power increases, the quantity of credit available also increases. This is due to the fact that every unit of economic power possessed affords the potential usage of another unit of credit (Knight 1921a, 313-75). The price of credit will also drop as the quantity of credit increases. The first reason for this price reduction is that economies of scale are enjoyed by lenders as the amount of borrowing increases. Here, costs associated with the valuation of a loan security, and application assessment, can be spread over a large amount of interest. An example of this cost differential exists in the interest rate spread which occurs between large and small corporate borrowers. Here, small borrowers are charged higher interest than large borrowers.

The second reason for the large borrowers accessing cheaper credit is the ability of the economically powerful to reduce the costs which result from uncertainty, by having better access to the stock of available market information. This means that lenders view larger borrowers as less risky, because of their greater capacity to contain the volatility of their earnings stream (Knight 1921a, 333).[9] All else being equal, we would expect that higher volatility of earnings will attract a higher credit charge, because of the increased probability of interest or principle default at any time during the loan period.

Economic Power - Conclusion

Knight argues that investment in human capital tends to assist those economic actors, in possession of surplus economic power, to reap the benefits of taking advantage of the opportunities presented by uncertainty. This assistance is in the form of both cultural and intellectual training, as well as access to credit. Such assistance is compounded by the fact that those economic actors, who lack a large enough surplus above basic needs, cannot take advantage of potentially profitable opportunities. This interrelationship, between the various forms of dynamic economic power, reveals the consanguineous relationship between economic freedom and economic power. A disproportionate level of substantive economic freedom provides the input to what we describe as the 'gearing mechanism' of dynamic economic power. If a surplus of substantive economic freedom exists, then both greater investment in human capital and a greater capacity to seize the opportunities presented by uncertainty, tend to combine in a cumulative fashion. This combination of factors provides the potential for a net increase in the imbalance of economic power, in the long-run. Knight outlines the way in which the imbalance of economic power increases throughout his work.[10]

Economic Efficiency

Introduction

Knight's general approach to efficiency is not significantly different to that of his contemporaries. However, Knight investigates the meaning of economic efficiency in a distinctive manner. Before discussing this feature of Knight's economic thought, we shall outline Knight's general approach to economic efficiency. This preliminary discussion involves the valuation of economic variables which is the procedure by which the individual evaluates the relative worth of one economic good, in relation to another economic good - subject to a budget constraint. Knight (1921a), along with his contemporaries, believes that this procedure forms the mechanism by which individuals maximise satisfaction. Due to the fact that wants conflict in the context of a limited budget, this procedure becomes a problem of evaluating the rate at which one good will be preferred to another (Knight 1921a, 59).

> Every valuation is a comparison, we have no conception of an absolute utility or an absolute standard of utility. The notion of value is meaningless except in relation to the alternatives of choice (Knight 1921a, 63).

This process of evaluating the relative value of commodities, in the context of a limited budget, is derived from Marshall's analysis (Marshall 1961). Knight's definition of efficiency is, therefore, quite similar to that of his contemporaries. As Knight says,

> In the utilisation of limited resources in competing fields of employment, which is the form of all rational activity in conduct, we tend to apportion our resources among the

alternative uses that are open in such a way that equal amounts of resource yield equivalent returns in all fields (Knight 1921a, 65).

However, this definition of efficiency is also influenced by J.M. Clark, who emphasises the fact that freedom to act often means freedom to act capriciously (Knight 1921a, 62). We can detect this influence on Knight at various stages throughout his academic career.[11] Although some economic actors may wish to act in a purely rational fashion, where all activities are achieved with maximum efficiency, some may not. In the case of economic actors who fail to maximise efficiency, Knight argues that they perceive the intellectual costs, associated with such an efficient outcome as being greater than the benefits derived from such outcomes.[12] The examination of these types of questions is characteristic of J.M. Clark, whose influence on Knight is borne out in Knight's criticism of positivistic economics (Hammond 1990).

Concentration on the powerful techniques of mathematical economics creates a false scientific confidence among economists in the earlier part of this century, according to Knight.[13] This confidence revolves around the methodological agenda which argues that the search for better mathematical techniques of analysing the real world (within a narrowly defined analytical framework) will result in better outcomes than a broad examination of the axiomatic premises of economic theory. Subjects, such as examining the theoretical underpinning of economic efficiency are, therefore, of little value to such an agenda. Knight, we argue, vehemently disagrees with such a methodological agenda.

The commitment which Knight has to the development of J.M. Clark's broad ranging, rather than mathematical, analysis tends to illustrate the distinction between Knight and his contemporaries. This distinction can best be demonstrated by analysing Knight's critique of the assumptions which underlie the standard notion of economic efficiency. This leads Knight to place economics within the broader social context; an aspect of his work which constitutes one of his contributions to economic theory. For instance, Schweitzer argues that Knight, "... was the first American economist who recognised in Weber's work the foundation for ... a social economics" (Schweitzer 1975, 280). However, Schweitzer goes on to say that, despite Knight's awareness of the possibility of a 'social' economics, he did not provide a systematic study of it (Schweitzer 1975, 292). In contrast to Schweitzer, we argue that Knight's critique of efficiency, when it is linked to his analysis of freedom and power, shows that he had begun to build a coherent philosophical alternative to traditional economic theory. While this alternative may not be what Schweitzer considers a 'social' economics, it did set out to integrate economic theory into the broader social setting. Unfortunately, Knight's analysis of this broadly based economics tends to be very terse. Nevertheless, Knight does outline a series of relationships which indicate a way of achieving this laudable, yet formidable, goal.

Assumptions Underlying the Orthodox Notion of Economic Efficiency

Knight identifies eleven micro assumptions about the social context of economic choice, underlying the standard analysis of economic efficiency. He proposes a taxonomy, consisting of three subsets, or categories. The first eight assumptions are classified by Knight, as 'idealising'. The ninth assumption is incorporated by Knight into the second category, which he terms the 'stability' category. The final two assumptions are classified by Knight under the heading 'analytic'. A summary of these assumptions is contained in figure one, below (Knight 1921a, 76-80).

Figure 2.1 Knight's Taxonomy of Assumptions Underlying the Standard Notion of Economic Efficiency

#	Group	Content
1	Idealising	Members of society ('MOS') are a random sample.
2	Idealising	MOS act rationally and deliberately.
3	Idealising	MOS are the final judge of his own welfare.
4	Idealising	Resources are perfectly mobile and divisible.
5	Idealising	Intercommunication, between MOS, is perfect.
6	Idealising	MOS are completely independent of each other.
7	Idealising	No interference in the relationship between MOS exists.
8	Idealising	Motives for the division of labour, and exchange, exist.
9	Stability	Inert technology, resources, and preferences.
10	Analytic	Pure exchange system; no productive property exists.
11	Analytic	Pure exchange system; only finished products.

(Source: Knight 1921a, 76-80).

Knight argues that the idealising assumptions of economic efficiency ignore the problem of dynamic instability; this is a recurrent theme in Knight's published works. For example, in his critical analysis of Pigou, Knight (1935c) argues that the idealising assumptions of orthodox theory exclude uncertainty. Such an exclusion ignores the incentives to monopolise which uncertainty creates within the economic system. These 'incentives to monopolise', which Knight identifies, operate in two ways.

First, as outlined earlier, if the size of the firm approaches the size of the industry, then the amount of knowledge which is acquired by the firm effectively transforms uncertainty into risk.[14] Broadly speaking, this tendency can be divided into two categories: (i) the more accurate estimation of risk, and (ii) the lower unit costs associated with insuring against risk. Addressing the first category, Knight contends that the ability of the firm to accurately estimate the relevant economic variables is constrained by the proportion of industry information to which the firm has access. The large firm tends to observe a higher proportion of industry transactions, which allows it to make more accurate estimates than the marginal (small) firm (Knight 1921a, 333). With regard to the second category, we note that the marginal (small) firm cannot cost-effectively access mechanisms which reduce financial risk, whereas the large firm can. For example, while the local grocer cannot hedge the price of orange juice, the global manufacturer of orange juice can easily hedge his risk in the commodity futures market. In addition, Knight argues that, in the case of the large firm, the costs of insuring against risk can be apportioned over a larger quantity of production. As a result, the fixed costs, associated with insuring against financial risks, become a smaller proportion of the overall unit costs. In other words, economies of scale apply to insurance costs, in a similar way to other costs.

Second, Knight argues that an increase in total sales, as opposed to a reduction in unit costs, also creates an incentive for firms to increases the scale of production.

> ... [if] two or more such agents combine so as to compete as a unit instead of separately, they can get the total product of that number of units at the lower end of the series, which is more than their separate marginal products. Therefore, under perfect competition, they will combine ... the same incentive will urge

> them to keep on combining until monopoly results [brackets added] (Knight 1921a, 191-2; Knight 1935c, 52).

An increase in total sales of any particular industry can be created out of what Knight terms 'human limitations'; when individuals assess the relative merits of goods they face the same sort of costs as firms do when they try to estimate the relevant demand and supply curves. Here, we argue that significant costs are associated with gathering and effectively evaluating the information which is required to assess the relative merit of goods; we call these information costs. Indeed, such information costs constrain, or block, consumption because so much effort is required to make an informed consumption choice. Information costs force consumers to save, rather than consume. However, if these costs can be reduced, then we would expect that consumption would increase; one way to reduce these costs is to reduce the available range of choice available to consumers (Knight 1921a, 191-2; Knight 1935c, 52). By constraining the range of choice, producers can reduce the information costs which block consumption; this reduces saving and increases consumption of the goods which are produced in the industry. In this way, the incentive to monopolise is, therefore, fuelled by the desire to maximise consumption, by reducing the information costs of consumers. In contrast, if perfect certainty were to exist, then we would not have to consider the information costs which constrain consumption. Here, all decisions would be made instantaneously and without regard to the effort required to gather and collate all relevant data. Variations in the quantity of choices available to consumers would have no effect on the quantity of consumption, or the level of saving. Human limitations, especially with regard to unequal ability to analyse and collate relevant data, provide an incentive for firms to monopolise.

By making it easier to consume, the firm can increase the general level of consumption in a particular industry. Some regulation of this incentive to monopolise is, therefore, required so as to prevent the complete monopolisation of all industries. For Knight, the crucial point is that perfect competition,

> ... is self defeating and could not exist in the real world. Perfect competition implies conditions, especially as to the presence of human limitations, which would at the same time facilitate monopoly, make organisation through free contract impossible,

> and force an authoritarian system upon society (Knight 1921a, 193).

Static Equilibrium Assumptions Underlying the Standard Notion of Efficiency

Knight also criticises the dependence of the standard notion of efficiency on the ninth assumption. Here, Knight emphasises that both partial and general equilibrium are static economic systems because both these analyses fail to take account of two aspects of the economic system. First, they both fail to take account of any change in the value of variables such as the overall concentration of economic power. Second, they fail to incorporate these variations into the assumptions underlying orthodox analysis. Knight emphasises his agreement with Allyn Young on the significance of increasing returns by arguing that such returns are not recognised in Pigou's model of partial equilibrium (Blitch 1983b; Hart 1989). Knight's critique of Pigou is similar in content to that which Young (1928) presents.[15]

On the topic of the static nature of partial equilibrium analysis, we note that the work of Young (1928), who provides an original and penetrating critique of Marshallian and Walrasian economic theory, from the perspective of classical writers such as Adam Smith. In particular, Young (1928) argues that increasing returns are evident in real economies; he argues that Marshall does not account for such returns. As Young (1928) points out,

> ... the mechanism of increasing returns is not to be discerned adequately by observing the effects of variations in the size of an individual firm or a particular industry for the progressive division and specialisation of industries is an essential part of the process by which increasing returns are realised (Young 1928, 539).

In order to account for such progressive specialisation, Young (1928) proposes that economics should reject the Marshallian division of the economy into 'industries', and adopt a new approach which views "industrial operations as a whole" (Young 1928, 539; Hart 1989). Knight's critique of Pigou's paper, *The Economics of Stationary States* (1935), demonstrates his agreement with Young on the inappropriateness of partial equilibrium as a mechanism of economic analysis. As Knight says,

> The notion of equilibrium is valid only with reference to an arbitrary fixation of all the fundamental features of the economic situation, including population in all its characteristics, and technology, as well as the supply of capital (Knight 1936, 393).

Knight's critique of Pigou, therefore, tends to parallel Young's critique of Marshall's system of partial equilibrium. In this case, we find that the partial equilibrium framework tends to exclude the study of economic progress: Young (1928) significantly develops this study and Knight incorporates it into his analysis. This, Knight hopes, would assist economists in their efforts to contemplate the long-run effects of economic progress on the survival of the free-market system.

In now turning to a consideration of general equilibrium, we note that Young (1928) recognises the theory's emphasis on the interrelated nature of an economy. Despite this praiseworthy feature, Young views general equilibrium as unsuitable for the study of the impact of increasing returns because this type of equilibrium cannot account for the, "... counter forces which are continually defeating the forces which make for economic equilibrium ..." (Young 1928, 533). On the one hand, forces exterior to the economy, such as inventions, create cumulative change throughout the economy. On the other hand, forces which are contained within the economy, such as increasing returns, call forth responses throughout the industrial structure so that change, "... propagates itself in a cumulative way" (Young 1928, 533).[16] Since the subject of increasing returns is inadequately treated by both Marshallian and Walrasian economics, one can argue that Knight laid the foundations for an analytical framework which focuses on the effects which increasing returns have on the economy. In particular, this framework focuses on the impact which increasing returns have on the distribution of economic power. Just as industrial change propagates itself in a cumulative fashion, so too do the benefits of such change accrue to the owners of industrial capital. This distributional aspect of Young's theory of increasing returns in part explains why Knight refers to the growth of power imbalance as 'cumulative' (Knight 1947a, 5-9; Knight 1951b, 295). The other reason for the growth of power imbalance being cumulative is peculiar to Knight, centres around his analysis of uncertainty. Investment in human capital, when combined with greater capacity to exploit the opportunities presented by uncertainty, results in an enhancement of the imbalance of economic power.

In summary, Knight argues that both partial and general equilibrium models are incapable of incorporating any change in the value of underlying variables, such as the concentration of economic power. Unequal capacities to deal with uncertainty prevent economic actors from attaining any form of static equilibrium. Instead, those increasing returns, which are mainly derived from the capacity to reduce the costs which emanate from uncertainty force the economy away from an equilibrium position: this point demonstrates that the incorporation of increasing returns into the standard analysis of efficiency, entails accounting for the distributional effects of such returns. Such an account is absent from the static framework within which the standard notion of efficiency is commonly analysed. A dynamic framework of analysis is vitally needed.

The Analytic Assumptions Underlying the Standard Notion of Efficiency

Of all the three classes of assumptions, which Knight identifies, this is the most repugnant to him. In order to identify economic efficiency as socially ideal, Knight emphasises, one must also implicitly assume that the initial distribution of goods, before exchange, is the best possible (Knight 1921a, 85-6). This assumption is untenable and represents a recurrent theme in Knight's academic career.

For example, in *Freedom and Reform* (1947a) he writes:

> The argument of the body of this paper has shown that an appeal to maximum freedom as a "standard" involves a fallacy. The result is a dogmatic acceptance of an existing distribution of power, which is an ethical proposition, a value-judgement in disguise, and an ethically indefensible one (Knight 1947a, 14).

Knight interprets the assumptions underlying the idealisation of perfect competition as a sort of sanctification of power imbalance.

> The principle [of maximum freedom] merely settles the ethical problem by decreeing fixity for all eternity of the *existing* distribution of means of enjoyment, as measured by a process the results of which also depend on the starting point. By a twofold *petitio-principii* it sanctifies *the status quo* [brackets added] (Knight 1947a, 5).

Apart from methodological considerations, Knight views the standard notion of efficiency (which embraces perfect competition), as a means of justifying social injustice. From an historical perspective the standard notion of 'economic efficiency' takes on the appearance of an apology for power imbalance.

> Regarding the precise extent to which classical economics and the pain-cost theory of value were, or are, consciously or unconsciously, formulated or taught for the purpose of apologetic, it is clearly useless to speculate. But viewing the matter historically one can hardly help watching the sanctity of property take the divine right of Kings as the main principle of social order, as the latter displaced ecclesiastical hegemony, with theorists shifting their ground as the fads change (Knight 1947a, 9-10).

Economic theory therefore, quite plainly makes the judgement on the rightness of the current power imbalance, according to Knight. Whether humans are able to devise a better way of diffusing economic power, other than by saying that the original endowments are the best is unclear (Knight 1947a, 9). In summary, we show that Knight is vehemently opposed to the acceptance of the existing endowments of economic power as representing the best possible distribution of power. According to Knight, this means that the standard notion of efficiency is based on an unacceptable theory of distribution which came into being because economics failed to grasp the distinction between economic freedom and economic power.

> The fatal defect in the utilitarian doctrine of maximum freedom as a goal of social policy is its confusion of freedom and power. Its advocates overlook the fact that freedom to perform an act is meaningless unless the subject is in possession of the requisite means of action, and that the practical question is one of power rather than formal freedom (Knight 1947a, 4).

Knight's Proposed Revision of the Notion of Value Used to Measure Efficiency

According to the idealising assumptions of Knight's critique, the standard notion of economic efficiency involves assuming a competitive structure which is highly unstable. This is so because the incentives to monopoly become magnified in the presence of uncertainty, rendering the perfectly competitive market a temporary state of affairs. Control of these incentives requires regulation by an authoritarian State. In a similar manner, the static system assumptions, which are contained in the standard notion of efficiency are rejected, because of their inability to incorporate other determinants of value into the economic system. In this case, the exclusion of increasing returns, and its resultant distributional effects, renders the standard notion of efficiency untenable for Knight.

In addition, the implicit analytic assumption, which is embedded in the standard notion of efficiency, is deemed inadequate by Knight. The standard notion of efficiency is rejected by Knight, because it is not supported by a demonstrably sound grasp of the philosophical issues which underpin the standard notion of efficiency. As elucidated earlier, Knight searches for an appropriate framework for the study of economic efficiency. Because Knight rejects the entire taxonomy of assumptions which underlie the standard notion of efficiency, he suggests that the standard notion of social welfare is deficient; a new conception of the 'social welfare function' is required. As a result, we must now develop the salient features of Knight's 'social welfare function': such a function requires a rigorous examination of the relationship between economic efficiency, economic freedom, and economic power. Each of these three goals, which hitherto have been treated as independent, are addressed in the following section under the heading of the 'Knightian Pyramid'.

Knightian Pyramid

Introduction

The 'Knightian Pyramid' is an explanatory device, which is developed to highlight the relationships which link the various elements of the economic problem: economic freedom, power balance, and economic efficiency. All three elements are to be treated as valid objectives which make claims on the structure of the economy, according to Knight. As we have observed throughout this Chapter, Knight visualises certain significant tensions between these objectives. The term 'pyramid' is employed so as to emphasise these important interrelationships, in a cohesive and sophisticated manner.

Rationale for the 'Pyramid' Structure

In order to outline this explanatory device, we ask you to imagine the apex of a pyramid representing the simultaneous optimality of economic freedom, balance of power and economic efficiency, throughout the entire economy. As these three elements of the economic desiderata depart from their optimal level, a tension begins to emerge between all three elements. As economic welfare deteriorates, the tensions between all three elements intensifies as we move closer to the base of the pyramid. The base of the pyramid, therefore, represents a situation of maximum tension between the three elements.[17]

In the below diagram, we represent Knight's social welfare function in three dimensional space. Economic welfare is conceptually measured by the vertical axis OO". As we note, the lowest possible level of economic welfare is located at the base of the pyramid, and this point is indicated on the vertical welfare axis at point O. Here, the incongruity between all three objectives is highest, and the majority of economic actors have little economic freedom while the minority of economic actors are super-wealthy. Tensions, between the majority of economic actors and the government, create a threat for the free-market system. Indeed, such tensions present a risk of the free-market system being overthrown by a highly inefficient authoritarian State. This is the scenario which Knight wishes to avoid (Knight 1935c, 310-11; Knight 1921a, 119-21; 1947a, 9-47; Knight 1960). In contrast, position A on the pyramid represents the point where the government achieves an optimal balance between all three objectives. Here, little, if any, incongruity exists between the objectives. Such an optimal position represents the highest level of economic welfare, which we represent as point O'' on the vertical welfare axis. In between these two extremes lies an example of the existing free-market economy, whose level of welfare corresponds to point O' on the vertical welfare axis. Knight is concerned that many free-market economies are concentrating on the achievement of economic efficiency, to the exclusion of the other two components of the 'social welfare function'. In the long-run, Knight argues that such polices will reduce economic freedom and enhance the imbalance of economic power; this has serious consequences for efficiency. The long-run outcome of such policies is the deterioration of economic efficiency because of the linkages which exist in Knight's 'social welfare function', but which are absent in the 'social welfare function' of orthodox economic theory. Policies which genuinely aim to increase welfare, therefore, unintentionally reduce economic welfare.[18]

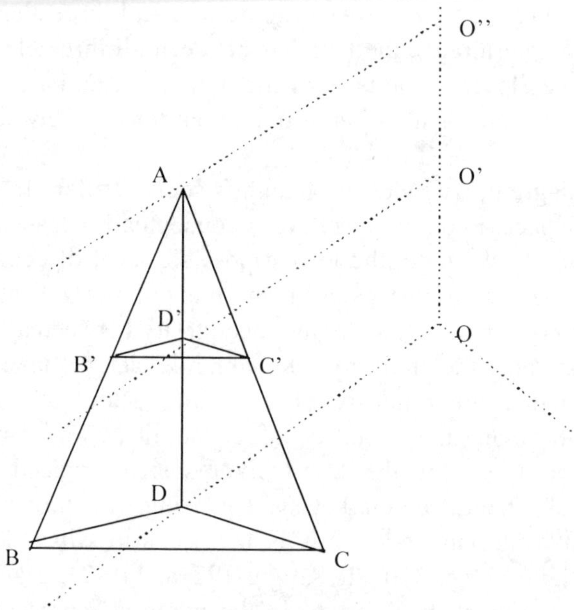

A = 'Optimal' Combination of Economic Power Balance, Economic Freedom and Efficiency

B = Lowest Possible Level of Economic Freedom

C = Lowest Possible Level of Economic Efficiency

D = Maximum Inequality of Economic Power

(Knight 1920a, 29-32; 1921a, 180-93; 1943c, 59-118;1947a, 5-14; 1951b 17-19; 1956a, 291).

Figure 2.2 The Knightian Pyramid: Knight's Conceptualisation of the 'Social Welfare Function'

This schema can be illustrated with reference to the imbalance of economic power. In this case, the more remote the balance of economic power is from its optimal position, the greater the effect marginal movements in the balance of economic power have on both the economic freedom and economic efficiency. Proximity to the base of the pyramid, therefore, tends to amplify the interdependence of the three elements. To briefly recapitulate, this analysis yields the proposition that the imbalance of economic power is increasing at an increasing rate. As the imbalance of power increases, we argue that a certain acceleration - away from optimality - occurs. Along with this acceleration away from optimality, it can be assumed that the remaining two elements will be forced away from optimality at a similar rate. The rationale for this assumption is explained by the significant tensions which exist between these three aspects of the economic system.[19]

> [The enterprise system] broke down precisely in failing to solve the problems which have arisen naturally out of progress, especially the *cumulative tendency towards inequality* [of economic power] [brackets and emphasis added] (Knight 1921a, 119-21; Knight1947a, 9-47).

It appears that Knight envisaged an unidentified mid-point between the extremes of power balance, as the optimal allocation of economic power in a given economy. Lack of sufficient detail on exactly what this mid-point consists of, or how it might be achieved, is not easily accessible in Knight's works. However, we conclude that this points to the innate complexity of the question. By highlighting these complexities Knight provides scope for subsequent generations of economists to enlarge and develop his analysis of the economic problem. Despite this lack of detail, it is possible to discern that, a conceptual framework is required to unify the analysis of this element of the economic problem with the other two elements, namely economic freedom and efficiency.

The essential point to note, in deriving this representation of Knightian economics, is the close interrelationship between all three parts of the economic problem. Without emphasising these important linkages it appears that the interpretation of Knight's contribution to economic theory is difficult, if not impossible. This approach expands the work of Kern, who suggests that a fundamental unity exists in Knight's work, which Kern expresses as *Knight's Three Commandments* (Kern 1987). In contrast to Kern, this thesis discerns the existence of the three elements in the 'social welfare function', as well as the existence of significant tensions between each element. Following Hammond's exposition, the present thesis shall incorporate Knight's normative approach to welfare economics (Knight 1933c; Hammond 1990). In addition, we re-examine the implicit value judgements made by orthodox economic theory (Knight 1947a, 14). It is this re-examination which best illustrates Knight's introduction of economics into a broader social context, as indicated by Schweitzer (Schweitzer 1975). Having outlined the rationale for the 'Knightian

Pyramid' we shall now seek to establish a more detailed account of the various linkages involved.

The Relation between Economic Power and Economic Efficiency

Perfect imbalance of power generates two significant problems: (i) a 'social problem' which is associated with a lack of economic freedom, and (ii) an 'efficiency problem' which is associated with a smothering of competition. First, the 'social' problem, as Knight describes it, tends to increase with the imbalance of economic power.

> Where incomes range from nothing up to tens of millions of dollars per year, it is idle to prate of equality, and the concentration of pecuniary power amounts in fact to the disinheritance and disenfranchisement of the great masses of people (Knight 1920a, 31).

This social problem results in a feeling of dictatorial control, on the part of those without substantive economic freedom (Knight 1943c, 105). This feeling, if left unchecked, may prompt well meaning reformers to call for radical change, thereby jeopardising current economic freedom. This threat to free markets constitutes the 'social problem' for Knight, where the existing system of exchange is firstly challenged by reformers and is then replaced by a governmentally controlled system. Claims that monopolies and business cycles are the instruments of hidden economic dictators are, according to Knight, manifestations of this romantic tendency which fails to confront the real problem of how to diffuse economic power in a responsible manner (Knight 1943c, 100-13). In the case of extreme power imbalance, the 'social problem' will intensify and consequently threaten the free-market. Measures which are aimed at controlling power imbalance, therefore, need to be instituted in order to prevent this situation from occurring.

Knight argues that the 'social philosophy' of utilitarianism blinds economists to this problem by focusing on formal rather than substantive economic freedom. Consequently, economic efficiency, as it is traditionally defined by economic history, does not yield an ideal or 'just' result. Even though free markets encourage economic progress Knight is arguing that those with economic power are more likely to constitute the group which reap the benefits of economic progress, due to, among other things, the investment in human capital.

> The conclusion that perfect competition would involve both maximum freedom and maximum efficiency, and ideal 'justice', as between given individuals, means only that the fruits of productive activity would be distributed on the basis of economic power ... possessed as any time by each individual ... (Knight 1943c, 114).

However, Knight argues that ill-conceived attempts to diffuse substantive economic freedom are even more dangerous than utilitarianism, which chooses to remain blind to the problem.

> But the current 'neo-liberal' reaction against this view, in the direction of Statism as a remedy for inequality, is political romanticism and even more dangerous (Knight 1943c, 80).

For Knight, 'Statism' as a remedy for imbalance of economic power is dangerous for three main reasons: (i) economic actors must be educated to wisely employ economic power (Knight 1943c, 81), (ii) although social institutions help bind society, they are also resistant to change, and (iii) Knight mistrusts economic reformers because he perceives their motives as usually being centred on their own self-aggrandisement, rather than on the common good (Knight 1947a). Indeed, Knight concludes his presidential address to the American Economic Association by expressing his contempt for economic reformers.

> ... I mistrust reformers. When a man or group asks for power to do good, my impulse is to say, "oh yeah, who ever wanted power for any other reason?" and what have they done when they got it? So, I instinctively want to cancel the last three words, leaving simply "I want power"; that is easy to believe (Knight 1951b, 29).

As Knight points out economic reformers, "... know nothing about economics ... have no idea what their own ethical ideals are ... and, ... they are also ignorant of the relations between economics and law and the cultural process ..." (Knight 1939e, 278-9). Knight's description of the delicate intricacies of the 'social welfare function', when combined with his awareness of the rashness of economic actors, delivers what Allyn Young calls 'social wisdom' to the debate on policy issues (Young 1927b, 25; Knight 1943a, 93). A fundamental incongruity, between the complexity of the subject matter and the impetuosity of economic actors, forces Knight to exercise prudence in exposing his ideas.

This means that neither social institutions nor economic actors can be rapidly transformed, without jeopardising either cohesion of society or the efficient usage of resources (Knight 1943c, 82). Social cohesion is also threatened by the steady growth in the size of the economy, because the difficulty of effective inter-communication tends to increase at an increasing rate (Knight 1943c, 86). This not only means that the imbalance of economic power will grow, but that the feeling of dictatorial control will also intensify. Ignoring the social problem which is largely caused by the imbalance of economic power would only result in risking the small amount of economic freedom which currently exists.

> ... private enterprise has, indeed 'worked' in the past, but it seems clear that it no longer works in even a relatively tolerable fashion, and is heading for complete collapse (Knight 1920a, 30).

Extreme imbalance of economic power leads to yet another problem which Knight describes as the 'efficiency problem', where competition is smothered (Knight 1947a, 81). This will ultimately create an economy which is unable to change or progress, because it will stifle any viable form of competition.

> In the absence of preventative measures, ... concentration of power ... would be inevitable and must before long smother the combative process in monopoly and other impediments to readjustment (Knight 1947a, 31).

In addition, Knight maintains that a reduction in uncertainty will ultimately bring a halt to economic process. This is caused by either a perfect diffusion of economic power (enforced by a communist-style government) or a perfect imbalance of economic power. In both cases uncertainty tends to decrease as a result of the rigid control of economic power. Consequently, economic actors will cease to invest in new ventures, the opportunity to significantly increase economic power having vanished: this would represent the end of economic progress for Knight (Knight 1921a, 333). In other words, rigid control of economic power tends to stifle the incentive toward economic progress.

Furthermore, the highly concentrated nature of economic power makes the large firm less likely to innovate or invent new products. Even if these innovations are successful, the relative increase in economic power is marginal when compared to the large portion of market power which is already enjoyed by the large firm. A preference for reliable - rather than potentially much more efficient - technologies emerges; the large firm becomes highly conservative. Further rigidities are caused on the demand side, where consumption patterns become inflexible due to the lack of opportunities for social mobility (Knight 1943c, 115-6). Consequently, consumption patterns become inflexible due to the lack of opportunity to increase economic power which then further stifles the incentive for entrepreneurial initiative. In general, therefore, the smothering of economic progress tends to reduce any incentive towards efficient action on the part of economic actors, both on the consumption and production side.

> [I]t goes without saying that very large incomes relax or destroy the incentive to efficient action [brackets added] (Knight 1920a, 31-2).

In turning toward a more detailed consideration of perfect balance of economic power, we first define this term as the situation where every economic actor controls an equal share of economic power. Such balance of economic power is broadly equivalent to that embodied in the traditional economic assumptions, especially the analytical assumptions, which are harshly criticised in Knight's definition of economic efficiency. Although perfect balance of economic power is conceptually attractive, this distribution of economic power suffers from much the same problem as a perfect imbalance of economic power (Knight 1920a, 31). A social problem arises in the case of a perfect balance of economic power, because of its dependence on the authoritarian State. In addition, an efficiency problem arises, because no allowance is being made for differential natural talent and effort.

Knight views the perfectly competitive as unstable, requiring governmental regulation. As shown above, this instability stems form an inadequate conception of the notion of value which underlies efficiency. Incorporation of economic freedom and power into this notion of value is required in order to remedy this inadequacy, thereby avoiding the need for such governmental regulation (Knight 1921a, 193). Acceptance of an authoritarian State - for the purpose of regulating the growth of economic power - is required if perfect competition is to be regarded as a stable economic arrangement. However, such a level of governmental intervention would lead us back into what Knight (1921a) terms the social problem. Just as large power imbalance causes feelings of coercion, so too would perfect power balance. In other words, Knight argues that we cannot escape some degree of coercive sentiment lingering in the community, however we must ensure that this sentiment does not get out of control.

Another problem which flows from a perfect balance of economic power is what can be broadly described as the 'efficiency problem' associated with perfect balance of economic power. If an authoritarian State were to maintain a perfect balance of economic power, then there would be no allowance for different levels of natural talent in the management of economic power. This is because economic actors have no incentive to develop and utilise capacities, as they cannot attain any more economic power than any other economic actor. Some degree of incentive, by way of rewarding meritorious effort with different levels of economic power, seems the most reliable means of encouraging economic actors to develop and utilise their diverse talents.

> Probably few would advocate complete equality [of economic power] ... A wide diffusion of power is ethically imperative, yet a certain concentration of power in the hands of those who can use it effectively is economically necessary [brackets added] (Knight 1920a, 31).

While investment in human capital can improve natural talents it cannot replace them immediately. By this we mean that the differential in natural talent for the management of economic resources, although relatively marginal (small), tends to be amplified by investment in human capital. In this regard those with human economic power are better able to manage economic resources, not because of a large differential in natural talent, but because of investment in human capital and the effects such investment has on economic character. Consequently, problems occur in attempting to quickly diffuse economic power, simply because it takes time to invest in human capital. In addition, a problem of granting incentives for effort is encountered. Differential levels of effort, Knight says, are neither rewarded nor penalised by the perfectly balanced allocation of economic power. Perfect balance of economic power, therefore, provides no inducement for economic actors to either develop dormant natural talents, or use existing talents more intensively.

Perfect imbalance of economic power gives rise to two major economic problems. First, is what Knight describes as the 'social' problem, which has already been discussed.[20] Secondly, economic freedom is jeopardised. In addressing the second question Knight emphasises that, ultimately, perfect imbalance of economic power tends to extinguish economic freedom (Knight 1920a, 31; Knight 1947a, 5-10). Extreme imbalance of economic power leads to a situation of 'unfreedom' for the average economic actor. By lacking surplus economic power the average economic actor has no capacity to increase his or her economic power over time, being unable to either: (a) invest in human capital, or (b) seize opportunities made available by uncertainty. In other words, each economic actor becomes the prisoner of his sociological environment, so that his ability to responsibly administer economic resources - his economic freedom- becomes fashioned within this environment. As Viner (1958) says, economic freedom is a 'cultural' phenomena where poverty 'breeds' poverty (Viner 1958, 134; Gill 1992).[21]

Perfect imbalance of economic power tends to specifically relate to 'the disenfranchisement of the great masses of people' (Knight 1920a, 31). Without the opportunity to invest in human capital or the financial capacity to take advantage of the opportunities which are presented by uncertainty, those who lack surplus economic power have little chance of attaining economic freedom at any future time.

> The property-less and ill-paid masses protest not merely against the privations of a low scale of living, but against the terms of what they feel to be unfair contest in which being defeated by the stacking of the cards against them is perhaps as important to their feelings as the physical significance of the stakes which they lose (Knight 1935c, 60).

On the other hand, Knight argues that the social problem which is generated by the presence of an authoritarian State would make the average economic actor unable to alter his or her substantive economic freedom. This is because all economic actors have freedom equilibrated by the State (Knight 1921a, 193). A problem of economic freedom, as outlined above, would also eventuate in this situation. Here economic actors have no ability to alter economic freedom because the State maintains a perfect balance of economic power through time. In this regard, the Russian revolution of 1917, and the subsequent communist arrangement of economic affairs, most probably influenced Knight. It is reasonable to assume that Knight viewed the high concentration of political power in Russia as a standard to which the capitalist countries might be tending: Knight is disturbed by this standard.

> The elevation of the separate contributions of individuals to the social total is overwhelmingly a matter of force and not of right and the inequalities tend overwhelmingly to reduce and not increase 'total satisfaction' (Knight 1947a, 8).

Even if all inequalities of economic power were to be removed by the State, then the average economic actor would still be denied the freedom to alter his economic position. In other words, by restraining the economic actor from enjoying an opportunity to improve his economic power there is no incentive to efficient action: whether the State or a highly concentrated balance of power imposes this restriction is irrelevant to this outcome. In this way, Knight reveals the possibility of a free-market economy which smothers any incentive to efficient action by failing to regulate the imbalance of economic power. Too little regulation of the imbalance of economic power can be just as dangerous as too much. Knight urges us to avoid both forms of regulation - only by challenging economic actors with an opportunity to seize the benefits of economic progress can we hope to promote sustainable economic efficiency.

The Relation between Economic Freedom and Economic Efficiency

A high level of economic freedom induces both producers and consumers to increase their respective levels of effort toward the more efficient usage of economic resources (Knight 1943c, 71). This pattern of inducement of efficient action has already been outlined, with regard to the relation between economic power and economic efficiency.[22] Economic freedom is the factor which is important for maximising efficient usage of economic resources and minimising the problems of power imbalance. This is why Knight views freedom as an important value in its own right (Knight 1951b, 17-9).

Despite the benefits which accrue from high levels of economic freedom, Knight (1921a) argues that the cumulative imbalance of economic power generates increasingly low levels of economic freedom upon the economy.

> In real life the possession of property is supposed to represent ... some contribution to social progress. But it is clear that there is no technical equivalence between these services of social progress and the right to their entire fruits in perpetuity, and to confer it on to one's heirs and assigns forever ... (Knight 1921a, 180).

While the practically highest level of economic freedom is consistent with the socially optimal position of maximum economic efficiency, the important thing to note here is that this optimal level of economic freedom is dependent upon the optimal level of power imbalance. This means that if the economy is not at this optimal level of power imbalance then the relationship between the two other dimensions becomes incongruous.

By way of illustration, it can be shown that bringing either economic freedom or economic efficiency closer to their optimal levels, when economic power is not at its optimal level of imbalance, has negative repercussions for the other two factors. On a more practical level, policies which are aimed at increasing efficiency - for example relaxation of anti-trust law when a large imbalance of economic power exists - will allow those with economic power to further augment their own power. This will drive the imbalance of economic power further away from its optimal position, reducing economic freedom as well. Conversely, Knight argues that the compulsory redistribution of wealth is highly problematic, because investment in human capital is required to ensure the permanence of such a redistribution. For example, the predisposition to spend must be altered by investment in human capital so as to ensure that redistributed wealth is not squandered.[23] However, Knight argues that such investment takes a significant period of time. In other words, Knight argues that the time-lags involved in investment in human capital prevent policy makers from permanently altering the distribution of wealth in a short period of time.

Even though this analysis of human nature can be criticised as being somewhat static, we view this analysis as generally being consistent with Knightian economics. This is because Knight's conservative approach to economic change is based on the proposition that the alteration of an economic actor's habits cannot be made instantaneously. Rather, a significant period of time is required so as to change the economic character of the impecunious economic actor. In this way Knight deals with the problematic issue of how economic expectations tend to be dampened by economic deprivation: sociological conditioning constrains the flexibility of economic character (or economic freedom in general). Poverty is, therefore, a 'cultural' problem which cannot be quickly changed (Viner 1958, 134). Rather than attempting to transform the economic system, by means of a radical shift in the diffusion of economic power Knight prefers to bring about change in a gradual and sustainable manner. For Knight, education is the instrument of this gradual cultural change (Knight 1956a, 291).

Conclusion

We conclude that the examination of Frank Knight's conception of welfare economics reveals the existence of what we term the 'Knightian Pyramid'. Knight's 'social welfare function' is not reducible to Pareto's notion of economic efficiency, rather it is comprised of the three components (economic freedom, the balance of economic power, and economic efficiency). This representation of his 'social welfare function' allows us to conceptually measure the value of economic efficiency in comparison to economic freedom and economic power. Instead of following orthodox economic theory, by emphasising the standard concept of economic efficiency, Knight's peculiar interest in economic power suggests a more integrated approach to economic policy. By highlighting the significant tensions between the various components of this 'social welfare function', we deliver a more objective framework for the policy maker. This interactive relationship between economic power balance, freedom, and efficiency forms the core of Knight's approach to economic policy (Knight 1935c, 353). As Knight says, "The question of *policy* is a question of alternatives, a purely relative matter" (Knight 1935c, 45).

This procedure is consistent with what other economists have recently discovered in Knight's works. For example, Kern (1987) referring to *Intelligence, and Democratic Action* (Knight 1960) describes this procedure as Knight's, 'three commandments';

> (1) compare the alternatives, beginning with an understanding of what they are, (2) appraise the alternatives, (3) act on the basis of the best knowledge and judgement that is to be had (Kern 1987, 639-40).

Another important feature of the 'Knightian Pyramid' is that it graphically portrays the significant tensions between all three components of Knight's description of the 'social welfare function'. Well meaning attempts to increase welfare, eventually cause unintended reductions in welfare. As the imbalance of economic power increases, the incongruity which exists with the other two components intensifies. Knight argues that this conflict may, at some stage, lead to the breakdown of the free-market system (Knight 1935c, 309).

> [The free-market system] broke down precisely in failing to solve the problems which have arisen naturally out of progress, especially the cumulative tendency toward inequality [of economic power] [brackets added] (Knight 1935c, 310-11).

The final feature of the 'Knightian Pyramid' is the way it assists in sharpening our perceptions of the overall social ideal. Without a clear understanding of what society desires we find that economists, being only part of society, have the invidious task of policy formulation for all of society. By explaining the significant tensions between the different components of the 'social welfare function', economists are better equipped to conceive of the overall social ideal: economists often conceive of this ideal somewhat differently to the general public (Young 1915, 214).

Simultaneously balancing economic efficiency with both economic freedom and the imbalance of economic power, is the daunting task which Knight assigns to economic theory. However, this ideal cannot be achieved immediately, rather it should be accomplished in a gradual and perspicacious manner. As Knight says, "All reflection on the problem of a society changing itself tends to emphasise the necessity of 'gradualness'" (Knight 1935c, 348).

If such a balance, between all three parts of the 'social welfare function' can be achieved then we will have found a way of preserving the free-market system: Knight (1935) argues that the free-market system is worth preserving because it is responsible for the, "... promotion of progress, to a degree undreamed of in any other region in history" (Knight 1935c, 310-11). Alternatively, if we continue to take a narrow approach to welfare economics, then the incongruities between different economic objectives will be exacerbated. In this case, the free-market system will suffer from what we believe is a preventable malady, until it is smothered (Knight 1947a, 311). In other words, broadening the scope of welfare economics, to include all three components of the 'social welfare function', cannot remain an option for economic theory; Knight regards it as a necessary condition for the preservation of the free-market system.

Notes

1 Knight gradually introduces the meaning of economic freedom in his two essays *The Meaning of Freedom* (1943c) and *The Ideal of Freedom* (1943c). These essays are contained *in The Philosophy of American Democracy* (ed) C.M. Perry (Knight 1943c).

2 This definition of economic freedom is similar to Berlin's definition of "negative freedom" (Berlin 1987, 123, 153). Negative freedom is, "... being free in the sense I mean not being interfered with by others. The wider the area of non-interference the wider my freedom" (Berlin 1987, 123, 153). While Berlin's definition contributes to the discussion of freedom, it represents only a small part of the debate on the subject; Knight is very much immersed in this ancient debate. For example, Knight refers to the philosophy of Hegel in his discussion of perfect competition being inherently self-contradictory (Knight 1921a, 193; Chamberlin 1933, 4). Hegel contributes to the debate by examining the question of whether freedom can exist in society, while Kant argues that freedom in a society might be best achieved through the clear specification of personal freedoms (Kolb 1986, 101). In this way, Knight's contrasting of individual with social freedom reflects the themes which are both relevant to a discussion of economic theory and an examination of the great philosophical texts. As Gildin (1983) points out in his discussion of Rousseau's *Social Contract*; "To enter political society means to abandon the right to act however one pleases, ... It means to be guided by the general will rather than by one's own will" (Gildin 1983, 156).

3 Consideration of these constraints imbues an extra layer of difficulty on the definition of economic freedom. Not only does Knight argue that deficiencies in economic power can constrain economic action, but he also contends that economic freedom is vacuous without economic power (Knight 1943c, 60). Orthodox theory does not address this contention, rather it chooses to sweep such difficulties under the rug. "The problem of defining freedom is found to be that of clarifying the relationship between desire to act and the power to act" (Knight 1943c, 64). Knight describes this relationship as a series of complex categories, which cloud the definitional issues, surrounding economic freedom.

> This complex mixture of categories, none of which can be clearly defined, makes the problem of defining freedom, for practical purposes, an extremely difficult one (Knight 1943c, 75).

4 On the one hand, we can say that potential benefits from trade come into existence, which are not available to the isolated Crusoe. On the other hand, Knight suggests that even these benefits limit the freedom of the

isolated economic actor. As we will discover in Chapter Five, the restraints on economic freedom emerge from differential access to market knowledge. Such differential access bestows differential benefits on economic actors from enhancements to economic efficiency.

5 We will not develop this aspect of Knight's analysis of economic freedom because Schweitzer largely provides an examination of this in his description of the influence of Weber on Knight (Schweitzer 1975, 280).

6 In other words, substantive economic freedom and economic power are interrelated. We develop this proposition in Chapter Two of this book. However, economic power and substantive economic freedom are not interchangeable terms because economic power does not take into account the sociological conditioning of the economic actor.

7 Since these factors are difficult to quantify, the incorporation of such factors into positivistic economics is problematical. See Hammond (1990) for a discussion of the relationship between Knight and positivistic economics.

8 Because of the economic actor's capacity to diversify his portfolio of investments.

9 This capacity stems from the large firm's ability to control the costs which emanate from uncertainty. We discuss these costs in Chapter Four and Chapter Five.

10 An example of this is Knight's essay, *Free Society, its Basic Nature and Problem* (1956a).

11 For example, Knight quotes J.M. Clark in *Risk, Uncertainty, and Profit* (Knight 1921a, 62).

> We carry some wants to complete satiety because it takes less effort than would be required to calculate accurately the most desirable place to stop when this point would be near the absolute satiety limit, as in the case of eating bread, for example. The fact may serve to illustrate the fundamental 'irrationality' of a perfectly 'rational' attitude to life. One of our most significant 'wants' is freedom from the bother of calculating things or making close estimates (Knight 1921a, 62).

12 We can include the cost of making an economic decision in the calculation of the optimal outcomes for economic actors. However, we argue that Knight introduces such costs for another more important purpose. We develop this argument in Chapters Four and Five. However, we point out at this stage that the cost of making decisions, as well as the accuracy of those decisions, is the general way Knight explains the differentiation of cost in imperfectly competitive markets.

13 In addition, we argue that the same false scientific confidence in mathematical economics re-merges after World War Two; it lead to the establishment of a highly orthodox approach to policy which seeks to restrain the role of government. Paradoxically, one of the leaders of this orthodox movement is one of Knight's students, Milton Friedman. As Miller (1962) says;

> The way in which Milton Friedman and other modern Chicagoans concentrate their attack on government interference with the market represents a major departure from the earlier Chicago [or Knightian] position [brackets added] (Miller 1962, 67).

14 More specifically, we argue that better access to the available stock of market information reduces the costs associated with uncertainty. We detail this procedure in Chapters Four and Five. In addition, we provide an explanation of how Knight came to conceive of this procedure in Chapter Three.

15 Young (1928) argues that increasing returns cannot be incorporated into Marshallian partial equilibrium (Hart 1989).

16 While Blitch notes that Knight and Young differ on the precise meaning and distinction between statics and dynamics, as these terms relate to increasing and decreasing returns, the relevance of Young's analysis on Knight's economic thought is, nevertheless, apparent (Blitch 1983b, 361-4).

17 In other words, the height of the pyramid allows us to conceptually measure economic welfare. If policy makers attempt to move any of the elements independently, then an unintended fall in economic welfare (as measured by the height of the pyramid) will result. Knight argues that any independent move of an element will create imbalance which will eventually force the other two elements lower. Over time, all three elements will be lower as an unintended result of the policy maker's actions. Only by simultaneously moving all three elements higher can a policy maker hope to improve economic welfare. Knight, therefore, forces the policy maker to recognise the requirement for a balanced approach to economic policy, rather than one which seeks to increase economic efficiency at all costs. In addition, the policy maker is forced to consider the broader social ramifications of policy in the medium to long-run, rather than the short-run efficiency effects.

18 Considering the work of Knight as a whole, I suggest that various policy combinations can be ranked. In the below diagram I illustrate an economy which attempts the fairly orthodox policy mix, which ranks efficiency ahead of moderating the imbalance of economic power and maximising overall economic freedom. Here, such an economic policy mix moves the

economy from the position BCD to BC'D, so that economic efficiency is promoted ahead of the other two objectives. However, according to Knight, the tensions which underlie the various components of the 'social welfare function' will create a situation where the benefits of such a policy mix will increase the imbalance of economic power and reduce the overall level of economic freedom. Hence the economy will tend to slide away from the 'optimal' policy mix (namely, point A); from BD to B"D". In addition, the social tensions which result from such a deterioration in the economy will force economic efficiency from C' to C". In other words, the long-run position of the policy mix which attempts to promote social welfare by narrowly focusing on one component of the 'social welfare function' will normally result in a reduction in all the objectives of the 'social welfare function' over the long-run.

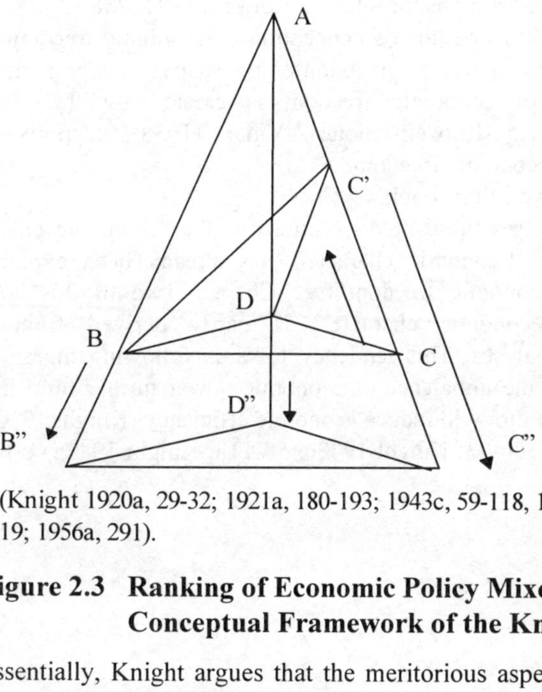

(Knight 1920a, 29-32; 1921a, 180-193; 1943c, 59-118, 1947a, 5-14; 1951b, 17-19; 1956a, 291).

Figure 2.3 Ranking of Economic Policy Mixes within the Conceptual Framework of the Knightian Pyramid

19 Essentially, Knight argues that the meritorious aspects of the free-market system tend to combine in such a way as to create some detrimental outcomes. Such a conclusion is shared with Berlin (1987), who notes that, "... not all good things are compatible, still less all the ideals of mankind" (Berlin 1987, 167). While Knight recognises the great prosperity which is generated by the free-market system, he also recognises that some problems exist in the distribution of this prosperity: a conflict of values emerges. On the one hand, there are those who argue that any tampering

with the free-market will jeopardise the prosperity generated by it. On the other hand, there are those who argue that the distribution of this prosperity is inequitable. In this respect Knight agrees with Berlin (1987), who argues that, "... it must be possible for all these values to live together, for unless this is so conflicts of values may be seen as an intrinsic, irremovable element in human life" (Berlin 1987, 167).

20 See Chapter Two of this book.

21 This conception of economic freedom can be contrasted to that of the modern Chicago school, as represented by Friedman (Friedman 1962; Friedman 1972). As Rotwein (1983) says,

> Friedman does not at all question whether market goods contribute to economic welfare. The question of human rationality is disposed of by the supposition that individuals behave as "responsible adults" (Rotwein 1983, 268).

The problem with Friedman's conception of economic freedom is that it ignores the way sociological conditioning shapes economic freedom; a heterogeneity of economic freedom is created by the sociological environment. As Rotwein notes, Viner (1958) supports Knight's conception of economic freedom.

22 See Chapter Two of this book.

23 Knight summarises these predispositions as the "economic character" of the individual. 'Economic character' has already been explained with reference to economic freedom (see Chapter Two of this book). The concept of 'economic character' is partly derived from Weber's sociological analyses. This tendency towards following ingrained habits will also force the imbalance of economic power further form its optimal position, and in turn will reduce economic efficiency (Knight 1920a, 29-32; Knight 1921a, 180-93; Knight 1943c, 59-118; Knight 1947a, 5-14; Knight 1951b, 17-9).

3 Intellectual Influences

Introduction

In seeking to explain the intellectual influences which underpin the development of the Knight's frame of thought we shall concentrate upon those authors who feature in Knight's first and most famous work, namely *Risk, Uncertainty, and Profit* (1921a). Although the theoretical conclusions which are contained in Chapter Two are derived from the totality of Knight's work, we will mainly limit our analysis of Knight's intellectual influences to this initial, yet highly persuasive work. This limitation is based on an assumption of continuity in Knight's work, which is consistent with the findings of Patinkin (1973a). Patinkin emphasises the strong continuity in Knight's thought on matters of ethics, individual freedom and the nature of the market system (Patinkin 1973a, 787-807). Patinkin comments on this continuity, with reference to a more limited examination of Knight, namely his lecture programme. Like Patinkin, we find a strong degree of continuity in a much broader examination of Knight's work.

> ... I remember characterising Knight's lectures at the time as being like a general equilibrium system - which could not be solved until the student was familiar with the set of Knight's articles that specified the relationships between the various parts of the lectures, and thus converted unknowns into knowns. And I still remember my feeling of satisfaction when I began to be able to see the system of equations as a whole - and things began to fall into place (Patinkin 1973a, 789).

In a similar vein, we propose that the analytical construct, which is described in Chapter Two, places Knight's arguments within a more structured framework of analysis. *Risk, Uncertainty, and Profit* (1921a) can be treated as providing the intellectual foundation from which Knight draws upon when developing his larger theoretical exposition.[1]

Generally, the underpinnings of the discussion in Chapter Two can be thought of as a revision of J.B. Clark's economics. In this revision Knight links the understanding of the industrialised economies of the late

Victorian age, with an analysis of the industrialised economies of the early twentieth century (Clark 1886, 1899). J.B. Clark is one of the predominant figures in Knight's intellectual development. However, he presents an apparent enigma to economists. Clark apparently changes his position on monopoly from a supporter, in his earlier writings, to a critic of monopoly, in the latter part of his career. Initially, J.B. Clark maintained the belief that that the economic system will evolve into a morally superior system; monopolies play an active role in forging this morally superior economy. However, with the advent of collusive behaviour, a more mature Clark came to realise that the system in general, and monopoly in particular, requires regulation. The purpose of this regulation is to enforce certain moral standards, which ensure that the economic system is not allowed to degenerate.[2] In order to arrive at 'fair' standards Clark is forced to seek a more adequate explanation of profit than that which is offered by orthodox economic theory. This explanation is necessary because 'fair' competition implies a 'fair' level of profit. Without a clear grasp of the economic basis of profit, the determination of both the existence and the level of profit becomes somewhat problematic. This is why Knight describes Clark as approaching the whole question of profit 'directly', meaning he sought to explain profit itself, rather than the "tendencies which other economists argue eliminate profit" (Knight 1921a, 22). Such an approach - although conceptually difficult - remains attractive to Knight.

This general approach of J.B. Clark's, however, only provides Knight with an initial orientation. The 'risk theorists', such as J.B.Hawley and I. Fisher, also contribute to the development of Knight's analysis. First, F.B. Hawley highlights the proposition that the information available to various economic agents is not homogeneous. Second, Knight modifies I. Fisher's interdisciplinary presuppositions; which involve the blending of economics with mathematics, statistics, and actuarial studies. Generally, he carries out this modification in his search for a more comprehensive understanding of uncertainty. More specifically, Knight shows how the confidence in estimating economic variables is a function of the firm's scale, relative to the scale of the market in which the firm operates.

Allyn Young's theory of increasing returns is also instrumental in Knight's development; Knight focuses on how decreasing the costs of operating in an uncertain environment can lead to increasing returns. The various aspects of this capacity are detailed in Chapter Eight of *Risk, Uncertainty, and Profit* (1921a). By expanding the scale of its operations, Knight shows that the firm is better able to reduce the costs associated with the control of uncertainty. In addition, Knight offers an explanation of how the scale of an industrialised firm can affect its capacity to reap the benefits from economic progress. Furthermore, we compare Knight and Young to Schumpeter, on the issue of monopoly regulation. Here, we conclude that Knight's analysis offers a substantial challenge to that of Schumpeter, and that Young's analysis tends to support this challenge.

Finally, we analyse the influence of J.M. Clark. Here, we show how Knight develops J.M. Clark's analysis of overhead costs, by demonstrating the effect scale has on production costs. Building on these analytical foundations, Knight concurs with J.M. Clark, on the requirement for government regulation of monopoly, which Clark later explores in his book *The Social Control of Business* (1925).

We conclude by noting Knight's special contribution to the revision of J.B. Clark's economics. In developing Clark's argument for a moral dimension in economics, we show how Knight re-defines the requirement for such a dimension. Knight's analysis of uncertainty allows this reappraisal because it focuses our attention on the connection between uncertainty and relative holdings of economic power. Knight indicates that the capacity to control uncertainty, on the one hand, and economic power, on the other, are positively correlated. Unequal capacities to control uncertainty create significant economic outcomes. For example, better control of uncertainty leads to a fall in the firm's volatility of earnings. As a result, credit rating agencies will improve the firm's credit rating, thereby enhancing the firm's access to credit. As opportunities arise, the firm will then be in a better position (compared to the larger firm) to participate in these opportunities. In this way, unequal capacity to control uncertainty translates, over the long-run, into an unequal participation in economic progress; some sort of moral dimension is required for economic theory to incorporate these significant outcomes within a coherent framework of analysis.

J.B. Clark

J.B. Clark - Introduction

J.B. Clark had three main influences upon Knight. All these influences demonstrate Knight's agreement with Clark on the general axioms which underpin economic theory. First Clark's lifelong interest in the moral dimension of economic theory becomes the central objective in Knight's economic analysis.[3] Indeed, Knight salvages Clark's argument for a moral dimension in economic theory. Here, Knight provides an innovative argument, which focuses on the implicit assumptions made by economic theory.[4] However, Knight avoids the problematic issues which Clark encounters in his attempt to define a moral dimension in economic theory.

The second major influence on Clark is that of analysing the inherent stability of the competitive system, upon the basis of existing imbalances of economic power. Like Clark, Knight is concerned that these imbalances might lead to instability in the competitive system. However, instead of basing his argument upon Clark's 'degraded' economic man, Knight sought to highlight the implicit distributive assumptions which are embedded in economic theory. These distributive assumptions indicate that 'efficiency' is not a descriptive noun, which is free of any distributive judgements. Rather, Knight argues that 'efficiency' has a strong normative basis, employing unacceptable distributive assumptions.

Lastly, and most importantly, Clark influences Knight in the analysis of profit as a permanent feature of economic systems. Once again, Knight disagrees with Clark, on the application of this idea to economic theory. Knight shows how Clark's economics, while arguing for the study of profit as a permanent feature of economic systems, avoids the discussion of uncertainty by employing the term 'friction'. Clark's explanation of profit is, therefore, shown to belong to the very orthodoxy which Clark opposes. In other words, Clark fails to appreciate the importance of the orthodox assumption that knowledge is assumed to be perfect. Knight challenges this assumption; only by accepting the presence of uncertainty can we account for profit. This is what Knight accomplishes.[5]

The Philosophy of Wealth

J.B. Clark's *The Philosophy of Wealth* (1886) provides us with a starting point from which we can evaluate his influence on Knight (Patinkin 1973a, 798; Stigler 1987, 57).[6] As part of a wide-ranging critique of the economic system J.B. Clark rejects what he perceives as, "certain leading principles of economic science" (Clark 1886, iii). An example of one of these principles is the definition which orthodox theory gives to 'economic man'. Clark argues that the economic man should be defined in a less selfish fashion than the way in which orthodox theory defines him. Clark argues that economic man seeks a somewhat "higher form of rational wealth" than that which is usually assumed of economic actors (Clark 1886, Ch. xi). In seeking a rationale for Clark's definition of economic man, we note Dorfman's analysis, which suggests that Clark is influenced by the English Christian Socialists of the 1850s (Dorfman 1949, 193). This religious theme in Clark's writing is developed in *The Philosophy of Wealth* (1886), where the economic actor is said to participate in the distribution of the, "highest forms of rational wealth" in a non-competitive fashion (Clark 1886, Ch. xi).

According to Clark we must recognise;

> ... the competitive struggle, wherever it survives, as the imperfect agent of moral law, a man may participate in it without taint. The bad effects of the contest he does not need to suffer; and to the lower levels, where the golden-calf worship is unhindered and blighting, he does not need to descend. It is his privilege to live on the mountain slope at the summit of which moral law reigns. He may buy, sell, and get gain, as well as give thanks and worship, with his eyes uplifted to the hills whence cometh his help (Clark 1886, 220).

In addition to the English Christian Socialists, Clark's analysis is influenced by the German Historical School. More specifically, one of Clark's most prominent influences, Karl Knies, makes Clark aware of the rich philosophical debate which surrounds the study of economics in Europe. The Hegelian tradition is evident in the work of Knies, who is an exponent of the German Historical School (Hildebrand 1955, 36). Apart from equipping Clark with a philosophical background - specialising in the branch of philosophy known as ethics - the German Historical School had a special interest in the moral underpinnings of economic theory. Dorfman (1955) detects this moral aspect of the German Historical School in John K. Ingram's speech to the British Association for the Advancement of Science in 1878. Here, Ingram argues that the Historical School opposes the proposition that wealth, "is the single ... object of human life" (Dorfman 1955, 21). Rather, the Historical School regards wealth, "as a means used by Humanity in its struggle towards moral ideals of life ..."(Dorfman 1955, 21; Hollander 1927, 1-5). Such an approach to the accumulation of wealth is deemed necessary, in order to avoid the equally unacceptable extremes of social revolution which tend to result in socialism and "rigid *laissez-faire*" (Dorfman 1955, 18-22).[7]

Clark's opposition to what he calls, the overly selfish assumptions of economic theory, can, therefore, be seen as attributable to the first axiom of the German Historical School (Clark 1886, 32-69; J.B and J.M. Clark 1912, 204). In addition, the tendency to study the historical development of economic phenomena, which is evident in Clark's study of the law of distribution, stems from axiom two of the Historical School (Clark 1886, 107-25). This tendency, to study chronological developments in economic variables, is especially prevalent in Clark's tracing of the historical growth of firms, or 'combinations', in Chapters Eight and Ten of *The Philosophy of Wealth* (Clark 1886, 107-48, 174-202).

Although the first two axioms of the German Historical School are evident in *The Philosophy of Wealth* (1886), Clark does not immediately emphasise the third axiom of the German Historical School (namely the right of the State to intervene) until later in his professional career (Clark 1899). This earlier position of Clark's is taken because, "the principle of cooperation" will eventually survive as the principle most suitable for society; such a principle is expressed in the form of industrial organisation termed 'profit sharing'. Clark thought that this form of organisation "may outlive" the other types of industrial organisation (Clark 1886, 187). For Clark, an evolution of industrial organisation exists; just as a better mechanical devise inevitably replaces an inferior one, so too will a better mode of industrial organisation (namely profit sharing) replace an inferior one (J.B. Clark 1886, 187). However, examples of market misconduct, such as the Standard Oil Case and the Tobacco Trusts, force a more mature Clark to abandon his earlier evaluation (Dewey 1958, 157). Instead of the 'fittest' form of industrial structure surviving, the trust problem erupted. In its path of large scale industrial collusion the trusts smothered the process of 'natural selection'. In addition, Clark's vision for a morally higher form of competitive process is smothered by the trusts. Frank A. Fetter expresses a similar conclusion in his speech, to the dinner in honour of J.B. Clark's eightieth birthday:

> In his twenties when young men can see visions, he [J.B. Clark] saw with his spiritual eye a finer, happier world, and in his *Philosophy of Wealth* he voiced his vision in the philosophy of optimism. Things have not moved exactly in the way, or perhaps the degree that he forecast them [brackets added] (Hollander 1927, 364).

Consequently, Clark began to recommend the third axiom of the German Historical School, namely government intervention so as to increase 'fair' competition.[8] This analysis demonstrates two main influences of Clark on Knight. Firstly J.B. Clark's economics shows a consistent pre-occupation with the moral underpinnings of economic theory. A similar pre-occupation with the moral foundations of economic theory is evident throughout Knight's work (Knight 1921a, 119-21; Knight 1935c, 611; Knight 1947a, 9-47).[9]

The second major influence of J.B. Clark's work on Knight flows naturally from the first influence. Given the attention Clark gave to the moral foundations of economic theory, an increasing imbalance of economic power suggests that the economic man was becoming somewhat 'degraded', and selfish (J.B. Clark 1899, 440). A stress upon the selfish acquisition of wealth, lead economic actors to accumulate wealth in such a way as to further accentuate the present imbalances of economic power; this atomises the fabric of economic society. As a result, Clark then began to question the long-run stability of the free market system. Indeed, Clark concludes that the competitive system may break down, in the absence of some form of regulation (J.B. Clark 1899, 440). Knight agrees with this conclusion, although his reasoning is somewhat different. However, Knight's rationale does not depend, as it did with Clark, on a notion of the 'degraded' economic man. Instead, Knight argues that a specific group of assumptions, in orthodox economic theory, form the basis of his conclusion. This group is what Knight terms the "analytic assumptions" of economic theory.[10]

For an economy to be described as 'efficient', we must, according to Knight, qualify this statement by the normative statement, "given the existing distribution of wealth" (Knight 1947a, 2-16). 'Efficiency' is, therefore, not a descriptive noun. Rather, it is normative and employs an implicit distributive assumption (Patinkin 1973a, 799; J.B. Clark 1907, 378). In this way, both Clark and Knight argue that power imbalance cannot be ignored when considering economic policy which is aimed at economic efficiency. According to both authors, economists will remain unable to adequately explain the operations of the economic system if they persist in ignoring power imbalance.

The third, and most important, influence of Clark stems from Clark's most famous work *The Distribution of Wealth* (1899). Here we find that Clark's association of profit with economic progress is utilised by Knight in *Risk, Uncertainty, and Profit* (1921a). In this book Knight apparently shows how the entrepreneur extracts a 'profit', from the other factors of production, because he bears uncertainty.[11] Uncertainty stems from both the supply and the demand side of the economy. On the supply side, a new process, which is employed by a rival, may threaten the entrepreneur's capital. Alternatively, on the demand side, a sudden change in consumer preference may threaten the entrepreneur's capital. Uncertainty, therefore, forces entrepreneurs to actively seek new ways to control uncertainty, and thereby ensure that their capital is not threatened. In this way we argue that the seeking of profit, the control of uncertainty, and the existence of economic progress are all interrelated.

> Considering, however, the universal recognition of the "tendency" of competition to eliminate profit, it is perhaps somewhat remarkable that the problem of profit itself has not, with one important exception [namely J.B. Clark], been attacked from the direct point of view adopted in this essay, of an inquiry into the causes of the failure of ideal competition to be fully realised in fact [brackets added] (Knight 1921a, 22).

Clark seeks to explain profit in terms of a dynamic deviation from a 'profitless' static state. It is this explanation of profit, as a result of dynamic change, which appeals to Knight. In the static state, given the absence of monopoly, exchange is taken place at a value equal to the cost of production (Clark 1899, 68-9). This value is in accordance with what Clark terms the 'older' theories of price, which equates the cost of production to the price which the consumer pays, as the 'natural' price (Clark 1899, 68-70). However, Clark renames this 'natural' price as the 'static' value of a product, with a view to emphasising the static-dynamic dichotomy in his work (Clark 1899, 68-70). This value equates what Clark refers to as the static standard of value; here profit does not exist except for the quantity of labour which is expended in 'supervision' (Clark 1899, 62-76). In addition, all types of change which promote economic progress are absent in the static state, which Clark regards as the normal position of the economy (Clark 1899, 77-94). Deviations from the static state, resulting from dynamic change, tend to result in what Clark describes as *temporary* profits. Entrepreneurs cannot permanently capture the abnormal (or super-normal) profit which emanates from their inventions or innovations because the standard of value adjusts over time, so that profit bearing inventions are ultimately reflected in these standards (Clark 1899, 408). If no 'friction' exists, and the standard of value is to adjust instantly, then no profit can ever occur. On the other hand, if friction exists, then profit will accrue to the entrepreneur for the length of time it takes the economy to adjust to the new value standard. For Clark, profit is, therefore, the ephemeral outcome which only occurs in the transition period between one standard of value and another. Once the transformation to the new standard is complete all profit is completely eliminated.

Knight, however, found the notion of perfect knowledge entirely unacceptable. Apart from this aspect of 'friction', Knight criticises its definition as being absurdly broad, mainly because it takes almost every imperfection in the process of capital readjustment into account (Knight 1921a, 34). Although J.B. Clark promises a dynamic theory of profit, he fails to deliver such a theory because he relies so heavily on the notion of 'friction'. Friction, along with profit, is unusual. Consequently, profit is not the 'norm', rather Clark deems it to be an ephemeral occurrence. Furthermore, rather than treating the progressive economy as the 'norm', Clark implicitly argues that it is only a temporary deviation from the static state, or the normal state of affairs. Knight concludes that this explanation did not assist the analysis of profit to any significant degree. Rather, it tends to obscure the whole question of uncertainty, and the crucial role it plays in explaining the permanent existence of profit. Knight (1921a) argues that 'friction' can be thought of as a situation which fills the gap between two states of perfect knowledge. In other words, Clark asks us to believe that 'friction' is the amorphous state in which we cross over, from one perfect state of knowledge to the next.

Exactly how long profit will last in the economy, depends on what Clark describes as 'friction', or the amount of time required to adapt standards of value from one static level to another. Although measured in terms of the time it takes the economy to adjust, friction is argued to be caused by imperfections in economic resources, such as the imperfect divisibility of economic resources. J.B. Clark argues that, if the static state had a zero level of friction, then "pure business profit would be annihilated as fast as it could be created ..." (J.B. Clark 1899, 410). However, this level of friction would be inconsistent with economic progress, because the firm would not have any incentive to risk its capital (Clark 1899, vii). In other words, zero friction implies perfect knowledge, as all firms are assumed to be able to instantly incorporate any technological change. However, zero friction means that firms will not innovate. Perfect knowledge thereby eliminates profit, and in so doing, effectively blocks investors from exploring the opportunities which ultimately promote economic progress. This means that we must question the notion of zero friction, or perfect knowledge, because it does not help us in explaining economic progress or the existence of profit. Indeed, zero friction means that the driving force behind economic growth, namely innovation and invention, will wither away because no incentive, in the form of profit, is available to firms.[12]

For Knight, the problem in this analysis, is that Clark did not distinguish between foreseen and unforeseen change, in the process of adjustment between two states of perfect knowledge. Each state of friction represents an example of unforeseen change. Consequently, Knight objected to the notion of a transition *between* states of perfect knowledge. To Knight, perfect knowledge never exists - either before or after - the incorporation of new technology into productive activity. Accordingly, Knight understands economics as an analytical superstructure which is based on a permanently incomplete stock of knowledge, rather than a set of immutable principles. Knight analyses how economic actors deal with uncertainty, rather than assuming that it never exists. On this basis, the transition, between states of perfect knowledge is, therefore, impossible because these states never exist.

> The fatal criticism of this [J.B. Clark's] procedure of taking changes in conditions as the explanation and cause of profit is that it overlooks the fundamental question of the difference between a change that is foreseen a reasonable time in advance and one that is unforeseen [brackets added] (Knight 1921a, 35).

J.B. Clark - Conclusion

The escalation of collusive business behaviour forces a more mature Clark to reconsider his youthful confidence in the evolutionary process of natural selection, which he initially anticipates will deliver a morally higher form of competition. These practices shook Clark out of what Fetter describes as his youthful optimism (Hollander 1927, 364). Clark struggled to adapt his moralistic economics, derived mostly from the German Historical School, to these new developments in the structure of industrialised economies. Re-casting of orthodox theory, in terms of statics and dynamics, is the way in which Clark attempts to meet this formidable task. Here, the dynamic transition - between static states - leads to a morally higher form of competition. Although this re-casting is shown by Knight to be a restatement of orthodox theory, it does lead to an important development - the causal linkage between profit and economic progress (Knight 1921a, 22). This causal linkage provides Knight with a course of study which would ultimately result in a coherent analysis of uncertainty and profit.

F.B. Hawley and I. Fisher - The "Risk Theorists"

F.B. Hawley and I. Fisher - Introduction

While J.B. Clark's economics assists Knight in its general orientation on the question of profit and its relationship with dynamic change, it nevertheless, fails to account for dynamic change itself. In his attempt to comprehensively incorporate dynamic change into economics, Knight studies the works of other theorists, who attempted to incorporate dynamic elements into their respective explanations of profit. F.B. Hawley's analysis, like J.B. Clark's fails, to appreciate the distinction between uncertainty and actuarially calculated risk (Knight 1921a, 46). Like Clark, Hawley interprets profit as another productive service, which can be analysed within the framework of marginal productivity theory. However, in order for this framework to be useful, a connection between the level of profit and the 'irksomeness' of bearing uncertainty must be established.[13] F.B. Hawley's analysis, it will be shown, can be described as a variation on the theme developed by J.B. Clark, namely where profit accrues to those who bear known risks. Hawley contributes to the development of economic theory by arguing that these risks can be actuarially determined, and that the capacity of economic actors to determine risk varies across the population. This means that differences in information processing capacity will lead to some economic actors being better able to estimate risks than others.

I. Fisher's influence is of somewhat greater importance because it highlights the sort centring of problems which Knight later attempts to solve. The problem with uncertainty, as it related to economic analysis, is that it is extremely difficult to conceptualise within any rigorous form of analysis. This is partly because economists, like Fisher, were only just beginning to understand the way statistical techniques could be employed so as to make uncertainty more tractable for economic analysis. We argue that Knight builds upon the mathematical foundation which Fisher assists in establishing. Fisher's work, therefore demonstrates the areas within statistical economics, which require further development.[14] Given the varying similarities and differences between the two authors, Knight is able to more adequately bring uncertainty within a richer and more coherent framework of analysis.

F.B. Hawley

Even though Hawley and Clark (1899) differ on the explanation of profit, both agree that it is a residual (Hawley 1901, 610). This indicates, as Knight shows, that both theorists regarded profit as being determined by imperfections in economic resources (Knight 1921a, 42-4). Rather than centring their analyses on the explanation of profit, which would involve a fundamental reappraisal of economic theory, both attempt to define profit in terms of orthodox theory.[15] In contrast to Clark (1899), Hawley argues that profit is the residual income, over and above the actuarial value of the risk, which accrues to the entrepreneur as a reward for assuming the 'irksomeness' of "being exposed to risk" (Hawley 1901, 610). Whereas Clark (1899) utilises the notion of imperfections in economic resources to explain profit, Hawley employs marginal utility theory to explain the differences in profit among economic actors. While some economic actors have the ability to accurately estimate profit, others can not, the cause of this being attributable to educational differences among economic actors.

Hawley parallels the analysis of the entrepreneur to the labourer, who will not bear the 'irksomeness' of labour unless he is adequately compensated. Whereas some labourers assess that some forms of labour are more 'irksome' than others, so too do some entrepreneurs assess that some forms of risk are more 'irksome' than others. In addition, while some labourers are more willing to labour than others, so too are some entrepreneurs more willing to take on risk than others. This arises from the fact that, according to Hawley, there is a cost which is associated with the bearing of risk, in the same sense that "there is a pain-cost to labor" (Hawley 1901, 616). Hawley maintains that the irksomeness of risk-bearing always ensures that the, "business man's subjective valuation of a risk is always greater than his actuarial valuation of the same risk" (Hawley 1901, 616).

In addition, imperfect information means that different entrepreneurs base their estimates on different information (or data sets). Even if their preferences are largely similar, each will end up making different actuarial valuations because of the different data sets on which those valuations are determined. In general, the difference between the entrepreneur's subjective valuation and his actuarial valuation of risk, will vary between entrepreneurs, such that those who are more risk averse will demand a higher premium over the actuarial valuation (Hawley 1901, 617). More specifically, however, the entrepreneur bases the decision of whether or not to engage himself in a particular venture, on the level of returns in excess of the actuarial valuation of the risks involved (Hawley 1901, 610-18). If the venture does not promise an excess return which is sufficient to satisfy the 'irksomeness' bearing capacity of the entrepreneur, then the entrepreneur will not engage himself in the venture. Uncertain income and returns, in excess of the risk assumed are synonymous, according to Hawley (Hawley 1901, 616-18). Uncertainty, therefore, cannot be distinguished from risk because all returns, both actuarial and excess, can be accurately foreseen and estimated (Hawley 1901, 616-18). This constitutes a fundamental point of disagreement between Hawley and Knight (Knight 1921a, 42). Unlike Knight, Hawley attempts to modify marginal utility analysis so as to account for the activity of the entrepreneur who, according to Hawley, can be analysed in much the same type of marginal utility framework as any other economic actor.

> What immediately concerns us here is to note that, since the obtaining of the unpredetermined residue is an inducement to assume the financial responsibility of any undertaking, the whole residue, when determined, must be the reward of the assumption of industrial risks; in exactly the same sense that wages are both the inducement to and the reward of labor, and interest both the inducement to and the reward of parting with capital ... (Hawley 1901, 619-20).

In order to accurately establish the sufficiency of returns, in excess of the actuarial valuation of risk, both the entrepreneur's calculation and the information upon which it is based must be extremely accurate. Such accuracy is secured by what Hawley describes as the 'professionalism' of the entrepreneur (Hawley 1901, 608). Such professionalism can be distinguished from speculation in the following manner.

> ... the professional class, - to which most speculators flatter themselves they belong, - who devote most or a large portion of their time to the careful study of market conditions, and, owing to their superior knowledge and judgment, are able, in the long-run, to make gains from speculation as great as, or greater than, the legitimate profit on the risks they assume, if they had assumed these risks as undertakers (Hawley 1901, 608-9).

Hawley posits that the professional study of the market enables the entrepreneur to achieve the requisite degree of accuracy in estimation, such that he can estimate his risks in an actuarial fashion. The distinction between the "professional entrepreneur" and the 'speculator' is one of education. Whereas the speculator enters the market on a whim, not having studied the market, the professional investor enters the market only after rigorous examination of it. Presumably, over a period of time, the speculator would become increasingly professional in his market related activities, eventually becoming a professional entrepreneur himself. Hawley (1901) implies that professionalism in entrepreneurship can render all future income streams knowable. However, this ignores the existence of uncertainty, by treating all income as foreknown quantities (Knight 1921a, 46). If uncertain outcomes are treated as unpredictable, as Knight suggests, then Hawley's procedure of calculating the marginal inducement to bear risk, as a premium over the actuarial value of risk, would be rendered quite useless. Calculation of actuarial estimates of economic variables would become impossible, unless other assumptions are made about the firm. This actuarial value is therefore *not* profit, because it relates to risk instead of uncertainty. Knight argues that Hawley, like Clark before him, attempts to exclude unforeseen events as he, "still treats uncertainty throughout his study as a known quantity" (Knight 1921a, 44). In this way Hawley's risk theory essentially reduces to that of J.B. Clark's, where economic actors operate under a set of parameters which are known to all of them, at all times.

Hawley, however, does modify J.B. Clark's analysis by introducing the idea that some economic actors are better able to estimate future economic variables, because of increased professionalism in estimation techniques. Hawley, therefore, introduces the conception of a heterogeneous spread of information, across economic actors, depending on the agent's skill. Knight expands this notion of heterogeneity in his analysis of uncertainty. However, he substitutes the relative size of the firm for Hawley's emphasis on the educational background of the economic actor, as the means of explaining information heterogeneity.

Uncertainty, although excluded by Hawley, can be made more tractable in economic analysis if it can be thought of in terms of actuarial estimation. However, Knight adds an important qualification to these techniques, maintaining that the relevance of these techniques depends on the relative access to market information. Whereas Hawley draws the distinction between the skills of the professional entrepreneur, and the speculator, in order to account for heterogeneity of access to market information, Knight accounts for it in terms of relative market power. In Hawley's analysis, the individual has the chance of transforming himself from a speculator to a professional entrepreneur. Given sufficient effort, in other words, any economic actor could gain the same access to economic information, as any other. In contrast, Knight argues that access to information is closely related to relative holdings of market power. Despite all attempts to become 'professional', some economic actors are always constrained, in their access to market information, by a deficiency in market power. Knight's innovation is to think of uncertainty as being relative to (or contingent on) the market power held by a particular firm.

I. Fisher

Knight's development of the mathematical theory of I. Fisher is central to his analysis. In fact, Fisher's mathematical inquiries hold the key to understanding Knight's theory of profit, especially its relation to uncertainty. Arrow's *Essays in the Theory of Risk-Bearing* (1970) offers an apt introductory remark:

> In Fisher's view, probability is simply an expression of ignorance; "*risk varies inversely with knowledge*". In the sense that the probability of an event is always measured relative to the available evidence, the proposition would be acceptable to virtually all schools of thought [emphasis added] (Arrow 1970, 10).

This suggests that the reliability of an economic estimate depends on both the quality and quantity of the evidence upon which it is based. In turn, this relationship corresponds to Knight's notion of uncertainty outlined in the previous Chapter (Knight 1921a, 47, 239).[16] In essence, this notion is based on statistical theory which concludes that the degree of reliability one can place on an economic estimate depends on the size of the sample data, relative to the total population of data. As the firm grows in size - relative to the total market - the reliability of its economic estimates increases, in a manner consistent with the statistical proposition of inference analysis. In this regard, Knight maintains that, while uncertainty exists, profit is derived from reducing the costs which uncertainty saddles on the firm. The core idea centres on the notion of consolidation, and how such consolidations can improve the firm's ability to accurately estimate economic variables, and thereby reduce the costs which are inflicted by uncertainty. In addition, if the costs which uncertainty imposes can be reduced, then the volatility of profit is likely to be reduced, thereby enhancing access to credit. As the access to credit improves, even greater consolidation can occur, leading to even greater expansion. In other words, by finding ways to reduce the costs which are associated with uncertainty, the firm effectively insures both higher levels of profitability and preferential access to credit.

> We shall show at length in our discussion of risk and uncertainty that if risk is measurable, but ... some ... consideration makes ordinary insurance inapplicable, *some other method of securing the same result will be developed* [emphasis added] (Knight 1921a, 47).

What is this other method? Knight maintains that it centres around the 'grouping' of economic activities. Employing Fisher's mathematical analysis of 'consolidation', he argues that, as firms increase market dominance, they are able to gradually move from a state of facing pure uncertainty towards a state where the firm can control most of the costs which uncertainty inflicts (Knight 1921a, 239). In other words, by increasing market share firms are able to increase the degree of confidence they have in their estimates of uncertain outcomes.

> The businessman himself not merely forms the best estimate he can of the outcome of his actions, but he is likely also to estimate the probability that his estimate is correct. The "degree" of certainty or of confidence felt in the conclusion after it is reached cannot be ignored, for it is of the greatest practical significance (Knight 1921a, 227).

Thus, as a firm's market share approaches that of the total market, its degree of confidence can also be said to increase. This process continues to the point where the costs which uncertainty inflicts can be gradually controlled. This line of argument explains Knight's disagreement with Fisher, regarding the purely subjective nature probability forecasts in economics (Knight 1921a, 227).

> We must, therefore, disagree with Professor Irving Fisher's contention, that there is only one estimate, the subjective feeling of probability itself ... A man may act upon an estimate of the chance that his estimate of an event is a correct estimate (Knight 1921a, 227).

Knight makes the distinction between the confidence in an estimate and the estimate itself, particularly because he believes that economic actors face heterogeneous information sets. In the case of the firm, this differential access to information is a consequence of differential market share. Consequently, all probability forecasts are not all of equal reliability. However, if we assume that economic power is perfectly equally distributed, then Fisher's contention, regarding the purely subjective nature of all economic estimates, may prove correct. In other words, Knight is arguing that different market share equates a significant differential in confidence, when estimating economic variables. We can demonstrate this aspect of Knight's analysis by means of a statistical illustration. This mode of expression assists us in demonstrating the interdisciplinary character of Fisher's influence on Knight (Schumpeter 1956a, 228-9).[17]

The Two Main Influences of Fisher (i) Demand for Information

According to Knight, for confidence to vary across economic actors, we must allow for differences of information among economic actors. The first source of heterogeneity is derived from the demand for such information. We argue that the poorer the economic actor, the less information he will demand, because of his incapacity to utilise such data. Even though the impecunious economic actor could profitably utilise some economic information, the threat of losing capital constrains him from acting on such information. Consequently, the possibility of losing capital therefore inhibits his demand for information, because such a loss threatens his capacity to pay for his subsistence needs. This idea of there being a relation between the quantity of capital possessed and aversion to risk is outlined by Fisher in terms of a "coefficient of caution" (Fisher 1906, 277).[18]

> The coefficient of caution expressed a feature of individual character ... The coefficient of caution ... varies with the same individual under different circumstances. Chief among these varying circumstances ... is the amount of capital of which the individual is possessed. The more capital a man possesses, the less is his chance of serious loss in any enterprise involving risk; and for this reason a rich man finds it possible to grow still richer (Fisher 1906, 277).[19]

The Two Main Influences of Fisher (ii) Supply of Information

As mentioned above, different levels of confidence in estimating economic variables, is attained by possessing greater access to the supply of information. While some economic actors have access to the supply of economic information, others are somewhat restricted in their access to information. Fisher analyses this issue - of access to information - in terms of, "comparative ignorance of the matter under consideration" (Fisher 1906, 268). Comparative ignorance stems from the degree to which an economic actor has access to market information. If firms can gain sufficient size, then Fisher claims that it should be possible for them to further enhance access to information. Essentially, the large firm becomes like an insurance company, which can specialise in the insurance of the uncertainties which threaten the firm's capital. Under this conception of the firm, large numbers of separate economic decisions can be treated as if they are a group of insurable events. As the number of events increases, the firm is able to offset the deleterious effect of one decision, against the beneficial effects of another. This process, of offsetting one bad result, against another good one, leads to a reduction in the level of costs which uncertainty inflicts on the large firm. Consequently, this process is not available to the marginal (small) firm, because it does not make enough separate decisions for the good effects of one decision to cover the bad effects of another; each decision which the marginal (small) firm makes can effect its entire existence. This means that the application of insurance principles is largely irrelevant to the decisions of the marginal (small) firm.

> Insurance involves the offsetting of one risk by another; that is, the consolidation of a large number of chances whereby relative certainty is, as it were, manufactured out of uncertainty (Fisher 1906, 291).

Whereas the marginal (small) firm faces the prospect of capital loss, because of the malodorous effects of one decision, this procedure of 'offsetting' one decision, against another, effectively insures the large firm against the prospect of capital loss. In other words, the large firm has a greater degree of confidence in its ability to retain capital, over time, than the marginal (small) firm. An example of a marginal (small) firm's greater potential for capital loss is the wrecking of a ship. Here, the firm may seek to insure against this event, at a cost, by insuring the ship. However, as the firm grows Fisher argues that firms can avoid the costs of insuring individual assets because, "the various risks insure each other" (Fisher 1906, 293).

> Thus, the North German Lloyd Shipping Company finds it profitable not to insure its vessels against shipwreck, because they have so large a fleet that their losses through a period of time can be counted on fairly well (Fisher 1906, 293).

Instead of bearing the cost of insuring the entire fleet of ships, a large company will accept the risk of shipwreck. This course of action is adopted because the cost of shipwreck, when assessed against the probability of occurrence, is less than the cost of insuring the entire fleet. This approach to insurance of vessels is not available to the marginal (small) firm, for two reasons. First, the marginal (small) firm will not be able to accurately estimate the probability of shipwreck, because it does not have access to the quantity of information required to make an accurate estimate of this probability. Second, the threat of capital loss involved in a shipwreck, to a marginal (small) firm, is proportionally much larger than the threat faced by a large firm. Indeed, in some cases, a shipwreck could bankrupt a marginal (small) firm. The marginal (small) firm can only escape the costs, associated with insuring its ships, by effectively allowing its capital to face the fortunes of the sea. In other words, the marginal (small) firm is forced to either face higher costs (through insurance) or face the risk of capital loss (through shipwreck). Either way the large firm has a comparative advantage over smaller firms.[20]

According to Knight, the costs associated with uncertainty can be brought under control by the expansion of the firm. In a similar manner to

Fisher, Knight shows how each decision of the large firm can be offset against every other decision of the firm.

> The possibility of thus reducing uncertainty by transforming it into a measurable risk through grouping constitutes a strong incentive to extend the scale of operations of a business establishment (Knight 1921a, 252).

In contrast to Fisher, Knight allows for differential levels of confidence in the estimation of economic variables. However, Fisher's work clearly creates a sound basis for this development, by outlining the limitations of contemporary analysis. Knight argues that by increasing the domain of its economic activity - in terms of market share - firms can enhance their access to the available stock of market knowledge. If such an increase in market knowledge can be attained then, as Fisher points out, risk will decrease. Errors made in the estimation of economic variables should, therefore, tend to vary inversely with the size of the firm, relative to the total size of the market (Knight 1921a, 239; Arrow 1970, 30).

F.B. Hawley and I. Fisher- Conclusion

Hawley's contribution to Knight is twofold. First, Hawley introduces the notion of differential access to information. Although Knight disagrees with Hawley's explanation of this heterogeneity, the initial influence remains intact. Second, Hawley introduces the application of actuarial techniques to the estimation of risk in economics. Again, although Knight disagrees with Hawley's application of this concept the influence is still apparent. Knight argues that as the firm grows its ability to access market information increases and this means that it can use actuarial techniques to a far greater extent than a smaller firm.

In concluding our examination of Fisher's influence on Knight, we note that Fisher's contribution assisted Knight mainly with his endeavours to think about uncertainty as a situation of supply and demand. This is not supply and demand in the normal sense - as defined by orthodox theory - but supply and demand of the stock of available market information. We argue that this insight is suggested by Fisher's distinction, between the estimate of an economic actor, and the confidence the economic actor has in that estimate (Fisher 1906, 266; Knight 1921a, 227). Fisher's work did not, however, significantly assist Knight with understanding the linkage between profit and economic progress. Although Knight employs J.B.

Clark's 'dynamic' theory, the term 'dynamic' has been shown to be an example of somewhat empty rhetoric on the part of Clark. It thus appears that Knight has not provided an account of how this theory of profit can be linked to economic progress. In closing his analysis of the theories of profit Knight remarks that;

> On the one hand, profit is in fact bound up in economic change (but because change is the condition of uncertainty), and on the other, it is clearly the result of risk, or what good usage calls such, but only of a unique kind of risk, which is not susceptible of measurement. The Clark school has confused change with a common but not universal or necessary implication of change, and both schools have followed everyday speech into the fallacy of treating risk as a substantially homogeneous category ... (Knight 1921a, 48).

In now attempting to explain how Knight incorporates dynamic progress into his analysis we now turn to his teacher and colleague, Allyn Young (Blitch 1983a, 5).

A. Young

A. Young - Introduction

Allyn Young took over the supervision of Frank Knight's Ph.D. thesis from Alvin Johnson, a former student of J.B. Clark (Dorfman 1949, 254). Initially, the thesis was entitled *A Theory of Business Profit* (Knight 1916b). However, it was "later revised with Young's help and published as *Risk, Uncertainty, and Profit*" (Blitch 1983a, 5). Young will be shown to be instrumental in the early stages of *Risk, Uncertainty, and Profit* as is Johnson (Knight 1921a, ix).[21] The relationship between Young and Knight is long and fruitful. Indeed, it is the subject of quite extensive literature.[22] The first of these influences is Young's analysis of increasing returns. The second, is Young's analysis of economic progress.[23] In seeking the origins of Knight's ideas on the large scale conversion of uncertainty into risk, we turn to Allyn Young's theory of increasing returns.

Increasing Returns

Allyn Young's conception of increasing returns centres on the idea that industrialised firms derive cost savings from increasing the scale of operations. In turn, this expansion depends on the size of the market in which they operate (Blitch 1983b, 367).

> The search for markets is not a matter of disposing of a "surplus product"... but of finding an outlet for a potential product ... it is partly a matter of augmenting profits by reducing costs (Young 1928, 537).

Young argues that this principle directly follows from Adam Smith's "famous theorem" that "the division of labor depends on the extent of the market" (Young 1928, 529). By increasing the size of a market a firm could reap the benefits which come from the division of labour. As Young says, "Taking a country's economic endowment as given ... the most important single factor in determining the effectiveness of its industry appears to be the size of the market" (Young 1928, 532).

The division of labour, according to Young, is not simply the increased specialisation of workers in increasingly narrow occupations. Rather it is, as Blitch notes, "something broader in scope than the pin-making example that Smith had used" (Blitch 1983a, 19). More specifically, Young emphasises that the division of labour, itself, does not yield the cost savings which underpin increasing returns. Rather these cost savings are mainly derived from, "capitalistic or roundabout" methods (Young 1928, 539).[24] Young is interested in explaining returns in terms of physical ratios: increasing returns, therefore, relate to an increase in the amount of output relative to the amount of input.

In contrast, Knight focuses on how monopolisation of access to market knowledge provides an incentive for the firm to expand the scale of production.[25] While both authors are interested in explaining the incentives for expanding the scale of the firm, they tend to concentrate on different aspects of a firms activity. On the one hand, Young concentrates on the effect which the scale of the firm has on increasing the physical ratio of input to output, without much attention to the influence of how uncertainty affects the transformation of input to output. On the other hand, Knight argues that uncertainty shapes the way a firm produces any output: firms must know the characteristics of both the demand and supply functions if they are to produce efficiently. By monopolising the access to such knowledge, Knight argues that firms can reduce the costs which uncertainty saddles on the firm (Knight 1921a, 48, 233-64). In this way, capturing access to market knowledge provides an incentive for the firm to expand the scale of production. Knight summarises this conclusion, where he argues that the;

> ... possibility of thus reducing uncertainty by transforming it into measurable risk through grouping activities constitutes a strong incentive to extend the scale of operations of a business establishment. This fact must constitute one of the most important causes of the phenomenal growth in the average size of industrial establishments which is a familiar characteristic of modern life (Knight 1921a, 253, 346).

Economic Progress

Allyn Young's theory of economic progress sheds light on the origins of Knight's theory of profit. More importantly, however, it gives us an insight into the dynamic aspects of Knight's theory of profit. If the large firm has an enhanced ability to estimate economic variables, then the large firm will also have an enhanced capacity to forecast the type of changes Young adroitly describes as causing a market to "lose its identity" (Young 1928, 538). In this way, the cost incentives described in the previous section give the firm an advantage in reaping profits which are generated in the process of economic progress.

> With the extension of the division of labor among industries the representative firm, like the industry of which it is a part, loses its identity. Its internal economies dissolve into the internal and external economies of the more highly specialised undertakings which are its successors, and are supplemented by new economies (Young 1928, 538).

As new markets are established, larger firms gain dominance by virtue of the lower production costs which they enjoy in the existing market. By reducing the costs which uncertainty inflicts, we will show that the larger firm reaps abnormal (or super-normal) profit.[26] In addition, we argue that these profits can be used to gain influence in the creation of new markets. In turn, these profits offer the large firm an opportunity to seize on what Young describes as, "the more highly specialised undertakings" which constitute a new market (Young 1928, 538). As the market in which the firm initially dominated 'dissolves', it is replaced with a set of new, more specialised, markets where the dominant firm retains its advantageous position. While marginal firms always exist in these new markets, their influence is gradually reduced in the long-run. Over time, markets are continuously created and dissolved: the large firm is in a better position to enjoy the benefits which result from this form of economic progress when compared to the marginal (small) firm. Knight echoes the concerns of Young in his description of, "... the quest for wealth ..." (Knight 1921a, 388; Young 1928, 531).

> In this long view ... the cumulative tendency [toward an imbalance in economic power] is ... intensified, by the role of uncertainty ... It is a situation which gives rise to a relatively permanent inequality ... and at least a tendency to its accentuation, in the absence of preventative measure [brackets added] (Knight 1943c, 115-16).

Economic Progress and the Concentration of Economic Power

As the process of economic progress continues, and the benefits of roundabout methods of production are translated into cost reductions, Young (1927a) then becomes concerned about the emerging concentration of economic power. Young examines this unfortunate side-effect of economic progress in a paper entitled *The Concentration of Wealth and its Meaning* (1927a). This essay is contained in his book *Economic Problems New and Old* (1927a). Young's concerns about the concentration of economic power are mainly derived from his analysis of economic progress, which focuses on the way markets are constantly being broken down into a series of new, more specialised markets. As this process of specialisation continues (resulting in a reduction in costs, at each successive level of specialisation) the owners of the large firm are able to increase their holdings of economic power. This is because increasing returns to scale tend to afford the owners of such large organisations a substantial advantage in terms of reaping the benefits of economic progress. Similar concerns have been expressed, more recently, by Samuelson (1967).[27] Young (1927a) expresses the idea, of how the scale of a firm effects its ability to participate in economic progress, rather cryptically in the following passage;

> ... the concentration of wealth that exists at any one time in a progressive society is in part an outcome of the circumstance that the productive army does not advance in even formation in its attacks upon new sources of wealth. There is an advance guard and there are laggards and stragglers (Young 1927a, 96).

This increase in economic power then affords greater opportunity to those with such power to accumulate even more wealth, such that the distribution of economic power becomes very uneven (Young 1927a, 102). While Young (1927a) is disturbed by this outcome, he treats this as merely the symptom of a much more serious problem, which in modern terms can be described as the "crowding out" of economic opportunity (Young 1927a, 97). Young is not advocating an equality of economic power. To the contrary, Young perceives a complete equality of economic power as "neither practicable nor desirable" (Young 1927a, 100-01). While economic progress promised, and indeed delivered economic benefits, Young argues that the majority of economic actors are unable to participate in the bulk of these benefits because of a lack of "competitive opportunity" (Young 1927a, 97-8). If this process of crowding out continues, then we can assume that economic progress would slow because the incentive towards economic progress is tied to the minority - rather than the majority - of economic actors. If we assume that talent for contributing to economic progress is evenly distributed between economic actors, then this problem is exacerbated. In this case, the majority of talented economic actors will be deprived of the opportunity to apply their talents, because the bulk of the benefits they generate are owned by the minority of wealthy economic actors. Consequently, Young (1927a) searches for a policy which will deliver greater, "equality of competitive opportunity" rather than "an arbitrary levelling down of fortunes, or to a revolutionary change in the structure of economic life" (Young 1927a, 96-7). Knight develops this aspect of Young (1935c).[28] Young's (1927a) concerns regarding the "crowding out" of competitive opportunity, stand in quite stark contrast to Joseph Schumpeter's analysis of economic progress. We shall now examine Schumpeter's analysis so as to provide a balanced comparison with both Young and Knight.

Schumpeter's Contrasting Explanation of Economic Progress

Schumpeter's analysis of the relation between monopoly and innovation is outlined mainly in *Capitalism, Socialism and Democracy* (1954a).[29] In his salient contribution to economics, Schumpeter (1954a) argues that the growth of the firm is a basis for perpetuating the process of innovation within the economic system. Schumpeter contends that a firm's capacity to devote a greater proportional outlay to innovative activities tends to increases with firm size. Innovative activities comprise mainly research and development of products, with a view to (i) increasing the volume of demand by modifying or creating new products, or (ii) reducing the cost of existing products. Over time, such innovative activities will secure a steady growth in productive efficiency. In turn, this process of innovation will reduce prices for existing products and expand the total output of the total economy by the addition of a new range of products.

> The competition that counts is "the competition from the new commodity, the new technology, the new source of supply, the new type of organisation (the largest-scale unit of control for instance) ... This kind of competition is ... the powerful lever that in the long-run expands output and brings down prices ..." (Schumpeter 1954a, 84-5; Chamberlin 1951b, 86-8).

In a manner akin to Knight and Young, Schumpeter (1954a) argues that economies of scale afford the large firm an opportunity to expand output and market share. A major difference between Schumpeter, on the one hand, and both Young and Knight on the other, exists in their assessment of monopoly. Specifically, Schumpeter argues that monopolies possess important positive attributes for any economic system, whereas Young and Knight concentrate on the negative attributes. A high concentration of economic power is the central negative attribute of an economic system, according to Knight and Young. The differences between these authors are best illustrated with reference to the two main reasons Schumpeter (1954a) proposes as providing a basis for the positive contribution of monopolies.

First Schumpeter (1954a) argues that an increase in the concentration of power will lead to an institutionalisation of innovation within the economic system. Once this occurs then Schumpeter maintains that the process of economic progress will be less subject to the vagaries of individual leadership or caprice. In fact, "[p]rogress becomes automated, increasingly impersonal and decreasingly a matter of leadership or individual initiative" [brackets added] (Schumpeter 1954a, 92). Innovation, by becoming part of the institutional process of production, thereby secures economic progress. Schumpeter refers to the process which ensures the institutionalisation of innovation as "the process of creative destruction" (Schumpeter 1954a, 76). We argue that Schumpeter proposes this system of economic analysis as a means of challenging the orthodox analysis of pure competition, which dominated the regulation of monopoly at this time (Schumpeter 1939, 358).

> Theirs [namely orthodox economists] is the ideology of a capitalist economy that would fill its social functions admirably by virtue of the magic wand of pure competition, were it not for the monster of monopoly or oligopoly that casts a shadow on an otherwise bright scene [brackets added] (Schumpeter 1939, 358).

Second, Schumpeter argues that an increasing concentration of economic power reflects the inherent differences in the capacities of economic actors to manage economic resources (Schumpeter 1939, 1044; Mason 1951, 90-3). Schumpeter refers to superior managers of economic resources as "supernormal brains" who are gifted with, "ability, energy and supernormal capacity for work" (Mansfield 1974, 19).[30] As economic progress creates a greater quantity of economic resources it is likely that the management of those resources will increase in complexity, thereby amplifying the skill differential between economic actors. This, inevitably, leads to an increased concentration of economic power as the mounting complexity of economic management tends to drive the ownership of economic resources toward those with superior economic skills. This rationale underlies Schumpeter's description of a paucity of "first rate" entrepreneurial ability. Such a paucity of talent is argued by Schumpeter to have lead only three to four hundred business concerns to create the bulk of American economic progress, in the late eighteenth century and the early nineteenth century (Schumpeter 1939, 1044).

In contrast, Knight (and to some extent Young) argue that the ability to manage economic resources is, to a large degree, a function of the investment in human capital. Although Knight acknowledges differences in talents, he maintains that the bulk of an economic actor's capacity to manage economic resources is derived from investment in human capital.[31] Just as investment in plant and equipment requires economic power, so too does investment in human capital. Indeed, without economic power, the economic actor is effectively excluded from access to human capital. Different levels of entrepreneurial skill are, therefore, largely explained by different levels of economic power, according to Knight.

On the basis of Knight's argument, which outlines the impact that investment in human capital can have upon the capacities of economic actors, we conclude that Schumpeter's analysis can be challenged by Knight. In other words, the capacity of an economic actor, while being dependent upon a degree of talent, is largely dependent upon investment in human capital. Capacity to manage economic resources is therefore a function of relative economic power. Schumpeter's argument, regarding the relative scarcity of entrepreneurial capacities, can therefore be attributable to the relative scarcity of economic power among economic actors.

Knight's analysis of the influence of economic power on the capacity of economic actors to invest in human capital draws on Young's analysis of what we have termed the eventual "crowding out" of competitive opportunity. Without competitive opportunity economic actors are not in a position to invest in human capital. This explanation of the investment in human capital provides a contrasting argument to Schumpeter's aristocratic conception of the distribution of entrepreneurial talent. In addition, Schumpeter's argument regarding the way a concentration of economic power ensures the process of economic development, is challenged by Knight. As the imbalance of economic power grows, the social tension which results then inflicts costs on the entire community. Indeed, such social tension provides a threat to the entire free market system. Knight's analysis, which evolves out of Young's concerns about the impact of monopolies, appears to more comprehensively incorporate the social impact of monopolies on society than that developed by Schumpeter. While the monopoly has some benefits to offer to the proposed society, which Schumpeter eloquently elaborates upon, Young and Knight challenge the reader to consider the broader social, and ultimately economic, consequences of monopoly. Whereas Schumpeter's analysis encourages us to challenge the ideology of pure competition, Knight's analysis points to the consequences of explaining the issue within the narrow confines of orthodox economic theory. Furthermore, while monopolies may increase efficiency (narrowly defined), Knight and Young highlight the costs that may occur as a result of increasing social tension.

A. Young - Conclusion

In conclusion, we argue that Allyn Young's influence on Knight can be seen to follow two paths. First, Knight adds to what Young describes in his famous paper *Increasing Returns and Economic Progress* (1928), as 'roundabout' methods of production. Knight's analysis of uncertainty revises Young's analysis of 'roundabout' methods, to give it a greater coherence. Increasing returns, are not simply associated with the relative scale of the firm's physical plant, but with the firm's ability to control the costs which emanate from uncertainty. Greater physical size of a firm's plant can lead to significant economies, in terms of increased specialisation and greater infusion of more and more intermediate stages of production. Associated with this physical expansion, however, is also the expansion of the firm's access to the available stock of market related information. As the firm expands market share, the total volume of transactions increases, to the point where it will be in a better position, than a marginal (small) firm, to estimate the relevant forces of demand and supply. Over time greater accuracy of estimating economic variables will, therefore, lead to an enhanced expansion path for the large firm.

In addition, Knight's theory of profit further develops Young's analysis of economic progress. The large firm has a greater capacity to estimate current economic variables, and, consequently, it has a better capacity to ascertain trends toward change in these variables. In Young's terminology, the large firm has an enhanced capacity to foresee the eventual dissolution of markets and their replacement with a set of more highly specialised markets. As part of Knight's theory of economic progress, it is evident that he is concerned with the consequences of an increase in the concentration of economic power.

These concerns, which are initiated by Young and developed in a more coherent fashion by Knight, can be contrasted to the more positive assessment of monopolies, expressed by Schumpeter. However, we argue that Schumpeter's assessment is based on the assumption that entrepreneurial talent cannot be acquired through education and that this skill is possessed only by a small sector of the community.[32] For this reason Schumpeter argues that only the large corporation with some degree of monopoly, has the requisite resources to shelter and cultivate such talent. Without such institutions Schumpeter argues that the economic system will flounder because the marginal (small) firm inefficiently detects and harnesses entrepreneurial talent. By way of contrast, Knight and

Young argue that economic power affords economic actors a greater capacity to invest in human capital. According to Knight entrepreneurial abilities largely stem from the ability of economic actors to invest in human capital. Such investment is, therefore, an important factor in the successful development of entrepreneurial talent, however the availability of such investment depends on the sociological environment which the economic actor finds himself in. To a large extent, Knight argues that the various 'talents' or skills of an economic actor are created within this sociological environment: entrepreneurial talent is nurtured within a particular sociological environment, or 'culture' (Knight 1935c, 60; Viner 1958, 134). In other words, the existing distribution of economic power has a large impact on the distribution of entrepreneurial talent. In this way we show that Schumpeter's aristocratic conception of the entrepreneur, and the implications this has for his assessment of monopoly, are challenged by Knight's analysis.

J.M. Clark

J.M. Clark - Introduction

J.M. Clark supervised Knight, in the period when Knight re-drafted his Ph.D dissertation. A metamorphosis then occurred, so as to produce *Risk, Uncertainty, and Profit* (Knight 1921a, ix). It is with J.M. Clark that we first find Knight developing the idea of controlling uncertainty, as an example of a firm's overhead costs. In addition, Knight draws on Clark's analysis of monopoly, with a view to demonstrating how his analysis of uncertainty explains the incentive for firms to increase the scale of operations. Finally, Clark's opposition to the use of perfect competition, as a policy standard is mirrored in Knight, being consistent with his analysis of uncertainty.

Williams (Unpublished) has noted the influence that J.M. Clark has on the work of his father: J.B. Clark. J.M. Clark encouraged his father to place greater emphasis on policy, rather than the theoretical analysis of monopoly. This approach involved a greater emphasis on reducing the negative effects of monopoly, rather than the promotion of perfect competition as a policy goal. Consequently, J.B. Clark's reliance on potential competition is revised, with the influence of J.M. Clark.[33]

J.M. Clark argues that potential competition is the necessary, but not sufficient, condition for ensuring that monopoly power is controlled. Revisions, primarily provided by J.M. Clark, in *The Control of Trusts* (1912), suggest that regulation of the imbalance of economic power is required, to ensure the preservation of the free market system.[34]

> To gain the end desired, the thing that must be prevented, whatever it takes, is the unified ownership or control of so much capital in a business that competition is extinguished as a result. The attempt to preserve active competition leads, then, to the need of *setting some limit* on the amount, or proportion, of capital that any one person or organised group of persons can control in any one business, by whatever method this control is exercised. It is to this policy that the enforcement of the Sherman Act is leading us [emphasis added] (J.B. Clark and J.M. Clark 1912, 145).

Thus J.M. Clark's concern about the imbalance of economic power is clearly evident in Knight's work, being, as we shall see, partially derived from J.M. Clark's analysis of overhead costs.[35] More specifically, Knight's unique conceptualisation of the conversion of uncertainty into risk, as a process which reduces the costs which uncertainty inflicts on the firm, represents an example of J.M. Clark's analysis of overhead costs.

In addition to his concern about the imbalance of economic power, it is evident that Clark also is concerned - like Knight - about the impact of this imbalance on economic freedom. While economists are trained to imagine economic actors as totally independent actors, where a range of alternative actions are always open, this is often not the case.[36] Thus, even though all economic actors are assumed to be independent, a lack of freedom exists in many facets of economic life. While the powerful maintain that everyone is independent, due to the opportunities that economic power bring, the powerless argue that a lack of economic power makes them dependent on others. Economic power, therefore, tends to distort the perception which economic actors hold, regarding their dependence on other economic actors. Clark (1927) shows that, in the case of the United States, a fundamental dependence of all economic actors, exists within the "Federal Reserve System" (J.M. Clark 1927, 59). This system protects "business men from ... other businessmen" (J.M. Clark 1927, 59). So, even though the powerful may imagine themselves as self-sufficient, within the economic system, none would refuse the assistance of the Federal Reserve, in a time of crisis (J.M. Clark 1927, 59). In this way

J.M. Clark seeks to highlight the dependence of all economic actors, powerless and powerful, upon each other. Given this dependence, the notion of perfect economic freedom becomes somewhat narrower than that developed in orthodox economic theory (J.M. Clark 1927, 59). Another factor, contributing to the inequality of competitive opportunity is "the system of inheritance" which "needlessly perpetuates our too great inequality of wealth" (J.M. Clark 1925, 49).[37] Clark's solution to the problem of power imbalance, like Knight's, points to a greater diffusion of power balance. However, like Knight, Clark does not call for complete equality of economic power. Rather, all Clark aims for is a significant reduction of power imbalance. The object, here, is "to avoid ... the proverbial corrupting effect of power that is unchecked" (J.M. Clark 1948, 151).

Clark's Theory of Overhead Costs

Clark presents his theory of overhead costs in *Studies of the Economics of Overhead Costs* (1923) and in an essay entitled *The Relation Between Statics and Dynamics* (1927).[38] Clark defines overhead costs as, "costs which frequently do not vary with the variation in the output, or not in anything like the same degree" (J.M. Clark 1927, 64). Essentially, Clark saw overhead, or fixed costs, as embracing the imperfections of the factors of production, namely imperfect divisibility and imperfect mobility (Dorfman 1949, 443). Because factors of production are imperfectly divisible and imperfectly mobile, those firms who can operate on larger scales are able to disseminate these imperfections in a less costly fashion than smaller firms. Accommodation of these imperfections involves the firm being able to either gain a better bargaining position for the supply of input, or being able to spread the costs of imperfectly divisible, or imperfectly mobile, input over a large quantity of production. In other words, the large firm can minimise overhead costs by either altering the supply of input, by either using its bargaining power, or by spreading the costs of imperfections in the supply of input over a large quantity of output. This can be contrasted to J.B. Clark's understanding of imperfections as mere 'friction'. Here, imperfections are seen as externally determined elements, which have no role to play in the determination of outcomes within the economic system, except from slowing the process of adjustment from one static state to the next. Consequently, the study of the costs that flow from these imperfections is not viewed as having any great impact, in terms of explaining the operation of the economic system. Nevertheless, J.M. Clark disagrees.[39]

According to J.M. Clark, increased scale gives firms a greater ability to actively manipulate overhead costs, so as to restrict the operation of potential competition. Clark shows how the large firm can restrict entry into industries by temporarily reducing price so that smaller entrants can only recover variable, as opposed to fixed, costs. In order to demonstrate this outcome Clark analyses the costs of production in such a way as to show that, as the scale of production increases, the amount of fixed, or overhead, costs fall per unit of production. Because fixed costs (per unit of production) are less for larger firms, a temporary reduction in price will mean only a reduction in profit, not a loss. On the other hand, the marginal (small) firm, who has higher fixed costs, per unit of production, will not be able to match the reduction in price, induced by the large firm. Over time, therefore, the marginal (small) firm is unable to survive, because it is only able to recover variable - not fixed - costs. This would enable the large firm to resume a policy which results in abnormal (or super-normal) profit; the large firm modifies the degree of competition so as to maximise long-run profit.

In addition, when overhead costs are viewed from outside the firm they can, "introduce doubt and ambiguity into the most essential economic service of costs" (J.M. Clark 1927, 64). This means that potential entrants will require information on the nature of costs which relate to a particular industry, in terms of them being either fixed, or variable. If the large firm can disguise the classification of these costs, so that potential entrants will be unable to establish the nature of the costs, then potential entrants will be unable to establish the potential viability of entering the industry. In other words, the large firm can manipulate information which relates to its costs of production, so as to prevent potential entrants from evaluating the viability of competition. Clark (1927) describes this restriction of information a blatant denial of a fundamental right: "... whether a given thing is economically worth doing" (J.M. Clark 1927, 64). Clark (1927) argues that all economic actors should have the right to evaluate the potential costs and benefits of all economic activities. However, such restriction of information prevents economic actors from enjoying such a right. Similarly, Knight notes that the increase in the scale of the average industrialised firm, is the structural change (in industrialised economies) which restricts the operation of potential competition (Knight 1921a, 252). In addition, Knight's analysis of profit leads to the conclusion that economies of scale are involved in the control of the costs which uncertainty inflicts on the firm. In this way, Knight (1921a) develops, and to some extent foreshadows, Clark's concerns about the way firms can manipulate information for their own ends. As the firm grows it essentially increases its knowledge of all costs, including overhead costs.

> When the technique of business organisation has reached a fairly high stage of development a known degree of uncertainty is hardly any uncertainty at all, for such risks will be borne in groups large enough to reduce the uncertainty to substantially negligible proportions (Knight 1921a, 47).

Knight's theory of profit can, therefore, be seen as a rather subtle development of the ideas which J.M. Clark expresses in his theory of overhead costs. While Clark maintains that the large firm is better able to reduce these costs, with a view to deterring potential entrants, Knight argues that the large firm is better able to control these costs, due to their disproportionate ability to control the costs which emerge from uncertainty. The large firm, therefore, has overhead costs which are both lower and more predictable than those of the marginal (small) firm. In addition, the evaluation of potential entry becomes more difficult, as the scale of the firm increases. In summary, we argue that scale provides the firm with (i) valuable information on the nature of its overhead, and variable, costs and (ii) greater potential to disguise this information amongst an array of accounting procedures (J.M. Clark 1927, 64).[40]

Social Control of Business

J.M. Clark's other major contribution to economic theory is his *Social Control of Business* (1925). Here, Clark sought to regulate free-market so that the advantages of large scale enterprise would not lead to an increase in the imbalance of economic power;

> [T]he control of large fortunes and of the unequal distribution of wealth is an ancient and ever new question which is becoming more and more acute as the masses gain a growing sense of their own political power [brackets added] (J.M. Clark 1925, 4).

This argument is premised upon, apart from other things, the above mentioned analysis of overhead costs. Here, the advantages of large scale enterprise lead to what Clark deems an unacceptable degree of imbalance of economic power. Clark's position on the control of business is also based on the realisation that, because of differential overhead costs, true *laissez-faire* is impossible.

> For, in essence, Clark was saying that, given the conditions of perfect competition, the theoretical structure of classical economics was correct; but - and here was the real intellectual blockbuster - contrary to the assumptions of perfect competition, the actual modern industrial order was characterised by all-pervasive and unavoidable frictions and rigidities [namely, overhead costs] which made any close approach to the theoretical competitive ideal impossible [brackets added] (Dorfman 1949, 46).

Knight's analyses of economic freedom, power and efficiency, are examples of these 'unavoidable rigidities'. These analyses are based on Clark's assessment of the scope for perfect competition in a real world economy. In addition, a further rigidity, namely the notion of a heterogeneity of information between economic actors is reinforced by Clark (J.M. Clark 1927, 58). Any attempt to bring the actual economy in line with an approximation to the ideal of perfect competition, which ignores these rigidities is, therefore, meaningless. Consequently, Clark's influence on Knight is mainly one of pointing out the irrelevance of perfect competition, as a means of evaluating the attributes of economic systems. As a result of this analysis, economists have no way to avoid the question of the distribution of economic power. Economists must, therefore, consider the moral issues surrounding the growth of firms, and contemplate what distribution of wealth is most conducive to the promotion of economic progress. If this consideration is ignored then the large firm is able to make full use of the advantages derived from differential overhead costs, as described in *Studies in the Economics of Overhead Costs* (J.M. Clark, 1923). Consequently, efforts to increase efficiency will result in the large firm increasing its market share. The inevitable result is an increasing imbalance of economic power, and a reduction in perceived economic freedom. Consequently, a new concept of competition is vitally needed. This is what J.M. Clark attempts to deliver in his famous paper *Toward a Concept of Workable Competition* (1940). Here, Clark conceives a policy orientated notion of competition, which avoids the 'undesirable' results which flow from the use of the notion of perfect competition, as an analytical framework within which policy proposals are evaluated.

> [Perfect competition] has seemed at times to lead to undesirable results, in that it does not afford reliable guidance to the factors which are favourable to the closest working approximation to that ideal, under actual conditions [brackets added] (J.M. Clark 1940, 241).

Clark wished to emphasise the unrealistic nature of perfect competition. Absence of one, or more, of the conditions of perfect competition, should lead to a rejection of perfect competition, as a policy standard (J.M. Clark 1940, 241). For similar reasons Knight views perfect competition as a dangerous standard, against which economic policy is to be evaluated against. Knight views the impact of uncertainty as a factor which compounds the problems examined by J.M. Clark (1923). Indivisibilities in factors of production, which give rise to the presence of overhead costs, also impact on the ability of firms to access information. Just as scale enables the large firm to overcome the indivisibilities in factors, Knight argues that scale can also overcome the difficulties involved in accessing information. As the firm's scale approaches that of either the input, or the output market, its ability to access information in each market will increase; the ability of firms to consolidate can result in the situation of almost total monopoly. Attempts to indiscriminately increase the freedom of firms will, therefore, allow dominant firms to consolidate to the degree where an authoritarian State is required to control them.[41]

> Perfect competition implies conditions, especially as to the presence of human limitations, which would at the same time facilitate monopoly, make organisation through free contract impossible, and force an authoritarian State upon society (Knight 1921a, 193).

We can discern the beginnings of this conclusion in Clark, who regards *laissez-faire* as, "an aspiration unfulfilled and unfulfillable ... a system of control fairly adequate for some purposes, but never self sufficient" (J.M. Clark 1925, 32). While Clark sought to outline the advantages which the large firm derives from overhead costs, Knight takes the argument one step further, by noting the informational advantages which the large firm enjoys. In this way, the conclusion of Clark, that perfect competition is an incorrect means of evaluating the outcomes of economic policy, is further emphasised by the work of Knight (J.M. Clark 1927, 58; J.M. Clark 1940, 241).

J.M. Clark - Conclusion

J.M. Clark's influence on Knight has been shown to have followed two main paths. First, Knight offers a subtle development, or anticipation, of Clark's theory of overhead costs. Here, Knight centres the discussion of overhead costs on the degree to which firms can accurately estimate these costs. Increased market share improves the quality of estimates, thereby increasing their accuracy; less economic resources are then required in the estimation process. These cost savings comprise of: (i) the costs of estimation, and (ii) the costs of bearing uncertainty. With regard to the first part of the process, the reason for this reduction in expenditure is found in the inherent accuracy of estimation, derived from the large firm's market share.[42] Here, the large firm has access to a relatively greater share of market transactions. This will mean that it has to expend relatively fewer resources - in the search for information - than the marginal (small) firm.[43] With regard to the second part of the process, larger firms are able to spread the costs of bearing uncertainty, over a larger volume of output, than smaller firms. The costs of bearing uncertainty, which are borne by all risk-averse agents, are therefore capable of being treated in the same fashion as other overhead costs.

Secondly, Clark's concerns regarding the imbalance of economic power and freedom, which brings in the requirement for government regulation of business, is evident in Knight's discussion. Clark's influence is especially evident with regard to Knight's analysis of economic power and the fallacies of using perfect competition, as a standard when evaluating alternative economic policies.

Conclusion

Knight's development of J.B. Clark's moral approach to economics lead him to significantly revise Clark's analysis of dynamic economics. At the same time, Knight adheres to the basic axioms of the German Historical School, which are broadly accepted by J.B. Clark. In performing this revision, Knight builds upon the conception of a heterogeneity of the information which is available to individual economic actors. Both Hawley and Fisher display interdisciplinary tendencies which Knight also incorporates in his analysis. In addition, Knight reviews the presuppositions of I. Fisher, with a view to explaining the impact of economic power on both access to market knowledge and confidence in estimating economic variables.

Another important element in Knight's revision of J.B. Clark's theory of dynamic economics is Knight's development of Allyn Young's theory of increasing returns. Young concentrates on how firms operate under conditions of certainty, by examining how firms decrease the ratio of inputs to outputs by increasing the scale of production. In contrast, Knight focuses on how the firm seeks to minimise the costs which uncertainty imposes upon it. Here, expanding the scale of production is aimed at monopolising access to the stock of available market information: such access holds the key to reducing the costs which uncertainty saddles on the firm. In addition, we argue that the large firm is in a better position to participate in the process of economic progress.

The final part of Knight's revision of J.B. Clark's economics mainly draws on J.M. Clark's analysis of overhead costs. Here, Knight shows the scale of a firm's operations can alter its costs. First, the costs of gathering information will drop as the relative size of the firm grows. Essentially, this is because information is attracted to the large firm, rather than the firm having to expend resources seeking information. Second, the costs of bearing uncertainty, which are borne by all risk-averse actors, can be spread over a much wider volume of production, so that these costs will fall, per unit of production. Both these cost savings can be thought of as another example of a large firm's capacity to derive competitive advantage from overhead costs. This advantage injects the requirement for social control, or government regulation of monopoly.

Knight's capacity to combine the relevant content, from the various authors described above, allows him to develop a powerful explanatory tool for economic theory. Instead of excluding uncertainty, Knight centres his analysis of imperfectly competitive markets on how uncertainty impacts on the cost function of the firm. After Knight, therefore, we can say that firms are no longer thought to compete under conditions of perfect knowledge. Rather, they compete for access to market knowledge. Markets fail to exist for setting a price for access to the stock of available market knowledge. However, as far as Knight is concerned, these costs shape the capacity of the firm to operate under uncertainty. In turn, these capacities fashion the ability of firms to participate in the expansion of wealth, which accompanies economic progress. Consequently, Knightian uncertainty forces a moral dimension upon economic theory; a conclusion shared with J.B. Clark, whose work forms the foundation of Knight's analysis.

Notes

1 This conclusion, is consistent with Patinkin (1973a), and other literature (See Howey 1983, 163-86; Johnson 1952, 227-28; Shils 1981, 179-86; Stigler 1987, 55-9).

2 This analysis of J.B. Clark is consistent with that of J.M. Clark, who argues that his father always sought to develop 'fair' standards of competition (Dorfman 1970, 16).

3 Such an influence stems from the German Historical School.

4 Patinkin supports this assessment of Knight, where he describes Knight's essay, *The Ethics of Competition* (1935c), as "among the most exciting things that I had read during my student days" (Patinkin 1973a, 798).

5 In probing the intellectual background behind Knight's revision of J.B. Clark, we will not attempt to enter the debate on the change in J.B. Clark's thinking, which is evident in the literature. Dorfman (1949), Jalladeau (1975), Henry (1982) and Williams (1989; unpublished) are examples of this debate, which we consider to be outside the scope of this book. In limiting our examination of Clark we do not wish to gag the discussion of Clark's eminent contribution. Rather, we seek to stress the influence of Clark on Knight.

6 (Dorfman 1970, 41).

7 1. The new [German Historical] school ... opposes ... the view ... that the production and acquisition of wealth by individuals is the single ... object of human life; wealth, it regards as a means used by Humanity in it's struggle towards moral ideals of life, and for the furtherance of universal culture. 2. It ... seeks to explain the present economic phenomena through the study of their historical development, and to ascertain them as accurately as possible through statistical investigations. It uses the knowledge of the nature of man's intellect and will for the rational explanation of economic facts, but does not construct the facts themselves out of one-sided assumptions respecting the nature of man. 3. It ... recognises the right of the State to positive intervention in the economic relations of the community, for the support of the weak and the strengthening of the public spirit. As the political economy of the last century applied itself chiefly to the liberation of the economic forces from antiquated and useless restrictions, so the new school specially meets the acknowledged need of new social arrangements, the need for social reform in opposition to social revolution on the one hand and to rigid *laissez-faire* on the other. 4. It takes up, therefore, a less isolated position in relation to other Moral and Political Sciences [brackets added] (Dorfman 1955, 21).

8 On this basis, we contend that J.B. Clark did not undergo a significant change of mind, on the subject of competition, meaning 'fair' competition.

At all times, we argue, J.B. Clark sought to offer a critique of the economic system, from a moral perspective: how competition could be transformed into a 'fair' competition. This proposition is consistent with J.M. Clark. Furthermore, this proposition is also consistent with the basic axioms of the German Historical School, described above. Accordingly, J.M. Clark notes that,

> "the continuing factor" linking both works [*The Distribution of Wealth* and *The Philosophy of Wealth*], namely the emphasis on the need of moralising competition by developing and enforcing standards of *fair* competition [brackets added] (Dorfman 1970, 16).

9 Corroborating evidence of Knight's continual interest in moral questions is available throughout the literature (Patinkin 1973a, 798; Shils 1981, 183; Stigler 1987, 57).

10 In Chapter Two we show that these assumptions are, in fact, implicit moral propositions, according to Knight (Knight 1921a). Consequently, Knight is quite vehement in his attack of these implicit propositions, and he expresses this attack somewhat trenchantly in *Freedom and Reform* (1947a).

> The argument of the body of this paper has shown that an appeal to maximum freedom as a "standard" involves a fallacy. The result is dogmatic acceptance of the existing distribution of power, which is an ethical proposition, a value-judgement in disguise, and an ethically indefensible one (Knight 1947a, 14).

11 We later show that this popular appreciation of Knight is misleading. Profit is not simply received as a *quid pro quo* for having to bear uncertainty, but also as a windfall reward for the firm which has succeeded to gain a large market share. See Chapter Four and Five of this book.

12 Knight exposes this argument as being without any rational basis, being based more on belief - or faith in the scientific nature of economics - than on fact. Clark's argument is the final expression of nineteenth century thinking, which based all its reasoning on the notion that economic phenomenon can be studied in the same way as the physical sciences. Uncertainty frustrates this study and, therefore, it is largely ignored by nineteenth century economists. By disagreeing with this approach Knight (1921a) single-handedly brings economic theory into the twentieth century, where we cannot ignore uncertainty. However, we argue that economists are still reluctant to consider the full implications of uncertainty for economic theory.

13 However, as Blaug notes, "no such connection exists" (Blaug 1962, 486).

14 Both authors, however, emphasise the gains to economics which can be made from a more interdisciplinarian approach, which is consistent with the influence of the German Historical School (Dorfman 1955, 21).

15 Clark argues that profit accrues to those who bear the "friction" which is involved in the movement of the "value standard" from one static position to the another (Clark 1899). Without "friction", or imperfections in the system, there cannot be any profit.

16 See also Chapter Two of this book.

17 Refer to the appendix for a statistical illustration of Knight's analysis of differential confidence.

18 Fisher enlarges on this relation between the quantity of capital and risk, in an appendix of *The Nature of Capital and Income* (1906). Here, Fisher argues that risk reduces as the quantity of capital increases.

> The wider the range of deviation considered, the less the chance that the actual dividends in any year will fall outside that range. Moreover, the chance decreases *far faster* than the range increases. This relation, which follows from the theory of probability, has very important consequences in the theory of distribution. From it follows as a corollary that the richer an individual, the less risk in *taking* risks. Being possessed of capital, he has a wider range within which he can safely afford to operate, and therefore he has a far greater probability of keeping within these limits of safety than his less fortunate competitors (Fisher 1906, pp 407-09).

19 This relationship, between economic power and the capacity of economic actors to seize opportunities, is discussed in Chapter Two. In addition, Rotwein (1983) cites Jacob Viner as identifying a similar relationship between economic power and capacity (Rotwein 1983, 272).

20 In this case the marginal (small) firm faces a permanent cost disadvantage when compared to the large firm, because of insurance costs. Knight incorporates these notions of Fisher in Chapter Eight of *Risk, Uncertainty, and Profit* (1921a): *Methods for Meeting Uncertainty*.

21 J.M. Clark, on the other hand, assists Knight in the more advanced formalisation of the arguments which Young initiates.

22 For example, see Dorfman (1949); Blitch (1983a; 1983b); Hart (1989). Rather than dwell on the nature of the relationship, which these other authors analyse, we will limit our examination to the more significant influences that Young has on Knight.

23 To briefly recapitulate Knight's theory of profit, we note that economic actors have differing capacities to evaluate the error involved in their economic estimates. As a firm's market share grows the relative access to

market knowledge also increases, thereby increasing the reliability of a firm's estimates.

24 The concept of "roundabout methods" is derived from Bohm-Bawerk, who defines it as the infusion of more and more intermediate stages of production, between the raw material and the finished good (Bohm-Bawerk 1923, 365-7). Bohm-Bawerk claims that increasing returns are derived from the addition of incremental stages of production, each more specialised than the previous stages of production. Greater specialisation allows for an increase in the substitution of capital for labour, which results in higher output and lower unit costs. In addition, increases in demand for capital goods creates new efficiencies in those industries which produce the capital goods, and those efficiencies flow back into the economy.

25 Knight outlines how firms control the costs associated with uncertainty in Chapter Eight of *Risk, Uncertainty and Profit* (1921a). Refer to Chapters Four and Five for a complete account of these costs.

26 We explain the way these abnormal (or super-normal) profits come into existence in Chapters Four and Five of this book.

27 Here, Samuelson (1967) notes the way scale reduces uncertainty and leads to an increase in the imbalance of economic power, as a process of reinforcement. Scale "permits reduced riskiness", and this "is only too likely to reinforce *other* increasing return factors", which will further increase "bigness and imperfection of competition" (Samuelson 1967, 724).

28 We analyse this development in Chapter Two of this book.

29 We limit our analysis of Schumpeter to the juxtaposition of Schumpeter, as against Young and Knight, on the issue of economic progress and monopoly. Although the analysis is brief, we argue that it highlights the major differences between these various authors. We argue that a larger exposition of Schumpeter's theories is outside the scope of this book.

30 We argue that Schumpeter derives the notion of "supernormal brains" from Nietzsche, who contends that man must replace false religious idols with his own "supermen". "Supermen" lead humanity forward along its cultural path, according to Nietzsche. In other words, Schumpeter's entrepreneur is to economic progress what Nietzsche's superman is to cultural progress (Bloom 1987, 200-10).

31 We give an outline of this argument in Chapter Two. Here, we note how Knight conceives capital in a broad sense, including the skills and training of labour. By adding to the skills and training of labour, or investing in human capital, the capital base of the economy expands, for Knight, in the same way as it would with the addition of any plant and equipment.

32 A parallel to these rare clusters of entrepreneurial talent exists in other fields. For example, musical talent is also rare, and it emerges - like entrepreneurial talent - from unpredictable natural factors.

33 Here, J.B. Clark maintains that the threat of potential competition is sufficient to ensure that industries would operate in an efficient manner, meaning that price would generally tend to reflect long-run marginal cost. With the advent of the trust problem, however, some industries were attempting to reduce competition, with a view to earning abnormal (or super-normal) profit. J.M. Clark emphasises the effects of the trust problem, to the point where he is able to force a revision of his father's views, on the adequacy of potential competition. As Williams (Unpublished) shows, this revision is evident in the 1912 edition of *The Control of Trusts* (J.B. and J.M. Clark 1912). In addition, the revision is also consistent with the influence of the German Historical School on J.B. Clark (Dorfman 1955, Letiche 1955, Hildebrand 1955).

> In contrast to J.B. Clark's earlier pronouncements that the threat of entry is sufficient to produce good results, a new Chapter is inserted entitled "What More is Needed". The preface of the new [1912] edition states that J.M. Clark "contributed most of the new material"- and new it certainly was [brackets added] (Williams, Unpublished manuscript, 14).

34 This conclusion is reflected throughout Knight's works; see Chapter Two of this book (Knight 1920a, 32; Knight 1921a, 193; Knight 1935c, 60; Knight 1947a, 8).

35 Refer to Chapter Two of this work.

36 For example, Clark describes the case of an employee who faces an employer. Here, the employer can more easily exploit workers when the labour market is depressed. In this case, the weak labour market compels the employee to accept almost any proposal which is put forward by the employer. As Clark notes, "There is real compulsion in such a situation ... competition is not perfect enough to prevent all compulsion of a more personal sort" (J.M. Clark 1927, 58-9). A similar lack of freedom flows through the system of standard contracts, which the less powerful economic actor agrees to, so as to avoid the legal costs which are involved in their amendment.

37 Knight's analysis of the inheritance system, as magnifying the inequality of economic power, parallels that of Clark (refer Chapter Two of this book).

38 (Hollander 1927).

39 Whereas J.B. Clark conceives of factor imperfections as exogenous to the economic system, J.M. Clark views them as endogenous determinants of economic activity. More importantly, however, these costs can be

manipulated by the large firm. The overhead costs, which accrue from the imperfections in factors of production, can play an important role in the deciding outcomes, especially as regards the relative opportunities available to the large firm. Of particular note is the way overhead costs tend to restrict the operation of potential competition; such competition, J.B. Clark argues, would ensure that competition would deliver acceptable outcomes. However, if potential competition is constrained in this way, then competition may well not deliver acceptable outcomes.

40 Without a reliable dissection of cost, into fixed (or overhead) and variable, the potential entrant cannot accurately determine his potential exposure to other uncertainties in the market. For example, a relatively small potential entrant may wish to test various demand scenarios. In the scenario where demand falls sharply, and supply adjusts accordingly, a reliable assessment of fixed costs will allow the potential entrant the chance to assess his cost structures. By this we mean that the potential entrant, in this case, will need to determine the minimum quantity which is to be supplied, so as to cover fixed as well as variable costs at the prevailing sale price. Consequently, the small potential entrant will require an accurate estimation of fixed costs, so that he can determine a level of production which will allow him to recover these fixed costs. If this information is not forthcoming, or can be disguised by the use of accounting treatments, then the entrant will find it difficult to evaluate the viability of entering the market. Both Clark and Knight argue that this information is restricted. However, Knight investigates the outcome of this restriction, in terms of its effect on the marginal (small) firm. By restricting information on fixed costs, the large firm can enhance the difficulties which are involved in entering the market and competing as a marginal (small) firm.

41 We outline this reasoning in Chapter Two.

42 Refer to Chapter Three.

43 This is because the large firm has better access to the limited stock of available market data, when compared to the marginal (small) firm. In addition, the large firm's dominance of input markets allows it to attract information from those firms who supply the various factors of production. In contrast, the marginal (small) firm has to expend resources in extracting this source of market knowledge.

4 Comparison of Knight with Chamberlin and Robinson

Introduction

Whereas Chamberlin and Robinson are widely regarded as the founders of the theory of imperfect competition, Knight's analysis of the subject remains somewhat obscure. Chamberlin and Robinson describe an unstable short-run position which is characterised by: (i) abnormal (or super-normal) profit, and (ii) a level of output which is less than that which is suggested by perfect competition. In the long-run, a largely orthodox equilibrium position exists: this position has three main characteristics. First, long-run equilibrium is described as being stable. Second, the long-run equilibrium output is usually lower than what is suggested by perfect competition. Third, abnormal (or super-normal) profit is absent in the long-run. Elimination of abnormal (or super-normal) profit usually occurs at a point before the minimum of the long-run average cost curve (LRAC) is reached. As a result, the firm operates at lower than what orthodox theory argues is an optimal level of capacity utilisation. These equilibrium characteristics are based on the central assumption of product differentiation (Harrod 1934, 463, 442).[1] These somewhat orthodox long-run outcomes are inconsistent with Knight's examination of imperfect competition.

In this Chapter we compare and contrast Chamberlin and Robinson's analysis of imperfect competition with Knight's. Essentially, Chamberlin and Robinson describe a multi-product model, with identical firm cost structures. This model reduces to a series of industries which are almost perfectly competitive. Indeed, as this product range is reduced we argue that Chamberlin and Robinson's analyses of imperfect competition tends to replicate the orthodox representation of perfect competition. In contrast, Knight focuses on cost differentials, which exist between firms in the same industry. This emphasis on cost - rather than product heterogeneity - does not reduce to perfect competition because it systematically considers how uncertainty impacts competitive outcomes.

We argue that Knight's description of imperfect competition is primarily based on his examination of how uncertainty influences the cost of production (Knight 1921a, 197-377). Here, Knight indicates that the costs - associated with the control of uncertainty - vary across firms within the same industry.[2] Inequality of uncertainty-control cost stems from: (i) different access to the stock of available market information, and (ii) the degree of independence used in deciding the value of present and future economic variables. Such inequality has two competitive outcomes. First, Knight argues that the competitive system will not reach an equilibrium because of the aggregate output volatility which is largely induced by the desire of the marginal (small) firm to capture the economic rents associated with market share. Such disequilibrium is the unintentional result of the attempt of the marginal (small) firm to minimise uncertainty-control costs; the output level never stabilises.[3] Second, Knight's analysis tends to disaccord with that of Chamberlin and Robinson, who describe a process which results in an absence of abnormal (or super-normal) profit in the long-run. In contrast, Knight conceives of abnormal (or super-normal) profit as accruing to the firm who can reduce uncertainty-control costs. Typically, this is the large firm who can derive economic rent from access to the stock of available market knowledge.[4]

While the economics profession is largely aware of the significant contributions of Chamberlin and Robinson, it remains largely ignorant of Knight's contribution to the analysis of imperfect competition. We argue that Knight provides a significant contribution to the analysis of imperfect competition by concentrating on the cost function of the firm. Indeed, Knight's analysis of firm costs represents almost a universally ignored development of early twentieth century economic thought; it is significant and worthy of further development. We argue that the reason for the lack of recognition of Knight's contribution is partly related to his perplexing writing style: he 'deliberately' makes his central reform proposals difficult to access.

E.H. Chamberlin and J. Robinson's Analyses of Imperfect Competition

E.H. Chamberlin and J. Robinson - Introduction

In order to describe Chamberlin and Robinson's analyses of imperfect competition we will first analyse the objectives of both authors. Second, we will investigate the major determinants of the transition to profitless equilibrium. Third, we will investigate competitive response under what we describe as a uniform level of uncertainty. Finally, we will examine the equilibrium position itself.

Objectives of Chamberlin and Robinson

Chamberlin's theory is influenced mainly by Allyn Young, J.M. Clark, and Frank Knight (Reinwald 1973, Skinner 1982). Allyn Young, in his role as Ph.D supervisor to Chamberlin, is credited with having a substantial influence on his doctoral thesis, which forms the basis of *The Theory of Monopolistic Competition* (Chamberlin 1933, xii). In addition, J.M. Clark influences the way Chamberlin analyses monopolistically competitive markets.[5] Here, Clark argues that the perfectly competitive model presumes that instantaneous change exists within the economic system. This type of change would mean that all firms are able to react - instantaneously - to any variation in market conditions. If firms could react this quickly, then it is highly unlikely that there would be any change in the pattern of resource ownership over time, from one firm to another (Chamberlin 1933, 4). In other words, Clark assists Chamberlin to question the notion of the firm reacting to market changes in a precise and instantaneous manner. Additionally, Clark inspires Chamberlin to look for a mechanism which allows for time-lags in the competitive reaction of rivals.

Another influence on Chamberlin is Knight. Chamberlin notes Knight as arguing that there is a, "Hegelian self contradiction in the idea of theoretically perfect competition ..." (Chamberlin 1933, 4). On the basis of this influence, we argue that Chamberlin develops the conception of uncertainty - initially proposed by Knight - in a manner which explains the dynamics of economic change: a peculiar knowledge set surrounds each producer. Because producers make such a highly differentiated set of goods, their knowledge of rivals becomes limited. Product differentiation, therefore, isolates each producer to such an extent that each producer becomes uncertain about the competitive reactions of rivals. Since the competitive group is characterised by a high degree of product differentiation, this uncertainty becomes uniform among producers: no producer has any better idea of what his rival will do than any other producer. Specific 'types' of uncertainty exist for each firm in the competitive group so that each firm is equally uncertain about the operations of every other group member; these different 'types' of uncertainty mirror the product differentiation which exists in the competitive group. Indeed, we argue that the uniformity of uncertainty - between firms in the competitive group - is the key to understanding Chamberlin's explanation of the transition to profitless equilibrium (Chamberlin 1933, 81-2, 302). As Chamberlin says;

> Out of this whole phase [of intellectual influence] ... came a number of critical distinctions, as between: pure and perfect competition, ... various *types* of certainty and uncertainty, ... time-lags ... and so on [brackets added] (Chamberlin 1933, 298).

Chamberlin argues that orthodox economics creates an unnecessary 'dichotomy' between monopoly and competition which distorts the analysis of monopolistically competitive markets (Chamberlin 1933, ix). This distortion is significant because monopolistic markets are the most common form of markets (Chamberlin 1933, xi). Accordingly, Chamberlin employs a 'hybrid' theory of price determination, which allows him to systematically incorporate product heterogeneity. According to this theory each seller is a monopolist.

> The recognition of each seller as a monopolist *in the full sense of the word* - as having control over the supply of a *distinguishable* product ... became the key to the whole analysis (Chamberlin 1933, 302).

Allowance for such a diversity of product within a competitive group, "... introduces forces, absent under pure competition, which materially alter the result" (Chamberlin 1933, 10). The objective of Chamberlin is to incorporate these new forces, so as to describe a new equilibrium position. Equilibrium is described as: (i) being perfectly stable, and (ii) free of abnormal (or super-normal) profit (Chamberlin 1933, 98). While this representation of equilibrium is broadly consistent with orthodox economic theory, it differs with respect to where equilibrium occurs. The position of stable equilibrium is usually not at the minimum point of the LRAC, rather it is usually somewhere to the left of this minimum point (Harrod 1934, 463).

In contrast to Chamberlin, Robinson does not explain the operation of imperfectly competitive markets by developing Knight's analysis of uncertainty. Instead, she draws on the orthodox school of English economics in an attempt to describe the equilibrium position which results from imperfect competition. Robinson's account of the state of economics, provides an explanation for why she attempts to modify economic theory (Robinson 1933a, v-vii). Here, Robinson indicates that Pigou attempts to transform orthodox theory, by finding a logical resolution for the inherent contradiction, between "internal economies and competition" (Robinson 1933a, v-ix). Pigou argues that internal economies of scale tend to decrease the costs of firms to a certain minimum cost, thereafter these costs rise continuously; this point of minimum cost represents an 'optimal' level of output (Robinson 1933a, v). At levels of production greater than this 'optimal' level of output we find that diseconomies of scale tend to offset economies of scale, so as to increase average cost. Consequently, all firms within any particular industry are supposed to operate at the level of production where average cost is at the minimum in the long-run; all resources are fully employed in the long-run. While some deviation from full employment is possible in the short-run, the depression years of the 1930's represents a challenge to this theory. Indeed, this period indicates that firms do not operate at anything like the point of production where all resources are fully employed.[6]

> Here we were, in 1930, in a deep slump, and this [Pigou's premise that all firms operate at optimal capacity] is what we were being asked to believe [brackets added] (Robinson 1933a, vi).

This clash - between real-world events and the theoretical explanation of these events - forces Robinson to consider the effects of an economic theory which proceeds from the premise that firms operate at a level which fails to employ all available resources in the long-run. As Robinson explains, she set out to describe a system of stable equilibrium in which, "more or less all plants were working part time" (Robinson 1933a, vi). This objective is similar to Chamberlin, in that it dismisses the model of perfect competition as not being applicable to the study of economies which experience long periods of unemployment (Robinson 1933a, vii).

While Chamberlin describes the actual transition, from disequilibrium to equilibrium, Robinson concentrates on analysis of equilibrium, without providing any detail of the transition.[7]

Although different emphases appear in the objectives of the two authors, it is clear that both authors agree on the general objectives of their analyses. We argue that this objective is threefold: (i) to demonstrate why perfect competition is inapplicable when describing stable equilibrium under imperfect competition, (ii) to demonstrate why profit (in excess of average cost) is regarded as being representative of unstable equilibrium, and (iii) to explain the transition to profitless equilibrium.

Transition to Equilibrium - Major Determinants: Product Differentiation

The dynamic transition - from a state of excess profit to profitless equilibrium - is conducted on the basis of a set of major determinants. In elucidating these determinants we will seek to establish a foundation for our discussion of Knight's theory of imperfect competition. Chamberlin defines product differentiation as, "any significant basis for distinguishing the goods (or services) of one seller from those of another" (Chamberlin 1933, 56). Differentiation can attach to the good (or service) itself, or to the conditions of sale surrounding the sale of the good (or service). Chamberlin argues that;

> ... virtually all products are differentiated, at least slightly, and that over a wide range of economic activity differentiation is of considerable importance (Chamberlin 1933, 57).

In order to emphasise the fallacy of treating goods as either perfectly substitutable or perfectly non-substitutable, Chamberlin compares the treatment of patents and trade-marks in economic theory. While we usually think of a patent as giving perfect monopoly power to a producer, this is rarely the case. Substitutes usually impinge on the specific monopoly rights endowed by patent. Conversely, trade-marks are not legally enforceable monopoly rights, as patents are. However, trade-marks do give producers some degree of monopoly power. On this basis Chamberlin argues that the distinction between patents and trade-marks is not clear-cut, rather it is one of 'degree' (Chamberlin 1933, 62). In other words, we should think of market structures in terms of monopolistic competition, where all goods have some degree of substitutability, yet remain imperfect substitutes for one another. This perspective on competition allows

Chamberlin to reject the notion that a market can be classified as being either perfectly competitive or as being perfectly monopolistic. Instead, Chamberlin invites the reader to think of markets as perennially 'monopolistic' where each market is but one in a, "network of related markets" (Chamberlin 1933, 69).

The Notion of the "Competitive Group of Firms"

Chamberlin assumes that the production of all commodities can be subdivided into a series of competitive 'groups' which comprise a number of firms. Furthermore, within the group, Chamberlin argues that: (i) a wide diversity of both products and cost functions exists, and (ii) each group has a large number of producers (Chamberlin 1933, 81). Consequently, the demand curve for each commodity, varies in both elasticity and position relative to both the X and Y axes (Chamberlin 1933, 81, 110-49). We conclude that the definition of a 'group' is based on relative substitution between commodities (Blaug 1962, 415). Consequently, a low degree of substitution between products would constitute an observable distinction between 'groups' (Chamberlin 1933, 1-81).[8] Blaug (1962) summarises these differences, in the relative substitution between products as "gaps in the chain of substitutes" (Blaug 1962, 415).

According to Chamberlin, entry to the competitive group is unrestricted. However, the impact of such entry varies across group members; consumer loyalty partly explains this variation (Chamberlin 1933, 82). In addition, Chamberlin assumes that firms overestimate consumer loyalty so that each firm thinks of itself as being in a uniquely defined market; each firm sees itself operating in its own competitive world. Here, each firm cannot know the competitive reaction of rivals. However, this overestimation proves incorrect because intra-group substitution broadens the effective incidence of competition, from the level of the individual product to the level of the competitive group. Consequently, the firm quite incorrectly estimates that: (i) consumer loyalty is high, and (ii) its own demand curve is relatively steep. It appears that these errors in estimation are treated by Chamberlin as being uniform throughout the competitive group; no firm is able to make better estimations than any other firm in the industry.[9]

Uniformity of Uncertainty between Members of the Competitive Group

Chamberlin characterises the entire competitive group as being uniform in several respects. First, Chamberlin notes that, "we ... proceed under the heroic assumption that both demand and costs curves for all "products" in the group are uniform" (Chamberlin 1933, 82). This 'uniformity' assumption, as Blaug (1962) calls it, appears to conflict with the first assumption, because it seems to contradict the main characteristic of the group, namely its diversity (Blaug 1962, 415).[10]

Second, Chamberlin argues that all members of the competitive group are uniformly uncertain with regard to the competitive reactions of rivals. Firms require knowledge of rival demand and supply schedules so as to formulate a competitive response when rivals alter price, or some other form of competitive challenge. Indeed, each 'gap' in the knowledge set of any one producer is sufficient to make each producer uncertain regarding the competitive reactions of rivals (Chamberlin 1933, 101).[11] We argue that Chamberlin characterises the uncertainty of the monopolistic competitors as being uniform; each firm faces the same deficiency of information, regarding the likely competitive repercussions of price changes.

We, being inspired by Knight, argue that the uncertainty (about the competitive response of rivals) which exists among members of the competitive group largely results from product differentiation. The distinction between products effectively limits producer knowledge to the subset of their own products within the competitive group. Every producer has a precise knowledge of the demand and supply characteristics which are exclusive to his product. Alternatively, each producer has only a vague idea about these characteristics for other products within the competitive group. Because the producer of one product is largely ignorant about the demand and supply characteristics of other products - within the competitive group - he will be uncertain about the competitive response of his rivals. In other words, productive diversity undermines the certainty of competitive response which can be argued to exist in the case of homogeneous production; diverse production is entirely consistent with uncertainty between members of the competitive group.

Uncertainty about the competitive response of rivals underpins Chamberlin's entire argument, and distinguishes it from both monopoly and perfect competition (Chamberlin 1933, 51). In the case of pure monopoly, the producer does not need to know the competitive response of potential rivals, because no rival exists. On the other hand, in the case of pure competition the producer has perfect knowledge of the competitive response of rivals, because his product is exactly the same as every other product in the group. When we mix pure monopoly with pure competition we attain a hybrid assumption regarding the knowledge of the individual producer. In this case, Chamberlin argues that: (i) the producer has rivals, because of the presence of a significant level of substitution linking all products into the group, and (ii) products of different producers are all heterogeneous. Consequently, the producer needs to know the competitive response of rivals, because consumer substitution away from his product threatens his existence. However, the producer is denied access to such knowledge; he does not know "what assumption to make" as to the conduct of his rival (Chamberlin 1933, 51). Every producer is put in an invidious position where his livelihood depends on information he cannot access: the monopolistic firm is perennially uncertain.

In addition, Chamberlin argues that "selling costs" enhance the uncertainty which exists between members of the competitive group (Chamberlin 1933, 145). "Selling costs" are aimed at reducing uncertainty, because each firm aims to 'fortify' itself against the invasion of his rivals (Chamberlin 1933, 154). However, all firms fail in this attempt because every firm in the competitive group incurs "selling costs", so that no firm is able to gauge the effectiveness of their own "selling costs" (Chamberlin 1933, 145).

Competitive Response under Uniform Uncertainty

Having discussed product differentiation and uniform uncertainty, we now turn to the linchpin of Chamberlin's analysis - the competitive response of rivals under uniform uncertainty. This analysis draws attention to the interaction between firms; a feature which sets Chamberlin apart from both standard economic analysis and J. Robinson's treatment of imperfect competition. We argue that Chamberlin's description of the competitive response of rivals centres on Knight's analysis of uncertainty; the essential outcome is that uniform uncertainty forces all firms to eliminate abnormal (or super-normal) profit. Because all firms are uniformly uncertain, competitive response will not be instantaneous: time-lags exist (Chamberlin 1933, 51-3). Price-leaders can exploit these time-lags (assuming that price (P) is greater than average costs (AC)) by attracting an increase in the volume of sales. Here, price-leaders attract a greater quantity of abnormal (or super-normal) profit in the short-run, than they would if they were to remain price-followers. As we shall see, these ephemeral profits provide a compelling reason for the bolder members of the competitive group to cut price, and eventually force the remaining group of price followers into a position of profitless equilibrium (Chamberlin 1933, 51-4, 101-3, 175).

Chamberlin explains this transition in terms of four components (Chamberlin 1933, 51-4). First, Chamberlin wishes to emphasise that competitors do not know who, "will make the first move". Even if a rival left his price unchanged, that does not ensure that other rivals will not attempt: (i) to alter their price, or (ii) further differentiate the product (Chamberlin 1933, 52). The issue of who moves first is fundamental to both the world of perfect competition and that of pure monopoly. However, in the case of monopolistic competition there is uniform uncertainty among the producers about which rival may "move first", and the effect this initial move will have on the competitive reactions of rivals (Chamberlin 1933, 51).[12]

Second, Chamberlin argues that uniform uncertainty (with regard to competitive response) emerges between rivals in assessing the time horizon or, "far-sightedness" (Chamberlin 1933, 52). Even if a rival determines that following a price cut is inconsistent with his long-run interest, he is still unsure whether or not other competitors share this time horizon. In this way, the firm is forced to shorten its time horizon because of the uncertainty surrounding the time horizon which is embraced by his rivals. Furthermore, competitors cannot determine the sustainability of competitive invasion, because of the limited nature of their knowledge. As Chamberlin says, "even though some can thus pursue their interests coolly, there may be others so eager for economic gain that they see nothing but the immediate profits from cutting under rivals" (Chamberlin 1933, 52). In pure competition there is no need to guess a rival's time horizon because all economic actors have perfect knowledge and homogeneous products. Alternatively, in the case of monopoly, there is no need to consider the time horizons of rivals because no rivals exist. In the case of monopolistic competition, however, the estimation of rival time horizon is crucial, because of its impact on both the timing and nature of competitive response.

Third, Chamberlin argues that uniform uncertainty enters monopolistic competition because firms cannot accurately estimate either the present or future number of firms in the monopolistically competitive group; the exact boundaries of the competitive group are unclear. This is because of the substitution which exists between all products. In addition, the entry and exit of firms to the competitive group creates further uncertainty as to the number of competitors. Here, Chamberlin and Robinson argue that a price change alters rival behaviour according to the number of rivals in the competitive group (Robinson 1933a, 50).[13] If the number of competitors is particularly small, as occurs in the case of oligopoly, then the effect of price changes on rivals is particularly large (Chamberlin 1933, 52-3). Conversely, a very large number of competitors diminishes the effects of price changes on rivals (Chamberlin 1933, 53). In contrast, producers in the monopolistically competitive group do not know the number of competitors and are, therefore, effectively prevented from estimating the competitive effect of a price change.

Fourth, Chamberlin argues that uncertainty leads to time-lags in the transition to profitless equilibrium. Chamberlin argues that these time-lags occur because of 'friction' in the working of the market (Chamberlin 1933, 53).

> The "immediate" effects of a price cut (i.e. those [profits] enjoyed before the rival also cuts) are not realised immediately in point of time, but with a delay the length of which is uncertain, depending upon the rapidity with which knowledge of the cut spreads and buyers are brought to alter established relationships [brackets added] (Chamberlin 1933, 53).

This final reason for uniform uncertainty encapsulates the essential outcome of uncertainty for the competitive response of firms under monopolistic competition. Time-lags tend to result from all three reasons listed above. In summary, the following three factors result in time-lags: (i) which competitor will cut the price first, (ii) what time horizon each of the rivals has, and (iii) the indeterminate number of firms in the group. These time-lags create an incentive for firms to cut price. Exploitation of short-run time-lags creates abnormal (or super-normal) profit for price leading firms. Firms cannot afford to ignore these time-lags because another competitor may exploit the situation. While price cuts are not in the long-run interests of all firms in the group, they are entirely consistent with wealth maximisation under conditions of uniformly uncertain competitive response. Indeed, failure to follow price cuts could lead to the failure of the monopolistic firm. In this way, uniform uncertainty compels the entire competitive group to adhere to a stable position of profitless equilibrium.[14]

Long-run Characteristics

Stable Equilibrium Although we have completed our examination of the transition towards profitless equilibrium, we have yet to examine the equilibrium position itself. Here, we focus on Robinson's analysis of imperfect competition.[15] Essentially, the equilibrium position is not substantially different from that given by orthodox theory. The major difference between equilibrium under imperfect competition, as opposed to perfect competition, is the location of equilibrium on the LRAC. Whereas perfect competition establishes that equilibrium occurs at the minimum of the LRAC, imperfect competition establishes that equilibrium usually occurs before the minimum of the LRAC is reached.[16]

Robinson argues that firms, will adjust production to the point where the marginal cost (MC) of production equates marginal revenue (MR) (Chamberlin 1933, 94).[17] When MR=MC the firm is said to be in "individual equilibrium" (Chamberlin 1933, 94). However, at this point, the average revenue (AR) curve may lie above the average cost (AC) curve. In this case, abnormal (or super-normal) profits are made, and the industry can be construed to be in a state of disequilibrium. At this point, Robinson argues that new firms enter the industry and, as a result of the increasing competition, each firm will reduce price. In turn, this price reduction will "lower the individual demand curve ... until it is ... tangential to the average cost curve" (Robinson 1933a, 94). Here, abnormal (or super-normal) profit has been completely competed away and there is no tendency for price to move either up or down. If, for example, price is increased, then the same process of competition, described above, would return price, or average revenue, to the point which is tangential with average cost.[18] In other words, the constant threat of new firms entering the industry keeps price equal to average cost, and this ensures that the long-run equilibrium position is stable.[19]

Normal Profit Chamberlin, as we noted earlier, provides a more detailed account of the transition toward profitless equilibrium. However, his diagrammatic account of the transition toward equilibrium is much the same as Robinson's. An initial state of abnormal (or super-normal) profit is firstly identified as ABCP', in the diagram below. Competition then forces the demand curve from dd to d'd', so that it is tangent to the LRAC.

Here, each producer only has knowledge of the demand and supply schedules which face his particular product. As a result, each producer is uncertain about the competitive reaction of his rivals to a price cut. This uncertainty generates time-lags in the competitive response of rivals. In an effort to exploit these time-lags, price leading firms attempt to attract additional profit by lowering price, because they know that competitive reaction will not be instantaneous. The process of price cutting then proceeds, starting from point C, along the DD line, to point E. If the price falls below E, then it will be below average cost.

As a result, firms will tend not to reduce prices below point E, because this will mean that producers are selling below the average cost of production. However, if price drifts back above E, the process toward E will recommence, and we will have something akin to a limit cycle. As a result, profitless equilibrium is essentially stable, according to Chamberlin because all firms are uniformly uncertain about the competitive response of rivals.

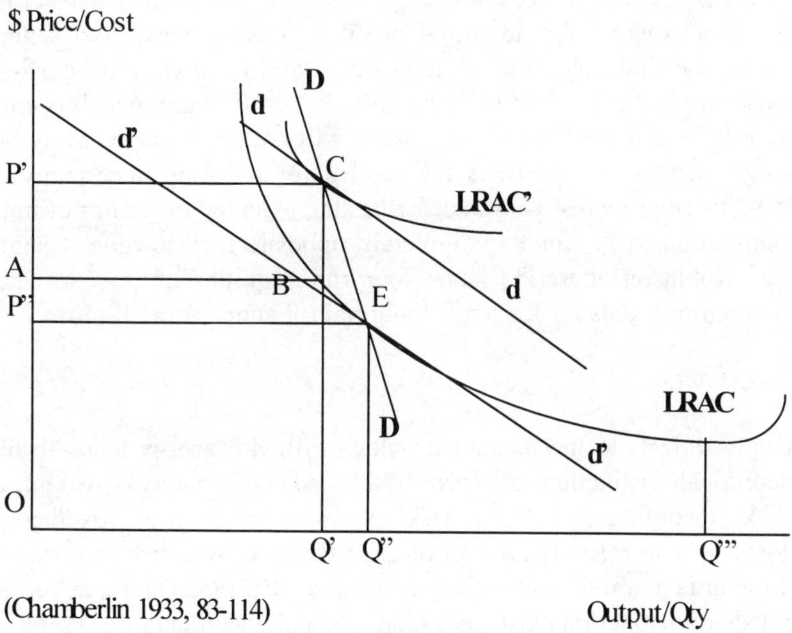

Figure 4.1 Chamberlin's Long-run Equilibrium Solution

Knight's Analysis of Imperfect Competition

Introduction

The final section in Knight's *Risk, Uncertainty, and Profit* (1921a) is devoted to his analysis of imperfect competition (Knight 1921a, 197-377).[20] Here, Knight defines the concept of uncertainty along with his disagreement with orthodox theory; orthodox theory fails to deliver a detailed distinction between risk and uncertainty (Knight 1921a, 268). Because uncertainty forces the firm to rely on forecasts of relevant economic variables, the firm incurs what we term "uncertainty-control costs". However, the large firm relies on a larger body of "sample data" when creating forecasts - such data is not available to the marginal (small) firm. As a result, the large firm enjoys significant cost advantages when compared to the marginal (small) firm.[21] When analysing these costs, Knight effectively divides the industry into two segments: the large firm enjoys access to market knowledge while the marginal (small) firm does not. The struggle for abnormal profit - between these two segments - forces the industry into a long-run state of disequilibrium.[22] Such instability is inconsistent with the notion of equilibrium which is embraced by orthodox theory. In addition, profit will not be competed away because Knight argues that profit is the reward for reducing uncertainty-control costs. In other words, Knight describes the essential outcomes of imperfect competition to be almost completely opposite to that which Chamberlin and Robinson describe: no long-run equilibrium occurs because competition exists for long-run abnormal (or super-normal) profit.[23]

Uncertainty

Knight objects to the manner in which orthodox theory tends to blur the theoretical distinction between 'risk' and 'uncertainty' (Knight 1921a, 233). According to Knight, 'risk' is employed by orthodox theory in a "loose way to refer to any sort of uncertainty viewed from the stand-point of the unfavourable contingency..." (Knight 1921a, 233). However, a clear and sharp distinction exists, between risk and uncertainty.

Risk refers to the description of a set of possible outcomes whose frequency distribution is discernible with the aid of statistical data. Firms are able to determine the distribution of possible outcomes on the basis of either: (i) *a priori* calculation, or (ii) statistical inference, derived from past experience (Knight 1921a, 233). Here, firms can measure the risk of economic action because each productive outcome is the result of a known frequency distribution of: (i) productive inputs, (ii) productive techniques, and (iii) demand characteristics. Although the individual outcomes of productive activity may vary within the frequency distribution, their average characteristics can be described by a set of summary statistics. If all demand and supply functions could be described in this way, then all production would be free from the costs which uncertainty inflicts on the firm. Knight disagrees (Knight 1921a, 233-5).[24]

In contrast, uncertainty refers to a situation where the frequency distribution of possible outcomes is unknown; statistical techniques cannot be applied to individual decisions, "because the situation dealt with is in a high degree unique" (Knight 1921a, 233). Knight argues that business decisions are rarely subject to the assignment of probabilities because each decision will cause, "a single unique outcome ..." (Knight 1921a, 234). According to Knight, individual business decisions lead to a set of possible outcomes which are not subject to mathematical statistics. Neither of these outcomes are equi-probable because of the unique nature of the circumstances which create such outcomes (Knight 1921a, 234).

While risk and uncertainty remain distinct in a theoretical sense, Knight's discussion of uncertainty shows that the containment of uncertainty-control costs is a necessary condition for the maximisation of profit. Here, Knight argues that firms asses the question of the "degree of uniqueness" between outcomes (Knight 1921a, 247). If the outcome is highly unique, then assignment of a probability to the range of possible outcomes will be difficult. On the other hand, if the outcome is not highly unique, then assignment of a probability is comparatively easy. Knight proposes that the "degree of uniqueness" inherent within the decisions of the firm varies inversely with the scale of the firms operations. In other words, as the number of separate decisions increases, the scope for assigning probabilities to the frequency distribution of outcomes also increases. In addition, the scale of the firm effects its access to the stock of available market knowledge.

> The outstanding fact is that the ubiquitous presence of uncertainty permeating every relation of life has brought it about that information is one of the principle commodities the economic organisation is engaged in supplying (Knight 1921a, 261).

Uncertainty-control Costs

The importance of the uncertainty-control cost becomes manifest when one considers Knight's understanding of the effect uncertainty has on the character of production. Without uncertainty, "man's energies are devoted altogether to doing things" (Knight 1921a, 268). Here, the process of production occurs in an "entirely automatic" manner (Knight 1921a, 267). In this case, all decisions are devoid of responsibility, because there is no possibility of error.[25] However, with uncertainty present, the 'execution' of economic activities takes a secondary role, and the primary function of economic activity becomes, "deciding what to do and how to do it" (Knight 1921a, 268). Here, the producer makes, "an entirely impersonal prediction of wants ...", which are unknown even to the consumer (Knight 1921a, 241, 268). The unknown nature of future consumption means that the function of foreseeing consumption, rests squarely with producers (Knight 1921a, 240-1). This assignment of foreseeing consumption is the, "most fundamental effect of uncertainty on the social-economic organisation" (Knight 1921a, 244). Furthermore, the function is difficult.

> It is notoriously impossible to tell accurately when entering upon productive activity what will be its results in physical terms, ... Second, the wants which the goods are to satisfy are also, of course, in the future to the same extent, and their prediction involves uncertainty in the same way (Knight 1921a, 238).

We argue that the level of accuracy, which is evident in such predictions, tends to effect the level of uncertainty-control cost of the firm. Uncertainty-control costs are comprised of two main components. First, we argue that an increase in the scale of the firm creates a lower volatility in the firm's earnings stream, because of its enhanced forecasting ability.[26] This reduced volatility of earnings will translate to lower interest costs from lenders, all else being equal. This occurs because interest charges are positively related to the volatility of a firm's earnings. Knight explains this reduction in interest cost in terms of a "reduction in the risk to borrowed capital", which is created by an increase in the scale of a firm (Knight 1921a, 246, 252).

Second, we argue that the large firm will enjoy cost savings as the incidence of forecasting error falls. As firms compete in uncertain circumstances they tend to rely on estimates - or as Knight puts it - "what they think of the future" (Knight 1921a, 273). Here, all the data upon which the firm makes decisions, "must be *estimated*, subject to a larger or smaller margin of error ..." (Knight 1921a, 276). This process of estimation has a parallel in the scientific examination of data, when 'experimentation' is conducted; an enhancement in the predictability of outcomes occurs if the amount of sample data is increased (Knight 1921a, 246, 272). Similarly, with regard to the firm, an increase in scale will increase the amount of sample data which is used to create forecasts; by increasing the scale of the firm a greater, "degree of constancy and dependability will be achieved" (Knight 1921a, 252). Consequently, we argue that greater predictability of outcomes will result in a reduction in the forecasting errors made by the firm (Knight 1921a, 272). As Knight says;

> ... there is a gain of large magnitude through the reduction of uncertainty by the principle of consolidation ... (Knight 1921a, 278-9).

We argue that the reduction in the size of forecasting errors will result in many cost savings for the large firm. For example, the large firm will need less stock of unsold goods because its estimates of demand constitute accurate predictions of actual demand. In turn, less unsold stock will mean lower interest costs because the large firm has to finance lower stock levels.[27] In addition, the firm will be better able to plan the usage of existing labour and plant. Here, the firm will be able to purchase inputs and apply these inputs through its plant and equipment in a more efficient manner than the marginal (small) firm. In other words, the large firm may achieve a smooth and continuous level of production, which minimises unused stocks of inputs and unsold output. In contrast, the marginal (small) firm endures a continuous series of misjudgments about inputs and outputs; production is discontinuous and sporadic.

The Relation between Uncertainty-Control Costs and the Scale of the Firm

Knight argues that firms can reduce uncertainty-control costs by increasing the scale of production because, "uncertainties are less in groups or cases than in single instances" (Knight 1921a, 238). Furthermore, Knight contends that even "true uncertainties" exhibit a tendency toward regularity, "when grouped on the basis of nearly any similarity ..." (Knight 1921a, 238-9). On this basis, we argue that uncertainty imposes a varying level of cost on firms, according to their scale; the ability to decrease uncertainty-control costs depends on the firm's ability to 'assimilate' one decision making situation with another assimilable situation (Knight 1921a, 245-6). When such assimilation occurs, a group of similar decision making situations can be analysed, so as to identify various sub-divisions within the group (Knight 1921a, 246). This procedure of analysing the group into ever smaller sub-divisions continues until each sub-division exhibits a set of outcomes which are "*equally probable*" (Knight 1921a, 246). In other words, the potential for a reduction in uncertainty-control costs encourages the firm to increase scale (Knight 1921a, 246-51).

> The possibility of thus reducing uncertainty by transforming it into measurable risk through grouping constitutes a strong incentive to extend the scale of operations of a business establishment. This fact must constitute one of the most important causes of the phenomenal growth in the average size of industrial establishments which is a familiar characteristic of modern economic life (Knight 1921a, 252).

The main difficulty in reducing uncertainty-control costs is the degree to which different situations can be 'assimilated' (Knight 1921a, 247). Here, Knight points out that different decision making situations are hardly ever subject to "really homogeneous classifications ..." (Knight 1921a, 246). However, no situation is totally 'unique' to the extent that different situations cannot be 'assimilated' in some way (Knight 1921a, 246). This means that almost all events lie somewhere between these two extremes. "The principle subject for investigation is thus the degree of assimilability, ... or, stated inversely, the *degree of uniqueness* of various kinds of business contingencies" [emphasis added] (Knight 1921a, 247). The possibility of attaining more reliable estimates is not dependent on the "degree of uniqueness" which is inherent in each type of decision. Rather, the uniqueness of decisions is malleable, because increases in firm scale lead to better access to the stock of available market information.

Knight illustrates this point with the example of the insurance industry, so as to demonstrate that a degree of assimilation can be achieved, "in the almost complete absence of scientific data ..." (Knight 1921a, 250). Knight argues that Lloyds of London can estimate an insurance premium on the basis of a wide variety of data. Insurance data, on which Lloyds establish their premium varies, "from something like the statistical certainty of life insurance at one extreme to almost guess-work

..." (Knight 1921a, 250). Knight argues that Lloyds are able to estimate these premiums because they have access to a large share of the insurance market, and the correspondingly large number of separate business decisions, or insurable situations. Whereas a small insurance company cannot insure the range of situations insured by Lloyds, the market dominance of Lloyds allows it better access to the data which underpins the actuarial assessment of insurance premiums. Greater scale thereby allows greater access to the total stock of market data, and this access creates, "a degree of constancy and dependability in the total results ..." (Knight 1921a, 252). Such access then allows Lloyds to assimilate separate business decisions and thereby reduce uncertainty-control costs in the long-run.

While increasing the scale of the firm's operations tends to lead to a more reliable set of data on which the firm can make estimates, specialisation of the decision making function also assists in reducing uncertainty-control costs (Knight 1921a, 256). Knight argues that the principle of specialisation is illustrated by the tendency of firms to separate the highly uncertain aspects of the firm from, "the stable and predictable aspects ..." (Knight 1921a, 257). Specialisation of uncertainty-bearing also generates skills which allow better management of uncertainty, and also results in lower uncertainty-control costs (Knight 1921a, 258). Better "knowledge and judgement" of the potential costs of uncertainty translates into a reduction in those costs, or as Knight terms it, "greater economy in the use of economic resources" (Knight 1921a, 259).

Because the level of cost in the large firm is always lower than the level of cost in the marginal (small) firm, it is a matter of truism that as long as smaller firms (producing essentially identical products) exist, prices will always be set at the level which allows the firm with the smallest scale to operate. In turn, this implies that the large firm will make abnormal (or super-normal) profit while the smallest firm makes normal profit. In the long-run, such abnormal profit inflates the imbalance of economic power between the large and the marginal (small) firm; this conclusion supports our discussion in Chapter Two.

Long-run Characteristics

Disequilibrium We argue that the variation of unit costs - across firms producing identical commodities - can be contrasted to the analysis of heterogeneous products (Robinson 1933a; Chamberlin 1933). Imperfect competition, according to Knight, is centred around the cost differentials which exist between the large and the marginal (small) firm, rather than the product differentials which exist between firms. Chamberlin and Robinson fail to effectively challenge orthodox theory because their analysis of a market which sells a multitude of heterogeneous products essentially boils down to a series of smaller sub-markets; each of these smaller markets can be analysed in the same manner employed in the model of perfect competition. In contrast, Knight challenges orthodox theory by arguing that uncertainty-control costs vary systematically from the large firm to the marginal (small) firm. Because of this systematic variation in cost, we can argue that the characteristics of long-run equilibrium are quite different from what Chamberlin and Robinson describe; their notion of equilibrium is perfectly consistent with orthodox theory. This is because - in their analyses - long-run equilibrium is both perfectly stable and is characterised by normal profit. In contrast, Knight argues that prospect of long-run equilibrium is destroyed by the existence of uncertainty; a fundamental inconsistency emerges between the idea of equilibrium and the presence of uncertainty.[28]

Uncertainty creates a long-run disequilibrium because, "productive arrangements are made on the basis of anticipations ..." (Knight 1921a, 272). Anticipation of consumption, especially in the case of the marginal (small) firm, is usually either too optimistic or too pessimistic when compared to the actual level of demand (Knight 1921a, 288). Disequilibrium is, therefore, the result of errors in the forecasting of economic variables, errors which Knight argues will not cancel each other out. Here, Knight argues that the marginal (small) firm, tend to follow the advice of so called 'authorities' so that the estimates of all marginal (small) firms can be swayed by these 'authorities' (Knight 1921a, 288). As Knight says, we must recognise the, "... importance of indirect knowledge [or] of fact through knowledge of others' knowledge ..." [brackets added] (Knight 1921a, 288). In other words, reliance on indirect knowledge shifts the responsibility of forecasting from the marginal (small) firm to the forecasting authority: a magnification of biased forecasts ensues.[29] Equilibrium fails to eventuate in the long-run because of the competitive struggle for access to market knowledge between the marginal (small) firms in the industry.

In principle, the large firm can eliminate the marginal (small) firm, because it produces goods at a lower cost than the marginal (small) firm. Knight is very concerned about the general trend toward monopolisation.[30]

However, we argue that the large firm is constrained from monopolisation by the regulatory sanctions which are largely instituted by J.M. and J.B. Clark.[31] Given the existence of regulatory sanctions, the cutting of industry price - by the large firm - is, therefore, inconsistent with the maximisation of long-run profit.

However, firms can avoid the application of the regulatory framework in three ways. First, they can expand on a global basis by increasing the scale of operations up to the maximum allowable limit in each country. By seizing the maximum allowable market share in each country, the large firm can reduce the scope for the marginal (small) firm on a global basis.[32] Second, the large firm can exert political influence on the government so as to relax the sanctions on monopolisation of industry. In Australia, the media and the steel industries are examples of such political power.[33] On this basis, we argue that the large firm restrains itself from destroying the marginal (small) firm not out of any belief in the 'fairness' of competition, but purely out of self-interest. Indeed, the large firm has an interest in promoting the existence of the marginal (small) firm so that industry price remains as high as possible.

Abnormal (or Super-normal) Profit

> Profit arises out of the inherent, absolutely unpredictability of things, out of the sheer brute fact that the results of human activity cannot be anticipated and then only in so far as even a probability calculation in regard to them is impossible and meaningless (Knight 1921a, 311).

Excess profit is not competed away, in Knight's conception of imperfect competition because profit accrues to the firm which bears a lower level of uncertainty-control cost by virtue of large size (Knight 1921a, 268). Because the large firm has the best access to the stock of available market information, the industry - as a whole - is not uniformly uncertain about competitive response to a price cut. Therefore, the large firm will not need to reduce price, because price is essentially set by the marginal (higher cost) firm; the large firm does not follow Chamberlin's transition to normal profit because they are not uniformly uncertain.[34] However, because the marginal (small) firm is uncertain about the competitive reaction of rivals, it will tend to follow Chamberlain's transition to normal profit - even though each producer sells the same product.

Abnormal (or super-normal) profits will attract entrants, however the information which is possessed by the large firm, creates a significant barrier to entry. Information about the market under consideration attaches itself to market share, and the firms who control that market share also enjoy the benefits which accrue to the owners of better information. In this way, access to market knowledge is proprietary in nature, it is not costlessly transferable to other firms. A potential entrant can seize access to this information by running losses for an extended entry period. However, such an entrant is usually frustrated by the monopolisation of access to market knowledge which large incumbents possess. In some unusual cases, it may be possible for a new entrant (or even an existing rival) to mount a successful challenge and thereby claim ownership of the large incumbent. Although unlikely, this change in ownership of the dominant firm will not alter the general industrial structure; the new owner will enjoy the same abnormal profit as the old owner and the marginal (small) firms will still compete in a way which contributes to the instability of the imperfectly competitive market. In this way monopolisation of access to market knowledge is never eliminated, even though ownership of such access may change.[35]

In contrast, such heterogeneity of information is absent under conditions of perfect knowledge because, "man's energies are devoted altogether to doing things ..." (Knight 1921a, 268). Forecasting, and the notion of being responsible for such forecasting, are entirely alien to those firms who rely on information which is completely accurate (Knight 1921a, 271).[36]

Knightian Analysis and Chamberlin's Transition to Profitless Equilibrium

Knight's analysis of uncertainty undermines the process by which Chamberlin establishes his dynamic transition towards profitless equilibrium.[37]

> Uncertainty, where present, as to (a) whether other competitors will hold their amount or their prices constant, (b) whether they are far-sighted, (c) the extent of the possible incursions upon their markets, and (d) in the case of a time lag, its length, renders the outcome [of monopolistic competition] indeterminate for the particular reasons indicated in each case [brackets added] (Chamberlin 1933, 54, 101).

First, Knight agrees with Chamberlin in that all firms will not be able to perfectly forecast the competitive impact of a rival's price cut. However, Knight argues that relative access to market knowledge modifies the amount of uncertainty-control costs which the firm incurs; forecasting ability increases with an increase in access to the stock of available market knowledge. On this basis, we argue that the large firm will tend to anticipate the price cutting activities of rivals more accurately than the marginal (small) firm, and that this favourable forecasting ability results in lower uncertainty-control costs for the large firm. These cost differentials mean that the large firm will be able to counter the competitive pricing pressures which are exerted by the marginal (small) firm, because its uncertainty-control costs are lower than that of the marginal (small) firm. As a result, the process of price-cutting which leads to Chamberlin's profitless equilibrium, will be frustrated by the cost differentials which exist in Knight's analysis of imperfect competition. Indeed, Knight's analysis suggests that the large firm will actively support the existence of the marginal (small) firm so as to ensure the derivation of abnormal profit

However, the marginal (small) firm, when grouped as an industrial segment, will tend to act as if it is uniformly uncertain about the competitive reactions of it's rivals. While each firm is assumed to sell the same product, these firms still exhibit the same sort of uncertainty encountered by Chamberlin's monopolistically competitive firm. This is because the marginal (small) firm produces such a small part of the industries output that it becomes just as deprived of access to market knowledge - and thereby uncertain - as Chamberlin's monopolistically competitive firm. As a result, price leaders within the group of marginal (small) firms will seek to maximise short-run profit by attracting the increased volume of sales which are associated with price cuts. In contrast, the large firm possesses access to market knowledge and, therefore, will not act like Chamberlin's monopolistic firm. The large firm will use its access to market knowledge so as to determine the benefits and costs of cutting industry price. If regulators prevent the monopolisation of markets, then we argue that the large firm will let the marginal (small) firm set industry price. In other words, government regulation prevents the large firm from creating a net benefit by cutting industry price. However, as long as industry price is above average cost of production the large firm earns abnormal profit.

Second, Chamberlin's contention that firms are uncertain, in gauging the time horizon of rivals is also subject to challenge. According to Knight, the marginal (small) firm will tend to behave in the way Chamberlin forecasts, because of the high costs which are associated with assessing these aspects of rival behaviour. On the other hand, the large firm will be able to assess the time horizon of rivals at a lower cost than the marginal (small) firm.[38] Consequently, the large firm will not shorten its time horizon, as the price-leader does in monopolistic competition. Rather, the large firm will only adopt strategies which are consistent with long-run maximisation of profit.

Third, Chamberlin argues that the indeterminate number of firms, in any monopolistically competitive industry, will prevent rivals from accurately estimating the extent of the competitive response. Once again, Knight's analysis of uncertainty suggests that the ability of the firm, to correctly estimate the sustainability of competitive invasion, is related to the relative access to market knowledge. As the scale of the firm increases the 'assimilation' of separate decision making situations, ensures that the large firm will be better able to accurately estimate the possible competitive ramifications of any competitive invasion. In addition, this estimate will tend to be made at a cost which is lower to that available to the marginal (small) firm (Knight 1921a, 246).

Finally, Chamberlin argues that firms are uncertain about the competitive response of rivals because they cannot accurately estimate the duration of the time-lags involved in competitive adjustment to price. Here, Knight suggests that the costs associated with these estimates are relative to the scale of the firm. Once again, the costs of accurate estimation are relative to what access to market knowledge the firm enjoys. In addition, as the amount of decisions made by the firm approaches the total amount of decisions made in the entire market, economies of scale accrue to the grouping of separate decisions: unit cost falls. In this way, the large firm can possess a better estimate of the time-lags (associated with competitive response), when compared to the marginal (small) firm.

Another way to present our argument, regarding the dynamic process toward equilibrium, is that Chamberlin assumes - in contrast to Knight - that all firms must operate under a uniform level of uncertainty-control costs. Our discussion of Knight's analysis, indicates that Knight saw a wide variance in uncertainty-control costs between firms of differing scale (Knight 1921a, 233-64). While some firms face high uncertainty-control costs, as Chamberlin depicts them, other firms face a lower level of such costs. Similarly, Fellner (1949) argues that the likelihood of firms knowing the competitive reaction of rivals depends on the scale of the firm, relative to the market (Fellner 1949, 42-6). As Fellner argues;

> ... the problem of fewness and co-ordinated action acquires significance as soon as certain firms grow to such a size in relation to the market that they affect one another to a noticeable extent by their individual policies (Fellner 1949, 44).

In addition, our conclusion regarding the dependence of profitless equilibrium on the uniformity of uncertainty is supported by Bain (1967). Here, Bain (1967) comments that if any degree of information about a rival's reaction to price cutting exists, then the process of price cutting - which leads to profitless equilibrium - is brought into question.

> When any seller is so situated that he knows that what he does will have a substantial influence on others and therefore may lead them to attempt to alter their present policies, he would be very short-sighted indeed not to take all of this into account (Bain 1967, 147-76).

If some producers are better informed than others, as Knight (1921a) and Fellner (1949) suggest, then we can expect the better informed firms to resist the price reducing practices of other firms. This resistance to price cutting will frustrate the process of competitive price cutting between firms which Chamberlin argues will conclude in a profitless equilibrium.

Conclusion

Both Robinson and Chamberlin depart from orthodox theory by showing that the old tools of orthodox theory, namely marginal analysis, can be applied in a new way when product differentiation is recognised. Chamberlin recognises a special type of uncertainty - uniform uncertainty - which regulates price adjustment in the context of the multi-firm industry with heterogeneous products. Here, Chamberlin explores the dynamic process of adjustment which transforms abnormal (or super-normal) profit into normal profit. Some producers realise that uncertainty will cause time-lags in the price adjustments of competitors, so that price leaders can enjoy transient increases in abnormal (or super-normal) profit as price is cut down to a level which equates the average cost of production. Indeed, such uniform uncertainty is required so as to be consistent with Chamberlin's notion of highly differentiated production; all the products in the competitive group are so different that every producer is effectively isolated in terms of gauging the competitive response of rivals. In this respect, Chamberlin's monopolistically competitive firm resembles the marginal (small) firm in Knight's analysis of imperfect competition; both are deprived of access to market knowledge and both are equally uncertain about the competitive reactions of rivals.

Consequently, Chamberlin completely rejects the notion of perfect knowledge which is embedded in orthodox theory. In this way, Knight's (1921a) analysis of uncertainty provides a starting point for Chamberlin's departure from the orthodox avoidance of uncertainty as an issue in economic theory. However, this is only a starting point. Paradoxically, Chamberlin's special treatment of uncertainty creates a competitive outcome which is generally consistent with orthodox theory's notion of perfect competition: abnormal (or super-normal) profit ceases to exist in a perfectly stable long-run equilibrium. As a result, we argue that the assumption of uniform uncertainty creates roughly the same competitive outcomes as the assumption of perfect certainty. Knight disagrees.

In contrast, Knight argues that the marginal (small) firm will compete in the same way as the monopolistically competitive firm, because it suffers from a similar deprivation of access to market knowledge. The source of the monopolistic firm's depravation is the highly differentiated nature of production, whereas the source of the marginal (small) firm's deprivation is lack of access to market knowledge. In an effort to seize access to market knowledge the marginal (small) firm creates a continuous variation in the general level of economic activity. Knight suggests that the notion of long-run equilibrium is inconsistent with the competitive tensions which underlie his analysis of uncertainty; a continual struggle for access to market knowledge prevents equilibrium from occurring. The large firm is constrained from eliminating the marginal (small) firm by government regulation, while the marginal (small) firm is constantly attempting to seize market share and the accompanying access to market knowledge. The marginal (small) firm augments its market knowledge by employing the assistance of an external adviser; this advice represents no substitute for access to market knowledge and results in marginal (small) firms having interdependent estimates. Such interdependence tends to increase the volatility of the marginal (small) firm's estimates: instability is thereby entrenched in the economic system (Knight 1921a, 164-233).

We argue that Knight's analysis of uncertainty-control cost provides the large firm with a systematic cost advantage when compared with the marginal (small) firm: something which both Chamberlin and Robinson fail to consider. This cost advantage will frustrate the process which leads to the elimination of abnormal (or super-normal) profit in the long-run. On this basis, therefore, we reject the notion that abnormal (or super-normal) profit will be competed away in the long-run.

Notes

1 While Harrod (1934) treats Chamberlin and Robinson's analyses as equivalent we argue that they are quite different; they develop different aspects of imperfect competition. Chamberlin revises the definition of markets in economic theory. This revision incorporates the notion of product heterogeneity which treats all products as if they were unique (Blaug 1962, 415) We argue that Chamberlin's main innovation is to describe why the competitive response of individual firms directs the industry toward a stable position of profitless equilibrium. In contrast, Robinson does not focus on the implications on competitive response; she concentrates on the mathematical description of the equilibrium (Robinson 1933a, 180-6). In other words, Robinson's analysis of imperfect competition fails to incorporate uncertainty; it is a highly orthodox form of analysis. This conclusion is consistent with other economists (Loasby 1991, 41; Rima 1991; Bharadwaj 1991; Levine 1991; Feiwel 1991). Consequently, we argue that the two analyses are complimentary; both are required to attain a coherent explanation of imperfect competition.

2 Hereafter we shall refer to the costs which are associated with the control of uncertainty as uncertainty-control costs. We provide part of our account of these costs later in this Chapter, however we can propose an initial definition at this stage. The term 'uncertainty-control costs' is not used to express the notion that the firm can 'control' uncertainty by incurring a certain level of costs. Rather, these costs are necessary to 'hedge' the firm against potential losses which can be inflicted by uncertain events. Essentially, Knight argues that the large firm can hedge itself against uncertain events more cost effectively - when compared to the marginal (small) firm - by dint of being large. More specifically, we note that an uncertainty-control cost is the difference in the cost of production which is incurred by the firm, under conditions of uncertainty, as compared to what these costs might be under conditions of perfect certainty (see Chapter Four of this work).

3 This analysis implies that markets which have a high proportion of marginal (small) firms will exhibit higher output volatility than markets which have a high proportion of large firms.

4 See Chapters Four and Five.

5 Both these influences are common to Knight.

6 While both authors succeed in making a positive contribution to economic theory, it appears that the intellectual background behind each of them is somewhat different. Robinson, on the one hand, draws on the English tradition in economic theory, in order to explain why firms may not operate at full capacity. This tradition focuses on economies and diseconomies of scale. This tendency of Robinson, to follow the English school of economic theory, is noted by other economists (Schumpeter 1934, 129).

> Everything about it [Robinson's *The Economics Of Imperfect Competition* (1933)] is Marshallian: the approach, the fundamental "conceptual scheme", the manner of reasoning, the starting points as well as the goals, even the general social vision (although somewhat more "modernised") which floats about it [brackets added] (Schumpeter 1934, 129).

Chamberlin, on the other hand, draws on the American tradition in economic theory, which J.B. Clark establishes and which is revised by both J.M. Clark and F.H.Knight. This tradition tends to be more interested in explaining the dynamic aspects of markets. We argue that Knight's analysis of uncertainty demonstrates this tendency. In addition, we contend that Knight's influence is most apparent in Chamberlin's discussion of uncertainty (Chamberlin 1933, 51-4, 81-2).

7 Moreover, when Robinson does attempt to provide an account of this transition it is somewhat vacuous, as she later concedes (Robinson 1933a, vi).

8 For example, a lack of substitution between food and clothing products would constitute a distinction between groups, because of the average consumer's inability to switch expenditure between product groups. Alternatively, a high degree of substitution between commodities would constitute a "group", such as a group of automobile producers (Chamberlin 1933, 1-81).

9 In contrast, Robinson defines the industry as, "any group of firms producing a single commodity", which is consistent with orthodox theory (Robinson 1933a, 17). Robinson initially acknowledges that some difficulties may arise in the correspondence of such an abstract notion to real world situations (Robinson 1933a, 17). Accordingly, in the 1969 preface to *The Economics of Imperfect Competition* (1933) Robinson adopts a concept of the industry which is more aligned with Chamberlin's "competitive group". This concept is based upon Chamberlin's notion of

product differentiation, where markets should not be thought of in terms of either perfect competition, or perfect monopoly (Chamberlin 1933, 69). In this later definition, Robinson argues that "the concept of industry" is "... amorphous and impossible to demarcate sharply at the edges" (Robinson 1933a, x). Consequently, we will adopt Chamberlin's definition of the competitive group.

10 This apparent contradiction is detected by Stigler, and is also reiterated by Blaug (Blaug 1962, 415; Stigler 1949, 297). We can, however, reconcile this apparent contradiction, by considering the level of abstraction which Chamberlin is employing in his analysis. Here, we argue that Chamberlin's "group" assumption allows us to see the distinction between groups, in terms of their broad demand and cost characteristics. Furthermore, this assumption does not imply, as Blaug suggests, homogeneous products with horizontal demand curves (Blaug 1962, 415). Rather, it is aimed at identifying variations in demand and cost, on a group by group basis (Chamberlin 1957, Ekelund and Herbert 1975, 492).

11 These "gaps" specifically relate to the absence of information on the competitive response of rivals in the competitive group. While such information is of critical importance it remains unavailable to the monopolistic firm. To a large degree, this problem emerges from the diverse nature of production; firms producing the same product have much less difficulty in gauging the competitive response of rivals. However, Chamberlin assumes that such knowledge is not available in the competitive group. Just as "gaps in the chain of substitutes" define the existence of competitive groups, gaps in the knowledge of firms can also define the existence of the competitive group (Blaug 1962, 415). In other words, the competitive group can be defined by the relative demand and supply of information relating to the competitive reaction of rivals. While members of the competitive group demand such information, the nature of each competitive group ensures that such information is never forthcoming.

12 Here, producers may attempt to offset the effect of a price cut - made by a rival who moves first - by increasing the after sales service on a product. In this example, the effect of such an offset is uncertain because each retaliating producer only knows the demand characteristics of his own product. This means that an initial price cut may induce a larger than expected substitution away from the rival, who then retaliates by increasing the quality of the product. As a result, the price cutter will benefit over the period in which his rivals under-estimated the demand which he generates through cutting price.

13 This occurs because the number of firms in the competitive group tends to determine the opportunity for abnormal (or super-normal) profit. Competitive groups with low numbers of firms tend to be associated with

higher levels of excess profit than groups with higher numbers. The intensity of competitive response to price change is, therefore, higher in the case of smaller competitive groups, because of the higher level of abnormal (or super-normal) profit they seek to protect.

14 Robinson's account of how firms actually follow the process of price adjustment, towards competitive equilibrium, is inconsistent and deficient in comparison to that of Chamberlin. An example of Robinson's inconsistency is where she initially argues that economic actors are completely certain about all the variables which are relevant to wealth maximisation. Secondly, she later argues that economic actors are uncertain, because the firm discovers "the conditions of demand for its product by trial and error ..." (Robinson 1933a, vi, 10-15). We argue that this process of discovering demand by trial and error would be otiose, if the firm were certain about the value of the variables on which it bases its conclusions; the assumption of perfect knowledge makes any form of "trial and error" entirely redundant. These sorts of inconsistencies, which centre around the treatment of uncertainty, lead Robinson to concede that her entire analysis lacks an account of the transition, from abnormal to normal profit. In other words, Robinson's analysis, as she says, "fudged" the appearance of giving an account of the dynamic transition towards profitless equilibrium (Robinson 1933a, vi).

> The whole analysis, which in reality consists of comparisons of static equilibrium positions, is dressed up to appear to represent a process going on through time (Robinson 1933a, vi).

15 Each author provides one essential aspect of imperfect competition. On the one hand, Robinson provides the detailed mathematical analysis of equilibrium, under imperfect competition. On the other hand, Chamberlin provides an account of the dynamic transition which transforms disequilibrium into profitless equilibrium.

16 Furthermore, Harrod (1934) argues that the equilibrium position can be at the minimum of the LRAC with firms earning abnormal (or super-normal) profit, however we consider that this is a rare circumstance (Harrod 1934, 456).

17 Marginal costs, "... represents the rate at which total cost increases as output increases" (Chamberlin 1933, 26). In other words, MC expresses the rate of change in the average cost curve, which Chamberlin defines as, "... the total cost of n units of output divided by n" (Chamberlin 1933, 26). Similarly, MR expresses the rate of change in the average revenue (AR).

18 See Appendix One to Chapter Four for a graphical representation of this long-run position.

19 In contrast, Chamberlin's analysis of equilibrium suggests that the stability of equilibrium, over the long-run, is ensured by the uniformity of uncertainty which exists between members of the competitive group. As long as all firms are equally uncertain about the competitive response of rivals, they will always keep price equal to average cost. If a firm raises price above the average cost of production, then it risks the erosion of market share within the competitive group. Moreover, the firm does not know whether rivals will be able to impinge on its market share. However, if some firms have better knowledge of competitive response, then all firms will not keep price equal to the average cost of production. In this way, non-uniform uncertainty creates the type of disequilibrium which Knight discusses.

20 However, a more detailed discussion exists in Chapters Eight and Nine (Knight 1921a, 233-90).

21 While we provide an initial explanation of these costs in this Chapter, we complete our explanation in Chapter Five.

22 Although in principle, the large firm can eliminate the marginal (small) firm by cutting industry price - so as to create a strict monopoly - we argue that existing regulation usually prevents such action. We discuss this in Chapter Four of this work.

23 We assume, for expository purposes, that products are homogeneous in our illustration of Knight's theory of imperfect competition. While Knight does recognise some degree of product heterogeneity, we abstract from this recognition so as to illustrate the impact of heterogeneous uncertainty on the costs of firms.

24 At this point, we should note the distinction between Knight's notion of the costs of controlling uncertainty, with the utility cost of bearing uncertainty which is borne by all risk averse economic agents in modern risk-bearing theory. Uncertainty-control costs refer specifically to the producer's inability to accurately estimate relevant economic data. If producers are unable to accurately forecast, then they will incur the costs which emanate from uncertainty. In contrast, the utility cost of bearing uncertainty refers to the relative discomfort, or exertion, which a firm expends in bearing uncertainty. In other words, Knight's notion refers to the existence of a forecasting capacity, whereas the notion of utility cost refers to the existence of some aversion to the bearing of uncertainty.

25 One could argue that no decision actually occurs in the case of perfect knowledge, because all the possible productive alternatives have definite values. In this case, the producer merely adopts the alternatives which maximise profit (Gordon 1974).

26 An enhanced forecasting ability is derived from the large firm's access to the stock of available market knowledge. Such access is analogous with

access to any other "database"; we explain this form of access in Chapter Five of this book.

27 Another way of reducing risk is given by modern portfolio theory, where a firm reduces risk by producing a diverse portfolio of products. Here, the risks which are involved with the sale of one product are offset by the diversified nature of the firm's total product portfolio. The problem with this strategy is that it does not take advantage of the reduction in uncertainty-control costs which are derived from being in a dominant market position, as the firm would produce only a small amount in each of the markets it services. In addition, normal economies of scale would remain unexploited. Here, the firm producing a diverse range of products would spread fixed costs over a small level of production which is smaller than if the firm produces only one product.

28 In addition, heterogeneity of cost directly contradicts Chamberlin's assumption, regarding the uniformity of cost, in the competitive group (Chamberlin 1933, 82).

29 Such a proposition tends to contradict the rational expectations theory. Here, rational expectations asserts that the forecasts of economic actors are both efficient and unbiased (Minford and Peel 1983, 16-7). Reliance on an external forecasting authority makes all marginal (small) firm forecasts interdependent. This not only magnifies errors, but also creates biased predictions.

30 Such concern constitutes a major theme of Knight's work: see Chapter Two of this book.

31 Examples of these sanctions are the anti-trust legislation in the United States and the *Trade Practices Act* 1974 (Cth) in Australia: see Chapter Three of this book.

32 Such a global analysis is considered to be outside the scope of this book.

33 Similarly, an examination of these industries is considered to be outside the scope of this book.

34 Because all firms sell essentially identical products, they all tend to be price takers. As mentioned in the earlier part of this Chapter, the large firm is prevented from eliminating the marginal (small) firm by the regulatory framework which prohibits the large firm from monopolising the industry. Given that the large firm cannot eliminate the marginal (small) firm, we argue that price cutting by the large firm is inconsistent with long-run profit maximisation.

35 In other words, the entrant faces an absolute cost disadvantage to the large incumbent firm. Contestable markets theory, in contrast, does not allow for any cost advantages. Entrants will not be able to enter the market and costlessly replicate the operations of the large firm (Baumol, Panzar, and Willing 1982, 332). Consequently, Knight's analysis of non-uniform

uncertainty leads us to reject the theory of contestable markets, because of the cost variations which such heterogeneous information delivers.

36 This responsibility is crucial to the future prospects of the firm, because it forms the driving force of competition, under conditions of uncertainty (Knight 1921a, 273). Competition is driven, not by the value of present economic variables, but by what firms "*think* of the *future*" (Knight 1921a, 273). Usually, a "twofold estimate of the future, involving both technological and price uncertainties ..." is involved in undertaking this forecasting function (Knight 1921a, 273). These forecasts effectively discharge the firms' "*liability of error*" (Knight 1921a, 276). Here, a potential liability faces the economic actor who forecasts the value of critical economic variables, on behalf of the firm. If the forecasts are wrong, then uncertainty-control costs will rise and this increase in cost may threaten the viability of the firm. In other words, the economic actor who is responsible for forecasting is liable to the firm, for any increase in uncertainty-control costs which emanate from his forecasts.

37 To briefly recapitulate our analysis of Chamberlin, we show how Chamberlin's transition to profitless equilibrium stems from his conception of product heterogeneity. Different products command distinct knowledge sets, which contain details of the supply and demand functions for each product. Each knowledge set surrounds and insulates each producer, to the extent that he becomes uncertain of the competitive response of rivals.

38 Here again, this is because the costs of these estimates will fall, as the firm's access to market knowledge increases.

5 Some Policy Implications

Introduction

We commence our discussion of Knight's policy response to imperfect competition with an outline of the policy response to imperfect competition which is given by Chamberlin and Robinson. Here, both authors describe how firms capture a degree of market power from their ability to differentiate products. As mentioned above, such power prevents firms from operating at the most efficient level of output, which exists at the minimum of the long-run average cost curve (LRAC). In other words, Chamberlin and Robinson describe a situation where unexploited economies of scale contribute to an efficiency problem. However, this problem proves difficult to solve. Bearing these difficulties in mind, we argue that the only available means of addressing such a problem is to eliminate the market power of the firm. However, this solution is inevitable within their analyses, because its basic axiom centres on the capacity of the firm to differentiate its product from other products in the competitive group.

As mentioned above, Knight suggests that market power stems from the capacity of the firm to capture more accurate market knowledge; the large firm possesses such a capacity. As a result, Knight argues that an inequality of production cost exists in the imperfectly competitive market, which leads to both a distribution problem as well as an efficiency problem. In developing solutions to these problems we illustrate the significant differences which exist between Knight's theory of imperfect competition and orthodox theory. While orthodox theory fails to recognise the distribution problem, we argue that Knight is not so nonchalant. Indeed the distribution problem is a central theme of Knight's contribution to economic theory. Second, we outline a solution to the efficiency problem which we argue is consistent with the policy objectives of orthodox economic theory. In contrast, we argue that Knight would oppose this solution, because it would inflate the distribution problem.

In contrasting the analysis of Chamberlin and Robinson to that of Knight we seek to correct some misunderstandings about Knight. For example, Stigler (1957) argues that Knight's criticisms of perfect competition prepares the way, "... for the widespread reaction against it in the 1930s" (Stigler 1957, 11; Buchanan 1968, 196). This reaction comprises, "... the doctrines of imperfect and monopolistic competition ..." (Stigler 1957, 11). Such an interpretation implies that Knight did not have a coherent theoretical alternative to the work which he criticises. Moreover, it implies that Knight's work is of a purely critical nature, having no distinct policy implications (Emmett 1989, Hammond 1990).

Policy Response to Imperfect Competition: E.H. Chamberlin and J. Robinson

Chamberlin (1933) and Robinson (1933a) both investigate the market power of the firm from a different perspective to Knight (1921a). Although differentiated, the products of the 'competitive monopolist' are constantly under challenge from existing and potential rivals, because these rivals introduce new and close substitutes into the market. Both authors define the LRAC to be tangential to the demand curve so that all abnormal (or super-normal) profits are eliminated. In addition, the incentive for entry, or introduction of new substitutes by existing firms, no longer exist; we can term this point of tangency a position of long-run equilibrium. In contrast to the orthodox perfectly competitive equilibrium, such an equilibrium does not occur at the minimum point of the LRAC, rather it usually exists to the left of this minimum point. Consequently, industry price will usually be higher than the marginal cost of production, but equal to the average cost of production. This means that firms do not derive any economic rent from their ability to differentiate production, but they supply less than they would if all products were homogeneous.[1]

In Chamberlin (1933) and Robinson (1933a), the main reason that firms cannot operate at the minimum point of the LRAC is because the demand, or average revenue curve (AR), is downwardly sloping.[2] Such a slope reflects the ability of each firm to differentiate its product from every other firm in the competitive group; consumers also prefer such diversity. In other words, consumers prefer a more expensive set of heterogeneous products, to a cheaper homogeneous product. As a result, the efficiency of production - under conditions of monopolistic competition - is usually lower than under conditions of perfect competition, because the average cost of production is not at its minimum.

Policy solutions for this 'inefficiency' are problematic because the difference between the marginal cost of production and industry price represents a payment for the creation of product diversity. However, it can be argued that producers seek to increase profit by adopting techniques which exaggerate the consumer's preference for a variety of products; Chamberlin (1933) defends the right of producers to proceed with such exaggeration.[3] Chamberlin argues that all producers have a basic right to create product differentiation. Product differentiation, in other words, reflects both the individual freedom of the producer to maximise profit and the individual freedom of the consumer to demand a diversity of production. If we withdraw the right of producers to differentiate production, we constrain the way in which a firm maximises its profit; a reduction in productive efficiency may follow. In addition, aggregate welfare may fall because a less diverse range of production will exist. Chamberlin, therefore, argues that the notion of an ideal output is questionable in the context of differentiated production. Consumer welfare is supplemented by the diversity of production. Attempts to solely increase productive efficiency cannot be considered because the notion of an ideal level of production is meaningless for industries which: (i) sell more than one (homogeneous) product, and (ii) where such diversity satisfies consumer demand.[4]

In addition to arguing that an ideal level of output is meaningless, Chamberlin (1933) argues that the number of firms in an industry does not indicate its relative efficiency. Rather, the number of firms in the industry is simply a, "... typical outcome of the free-market system" (Chamberlin 1933, 213). While an excessive number of firms may cause some loss in productive efficiency, the competitive activity of building up, and defending, product differentiation remains a basic right of free-market (Chamberlin 1933, 213-4). In other words, government policy makers should employ a wider range of considerations than "productive efficiency", when assessing the relative merits of policy proposals. For these reasons, Chamberlin argues that no efficiency problem exists in monopolistically competitive markets.

Similarly, Robinson (1953) is reticent to suggest policy solutions because consumer demand is more complex than is assumed by orthodox theory. Robinson argues that: (i) a downward-sloping demand function represents the normal slope of demand function, instead of the horizontal demand function assumed by classical economic theory, and (ii) the complexity of consumer demand is merely indicative of the complex nature of the entire economic system. Such complexity renders simplistic objectives, such as the maximisation of efficiency, somewhat obsolete (Robinson 1953, 586-9). Accordingly, Robinson argues that policy makers should increase the range of variables under consideration when deciding on economic policy: allocative efficiency is not the only consideration. In order to adequately take these various considerations into account, Robinson (1953) argues that economics should study the ways in which entrepreneurs actually make decisions; ignoring such complexities can cause problematic outcomes. For example, policies which seek to solely increase the efficiency of production will ultimately lead to the domination of each industry by one monopoly. Robinson describes such a situation in terms of, "... a world of monopolies..." which contains severe distributional effects for all those who inhabit it, except the owners of the monopolies (Robinson 1933a, 307-26).

> We find in comparing a world of monopolised industries with a world of imperfect competition that there may be very considerable improvements in the technique of production when the unit of control in industry increases in size. But we find that an increase in size of the unit of control will lead to an increase in the inequality of the distribution of wealth. The problem of the world of monopolists thus resolves itself into the familiar dilemma between efficiency and justice (Robinson 1933a, 324).

Similarly, Knight argues that the adoption of economic efficiency as the objective of economic policy has severe consequences for the distribution of economic power and economic freedom. Knight, however, approaches the problem of analysing the firm from a different perspective from both Chamberlin and Robinson. Indeed, Knight approaches the problem in the way which Robinson suggests; by studying the way entrepreneurs actually make decisions (Robinson 1953, 586-9). Knight suggests that entrepreneurs seek to reduce the costs which flow from uncertainty. We extend this proposition and argue that entrepreneurs do not profit from bearing uncertainty, but rather from minimising the costs inflicted by uncertainty. Domination of access to market knowledge is the central means of bringing about this reduction of costs.

In addition, Knight's underlying analytical intention can be contrasted to that of Chamberlin and Robinson. We argue that Knight's major objective is to explain imperfect competition, in terms of how firms usually go about maximising profit, under conditions of uncertainty. In contrast, Chamberlin and Robinson mainly provide an explanation for the unemployment (of both labour and capital) which is evident in the 1930s. For Chamberlin and Robinson, explaining imperfect competition is only a means to achieving this timely end. We contend that this objective leads both Chamberlin and Robinson, as well as most of their contemporaries, to become pre-occupied with: (i) excessive productive capacity (hence the search for an explanation of why the long-run level of production is lower than that which minimises average cost), and (ii) the shape of the demand curve. As a result, the demand function dominates their description of how the firm determines the optimal level of output; product differentiation - rather than cost differentiation - becomes the focus of their analyses. In contrast, Knight suggests that the firm's cost of production should be the focus of an analysis of imperfect competition. In other words, Knight directs us toward the central means of explaining the activity of those firms which face uncertainty, whereas Chamberlin and Robinson are distracted from this consideration by the unemployment problems of the 1930s.

Policy Response to Imperfect Competition: F.H. Knight

Introduction

Knight's policy response to imperfect competition is shrouded in misunderstanding and misapprehension. The failure to appreciate the significance of the link between costs and uncertainty has been a major contributing factor, along with Knight's prudently obscure writing style.[5] We argue that the costs which stem from uncertainty provide a new appreciation of Knight's analysis of imperfect competition, along with a new appreciation of the policy response which is appropriate.

For Knight, imperfect competition is centred on access to market knowledge; preferential access to market knowledge is proposed to act as a means of reducing the costs which are generated by uncertainty. Such a proposition is absolutely fundamental to understanding Knight's explanation of imperfect competition because it also underpins Knight's policy response to imperfect competition. However, we argue that Knight fails to complete this idea, and that such a failure is intentional. Instead, Knight provides us with most of the surrounding material - leaving his students to piece together the various segments of his discourse; we are left to fill in the gaps.[6] By enlarging Knight's description of the essential elements of imperfect competition (which we initially outline in Chapter Four) we attempt to fill this gap as comprehensively as possible. The main elements of imperfect competition are: (i) a definition of the economic resource of market knowledge, and (ii) a definition of uncertainty-control costs.

Our discussion of these elements leads us to recognise two policy problems. First, if such preferential access to market knowledge is costless, then such access allows all non-marginal firms in the industry to receive some economic-rents; this represents a distribution problem for governments. We argue that, under certain assumptions, governments can act to re-distribute these economic rents by the imposition of taxes on larger firms. By judiciously employing the revenue of these taxes to alleviate the 'culture' of poverty (Viner 1958; Gill 1992), Knight aims to enhance the aggregate level of socio-economic welfare (Knight 1956a). In addition to this welfare problem, we argue that an efficiency problem arises. We argue that the efficiency of production is maximised - as J. Robinson (1933a) suggests - when each industry is dominated by one firm. Here, uncertainty-control costs are at their lowest level for the industry as a whole. However, such an industrial structure is inconsistent with Knight's conceptualisation of what we now define as the 'social welfare function'.[7]

General Character of Knight's Policy Response

Raines and Jung (1988) argue that Knight accepts monopoly as, "... a mechanical defect ..." in the free-market system (Raines and Jung 1988, 141-3). The authors contend that some degree of monopoly power is possessed by all producers, "... as a result of the innate distinction among products from different suppliers" (Raines and Jung 1988, 136). These 'innate' distinctions only generate "temporary competitive advantage" for producers; the problems associated with monopoly are short-run in nature (Raines and Jung 1988, 143). These problems are outweighed by the long-run efficiency benefits which are delivered by monopoly, according to the authors (Raines and Jung 1988, 143). We disagree with this proposition for three reasons. First, we argue that their interpretation of Knight (Raines and Jung 1988) is inconsistent with other studies of Knight. For example, Stigler (1987) remarks that, "... time and time again he [Knight] returned to the two forces which made liberalism intolerable: the cumulative growth of monopoly and increasing inequality of income ..." [brackets added] (Stigler 1987, 59). Second, and more importantly, we argue that the interpretation of Raines and Jung (1988) is inconsistent with Knight's conceptualisation of the 'social welfare function'.[8] Third, we argue that Knight considers the issue of monopolisation of economic power as a serious threat to the operation of the entire free-market system. Knight, therefore, rejects the notion that the existing distribution of economic power is optimal; such conservatism still constrains the sort of inquiry which is necessary to adequately critique the free-market system.[9]

> The result is a dogmatic acceptance of an existing distribution of power, which is an ethical proposition, a value-judgement in disguise, and an ethically indefensible one (Knight 1947a, 14).

In addition, Raines and Jung (1988) maintain that government intervention is problematic for Knight, saying that he sees a very limited role for government intervention (Raines and Jung 1988, 140-1). For example, the authors argue that Knight sees social reformers as presenting a major difficulty for government intervention, because their attempts to formulate policies are usually ad-hoc and self-serving.[10] At the same time, a more consistent central planning approach is strongly opposed by Knight, because central planning constrains the operation of free-market (Raines and Jung 1988, 140-1). We disagree with this description of Knight's approach to government intervention as misleading, because it only represents two extreme forms of governmental intervention. While most social reformers lack any cohesive policy, central planning presents almost total control of all economic activity: both are extreme forms of intervention. Even though Knight has grave doubts about the effectiveness of such extreme forms of intervention, we argue that government intervention can judiciously avoid both extremes; prudent government intervention is something which most economists - including Knight - condone. We should not interpret Knight's condemnation of the impetuous approach to economic policy as a denunciation of all government intervention. Indeed, government intervention, which is designed to promote the long-run survival of the free-market system, is the backbone of Knight's entire contribution to economic theory. In other words, we argue that Knight is an advocate of perspicacious government intervention.[11]

Another example of the misinterpretation of Knight is that presented by Le Roy and Singell (1987). Here, the authors note the title of part three of *Risk, Uncertainty, and Profit* (1921a), which contains Knight's analysis of imperfect competition entitled "Imperfect Competition through Risk and Uncertainty" (Knight 1921a, 197-376). Le Roy and Singell (1987) argue that such a title is 'puzzling', because it associates both risk and uncertainty as causing imperfect competition (Le Roy and Singell 1987, 403). The authors maintain that risk should be excluded from the analysis of imperfect competition because: (i) uncertainty, not risk, is the distinguishing feature of imperfect competition, and (ii) uncertainty, not risk, generates profit. According to the authors, profit is the reward for bearing uninsurable hazards (Le Roy and Singell 1987, 397).[12] Risk is, therefore, otiose in terms of analysing imperfectly competitive markets, according to Le Roy and Singell (1987). In contrast, we argue that Knight's reference to risk indicates a different proposition; namely that as the size of the firm increases, it progressively reduces uncertainty-control costs by gaining better access to market knowledge. Imperfect competition is, therefore, competition for access to the economic resource of market knowledge; such competition rests on the existence of a certain tension between risk and uncertainty. Both risk and uncertainty are important in Knight's analysis, because large market share provides a lure to the marginal (small) firm in the form of lower uncertainty-control cost; such a lure urges the marginal (small) firm to try to expand the scale of production. The mixture of risk with uncertainty, therefore, generates a competitive tension between the large and the marginal (small) firm.

Secondly, we disagree with Le Roy and Singell's (1987) proposition that uncertainty generates abnormal (or super-normal) profit, because Knight suggests that the large firm essentially transforms uncertainty into risk.[13] By gaining access to market knowledge the large firm reduces the costs which they incur as a result of uncertainty (in our terminology, the large firm reduces uncertainty-control costs). In contrast, the marginal (small) firm faces pure uncertainty and, consequently, it becomes saddled with a relatively high level of such costs. Since Knight does not emphasise product differentiation, we deem the marginal (small) firm to be a price taker for the illustrative purposes of our analysis.[14] As a result, industry price is set at the level which just allows the marginal (small) firm to operate; it earns only normal profit.[15] In contrast, the large firm is able to use its superior market knowledge to reduce uncertainty-control costs; it enjoys abnormal (or super-normal) profit. In other words, Knight does not argue that abnormal (or super-normal) profit is generated by uncertainty; he suggests that abnormal (or super-normal) profit results from the transformation of uncertainty into risk, through the large firm sheltering itself against the costs which flow from uncertainty.

Accordingly, we argue that Knight's critique of imperfect competition seeks to correct a new form of monopolisation - monopolisation of access to market knowledge. However, Knight fails to spell out an explicit policy remedy for this aspect of imperfect competition, even though he hints at such a response throughout his published works.[16] We argue that Knight refrains from giving an explicit policy response to imperfect competition for four main reasons. First, Knight regarded himself as an academic, who is not obliged to give detailed policy prescriptions. This means that the application of Knight's theoretical insights is left to either policy makers, or theoreticians interested in following his line of reasoning. As, Stigler observes;

> He [Knight] was not a consultant to great or small bodies; whether public or private; he did not ride the lecture circuit; he did not seek a place in the popular press. He conducted himself as if the pursuit of academic knowledge was a worthy full-time career for a first-class mind [brackets added] (Stigler 1973, 519).

Second, Knight never developed a group of disciples (Gordon 1974, 577). This meant that the policy implications of Knight's theoretical insights had little chance to be developed by other economists, either during his lifetime or after. We propose that Knight's failure to develop a following is mainly the result of his questioning of the notion that the existing balance of economic power is optimal; this topic remains an unpopular one.[17]

Third, we argue that Knight's questioning of the existing imbalance of economic power is associated with his development of a moral dimension to economic theory. However, any concern for the moral dimension in economic theory ran contrary to the then accepted approach to the social sciences, which excluded ethical considerations.[18] Although Knight possesses a particularly erudite understanding of the philosophical underpinnings of the social sciences (especially with his knowledge of Max Weber) his argument for a moral dimension in economic theory still remains otiose to accepted economic theory (Knight 1950 a; Schweitzer 1975).

Fourth, Knight wishes to conceal his proposals for economic reform from zealous reformers; he intentionally adopts what Patinkin (1973a) describes as a discursive writing style. In doing so, Knight can proceed with his 'radical' critique of the free-market system while appearing to be an arch conservative.[19] A fundamental incongruity prevents Knight from openly revealing his most important proposals for reform; a certain fastidiousness is required so as to fully comprehend Knight's more shocking reform ideas - a fastidiousness which is lacking in most economic actors, especially economic reformers. In addition, Knight mistrusts economic reformers, because he asserts that they often seize on economic reform as a vehicle to liberate themselves from the confines of their own sociological environments (Knight 1935c; Knight 1947a).[20] Indeed, Knight poignantly concludes his presidential address to the American Economic Association by pointing out his contempt for economic reformers.

> ... I mistrust reformers. When a man or group asks for power to do good, my impulse is to say, "oh yeah, who ever wanted power for any other reason? and what have they done when they got it?" So, I instinctively want to cancel the last three words, leaving simply "I want power;" that is easy to believe (Knight 1951b, 29).

As Knight points out economic reformers, "... know nothing about economics ... have no idea what their own ethical ideals are ... and, ... they are also ignorant of the relations between economics and law and the cultural process ..." (Knight 1939e, 278-9). Knight fears that the free-market system may be irrevocably damaged by the self-centred efforts of economic reformers.[21] Knight, therefore, is prudent; a fundamental incongruity between the complexity of the subject matter and the inveterate romanticism of economic actors forces Knight to exercise prudence in exposing his ideas.[22] Knight, therefore, writes in a way which requires very detailed reading. In contrast, zealous reformers will find little to fuel their desperate ambitions. In this respect, Knight resembles many of the great thinkers of the past, who are forced to conceal their original ideas because they fear either misunderstanding or persecution. For this reason, we argue that a parallel exists between Knight's style of writing and that of other great authors. Strauss (1952) illustrates this style of writing as follows:

> Persecution, then, gives rise to a peculiar technique of writing, and therewith to a peculiar type of literature, in which the truth about all crucial things is presented exclusively between the lines. That literature is addressed, not to all readers, but to

> trustworthy and intelligent readers only. ... The fact that makes this literature possible can be expressed in the axiom that thoughtless men are careless readers, and only thoughtful men are careful readers. Therefore an author who wishes to address only thoughtful men has but to write in such a way that only a very careful reader can detect the meaning of his book (Strauss 1952, 25).

In summary, therefore, we argue that Knight is not prepared to simply comply with the existing academic orthodoxy, nor is he an academic showman or a flatterer of the powerful. Instead, Knight prudently complies with the serious obligations which pertain to the subject matter under consideration. Bearing Knight's prudence in mind, we will now elaborate Knight's analysis of imperfect competition, so that we can better understand why he approached economic theory from such an unusual perspective.

The Main Elements of Imperfect Competition, According to Frank Knight

Market Knowledge as an Economic Resource Market knowledge can be conceptualised as a type of transactional database; every industry contains a series of transactions, some for the purchase of inputs and some for the sale of outputs. Comprehensive knowledge of this database tends to reduce production costs because it will make less forecasting errors. Firms enhance their knowledge base by competing with each other so as to capture market share. This procedure can be seen to be akin to a statistician's enlargement of his sample size, so as to improve the accuracy of the estimates of population parameters. In other words, the large firm, which supplies a large portion of the industry, has a more comprehensive knowledge of the market 'database'. In contrast, the marginal (small) firm, whose market share is small, has less comprehensive knowledge. Consequently, their conjectures have a larger margin of error than those which are made by the large firm. Market knowledge, we propose, reduces production costs by reducing the costs which arise from deficiencies in knowledge. In other words, the reduction of uncertainty-control costs gradually transforms uncertainty into risk.

We define an economic resource as having two major characteristics. First, an economic resource is used, "... to produce goods which can be used to satisfy wants ..." (Mansfield 1979, 8). Second, economic resources command, "a non-zero price ..." (Mansfield 1979,

8).[23] Although market knowledge satisfies the first criterion, it is difficult to say whether or not it satisfies the second. With regard to the first criterion we note the economic value of market knowledge is illustrated by the fall in production costs which it delivers. However, with reference to the second criterion, we note that the economic resources of preferential access to market knowledge does not command a market price - not because preferential access lacks any value - but because governments remain unaware of such value. Firms acquire preferential access to market knowledge as a consequence of a superior business talent, or pure luck.[24] Upon acquisition of such preferential access, a virtually perpetual stream of low uncertainty-control costs assists the firm to maintain, and expand, such preferential access.[25] In other words, preferential access to market knowledge provides the holder with a significant piece of competitive armour; such armour protects the large firm from most forms of competitive challenge (Knight 1921a, 372-3, 347). Here, Knight (1921a) seeks to explain how preferential access to market knowledge amplifies the existing imbalance of economic power. In the long-run, such accentuation tends to constrain the marginal (small) firm from mounting any significant challenge to the large firm; such an obstacle to competition inhibits economic progress. Knight vividly illustrates this problem as follows;

> In the existing system, the serpent's tail is always in his mouth; all the inequitics of the system aggravate themselves cumulatively around an unbreakable vicious circle (Knight 1920a, 32).

A way of illustrating the nature of market knowledge as an economic resource is by drawing a parallel with other intellectual resources. For example, a patent is an intellectual resource possessing contrasting characteristics. Knight argues that patents are an ephemeral economic resource, which are specifically designed to stimulate economic progress through the creation of new products or methods of production (Knight 1921a, 341-2). Patents have a limited life because the idea, which forms the basis of the patent right, becomes common over a defined period of time. Eventually, the once patentable idea becomes a, "... superabundant element in production, a free good" (Knight 1921a, 342). However, during its limited life, market participants pay a specified fee for the use of the patent's special knowledge; the market value of the patent, therefore, falls over its limited life. While the initial value of a patent is high, its value will tend toward zero at the conclusion of its useful life. In contrast, the value of market knowledge - as an economic resource - does not fall over time, rather it grants those who have access to it a virtually perpetual stream of low uncertainty-control costs. Indeed, the value of this form of intellectual resource tends to increase - rather than decrease - over time. While patents are characterised by having a limited life, with a well defined set of fees for usage, access to market knowledge remains undefined in terms of both its duration and the fees which attach to its usage.

Uncertainty-Control Costs We define the value of market knowledge as the difference in uncertainty-control cost between the marginal (small) firm and the dominant (large) firm in any industry.[26] Generally, we find that economic actors wish to insure themselves against any unforeseen changes in economic conditions; Knight contends that the costs of such insurance are differentially spread throughout the industry. More specifically, we argue that two examples of uncertainty-control costs exist. First, the average level of stock (per unit of output) is higher for the marginal (small) firm as opposed to the large firm. Second, interest costs are higher for the marginal (small) firm.[27]

We argue that the marginal (small) firm has a higher level of stock (per unit of output) as compared to the large firm, because of its inability to accurately assess critical market variables. The marginal (small) firm attempts to estimate supply conditions from such a small sample of data, that the reliability of this estimate is low.[28] For example, over-estimation in the output market may lead the marginal (small) firm to reduce its output. On the other hand, if the marginal (small) firm increases its demand for input, then such demand may either not be met with a sufficient amount of supply, or may be met at a higher input price. In order to insure against the occurrence of such outcomes the marginal (small) firm will prefer to keep higher stocks of inputs and outputs, compared to those kept by the large firm. We argue that these stocks, in excess of what the large firm would normally keep, represent a form of insurance premium; without such insurance, the marginal (small) firm could be sent out of business by unforeseen variations in supply conditions.[29]

Interest rate differentials are another example of uncertainty-control costs. Here, we argue that uncertainty impacts on the activities of lenders. Lenders require compensation for uncertainty, either in the form of profit or in the form of a higher rate of interest. If a prospective borrower enjoys abnormal (or super-normal) profit, then such profit provides potential lenders with compensation for uncertainty, because it reduces the risk of loan default. Similarly, high interest rates provide lenders with an amount of compensation for default risk. The profit margin of the marginal (small) firm is generally lower and more volatile than the profit margins which the large firm enjoys: the marginal (small) firm represents a riskier borrower - compared to the large firm. To insure against this magnified risk, a potential lender will charge the marginal (small) firm a higher rate of interest. Accordingly, we can say that uncertainty-control costs: (i) reduce the degree of default protection which is available to lenders, and (ii) increase the rate of interest charged on loans.[30]

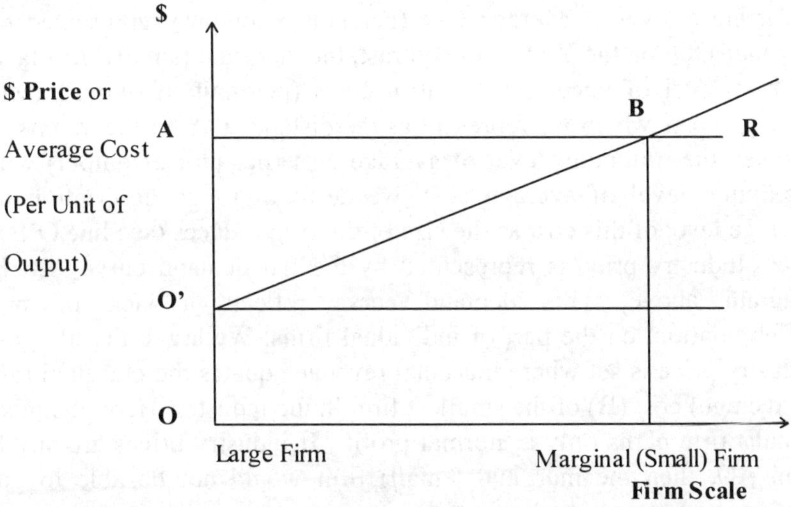

Figure 5.1 Cost Variations across the Imperfectly Competitive Industry

The Distribution Problem Uncertainty-control costs display a pattern of variation across firms; we can best illustrate this pattern diagrammatically, arranging firms in descending order of size. In the above diagram, the horizontal axis denotes the largest firm as being closest to the point of origin; smaller firms are placed to the right of this firm. As we traverse the horizontal axis we find that firms diminish in size until we encounter the marginal (small) firm; smaller firms could (in principle) exist in the industry, however the industry price is too low to allow these firms to operate. The vertical axis denotes product price and average cost. Because we are concentrating our analysis of imperfect competition on costs, we assume that all products are virtually homogeneous.[31]

In contrast, production costs are heterogeneous. Here, we assume that the central cost variable is uncertainty-control cost - which varies with firm scale. This means that the average cost (per unit of output) of the large firm is the lowest in the industry; we represent the average cost (per unit of output) of the large firm as the distance between the point of origin and O'. We assume that all firms in the industry produce an output level which maximises profit; each firm sells a quantity of output which equates the marginal cost of production with marginal revenue. This means that the largest firm sells what it considers to be an optimal amount of output by incurring a level of average cost (per unit of output) represented by the distance OO' on the Y axis. In contrast, the marginal (small) firm faces the highest level of uncertainty-control costs (per unit of output) incurring average costs which we represent as the distance OA on the Y axis. If we connect the minimum level of average cost (per unit of output) with the maximum level of average cost, we derive a rough description of the average level of this cost as the size of the firm reduces (see line O'B).

Industry price is represented by the flat demand curve AR, in the diagram above. This demand curve reflects a lack of product differentiation, on the part of individual firms. We argue that the level of industry price is set where marginal revenue equates the marginal (as well as average) cost (B) of the smallest firm in the industry. Here, the marginal (small) firm earns only a 'normal profit'. If industry prices are any lower than AO, then the marginal (small) firm would not be able to operate because price would be lower than average cost.[32]

In the above diagram we represent the abnormal (or super-normal) profit (per unit of output) which flows to all non-marginal firms in the industry, as the triangle O'AB. Here, a high level of abnormal (or super-normal) profit (per unit of output) is enjoyed by the large firm. We represent this profit (per unit of output) as the distance AO'.[33] The abnormal (or super-normal) profit, which is derived from preferential access to market knowledge, is only distributed among non-marginal firms in the industry; it represents a form of economic rent. We argue that such a distribution of economic rent presents a policy problem for the government.

The main cause of the distributive problem for the government lies in the fact that the above-mentioned distribution conflicts with Knight's conceptualisation of the 'social welfare function'.[34] In Chapter Two we argue that economic policy should aim to judiciously balance efficiency with equity issues. Specifically, we argue that the government should pursue an economic policy which seeks to enhance three objectives in tandem, these are: (i) economic efficiency, (ii) an acceptable balance of economic power, and (iii) economic freedom. By allowing the large firm to enjoy economic rent the government fails to achieve the latter objectives; a distribution problem emerges. However, we propose that an amendment to the existing corporate taxation system can mitigate this problem, by taxing away the economic rent which the non-marginal firm enjoys. Knight hints at such a solution, however he fails to examine these issues in any detail. As Knight (1921a) says,

> The writer is much more optimistic as to the possibilities of a drastic program of taxation for securing a greater degree of economic equality than over most proposals for social interference in contractual relations (Knight 1921a, 194).

In deciding the exact form of this taxation program we are faced with two main alternatives. First, we could introduce a progressive taxation of firms, so that the large firm pays more income tax than the marginal (small) firm. Here, the income taxation differential would reflect the differential access to market knowledge, which exists between firms. Second, we could impose a lump-sum tax on the large firm, according to market share. Here, the lump-sum amount would reflect the benefit which the large firm receives from preferential access to market knowledge, over a specified period of time.[35]

Addressing the first alternative, we argue that such a taxation policy will have to satisfy an onerous set of assumptions. First, we must assume that by taxing larger firms at higher rates we would not reduce the market share of the largest firms in the industry. We make this assumption because the large firm is the most efficient user of market knowledge; any redistribution of production away from it to the marginal (small) firm (who is less cost efficient) will increase the average cost of production for the entire industry. In addition, we must assume that, by decreasing the tax on the marginal (small) firm, it will not expand market share and thereby reduce its uncertainty-control costs. Instead, we assume that the marginal (small) firm behaves as if it were in a situation of monopolistic competition (except that all marginal (small) firms sell the same product). Here, price leaders - within the group of marginal (small) firms - will seek to maximise short-run profit by reducing industry price down to a level which fully reflects any reduction in marginal (small) firm taxation.

However this is a problematic set of assumptions and, therefore, this form of progressive taxation does not seem very appealing.[36]

In contrast, we argue that a lump-sum tax may avoid the problem of reducing the size of the largest corporations in the industry. Here, we argue that the government could impose a lump-sum tax on a large firm, based on an estimate of the benefits received from preferential access to market knowledge, over a specified period of time. By imposing the tax on a lump-sum basis (in return for access to market knowledge) over a certain period, the large firm will only incur periodic reductions in net-earnings. Here, the intention is to tax away the economic rent which the large firm enjoys, without altering its marginal cost curve, or affecting its level of output.[37]

In summary, we note that the large firm reduces uncertainty-control costs, and thereby increases economic efficiency.[38] Economic rents are earned, because the large firm sells at a price greater than average cost. We then propose that these rents can be taxed away by means of a lump-sum tax; orthodox economic theory is indifferent to such a policy proposition because this policy does not change economic efficiency. In contrast, we argue that Knight would be supportive of such a tax for two main reasons. First, by failing to tax these rents we fail to consider both the imbalance of economic power and economic freedom. Failure to tax such rents will result in the enhancement of existing power imbalances, which will inhibit the substantive economic freedom of society as a whole. As Knight says,

> The evaluation of the separate contributions of individuals to the social total is overwhelmingly a matter of force and not of right, and the inequalities tend to reduce and not increase "total satisfaction" (Knight 1947a, 8).

Second, by applying the lump sum taxes to increase the investment in human capital (particularly the human capital of the economically powerless), we achieve the objectives which we identify in our discussion of Knight's conception of the 'social welfare function'. We, therefore, argue that expenditure of the revenue from lump-sum taxation towards improving the investment in human capital, available to the economically powerless, is a natural extension of Knight's logic.[39]

Knight's analysis of imperfect competition represents an example of his attempt to introduce a moral dimension to economic theory. Uncertainty has prevented, and always will prevent, the achievement of perfect competition. This means that, on the one hand, we cannot treat the attainment of perfect competition as a goal for economic policy. On the other hand, in the context of imperfect competition, governments cannot presume that market outcomes are either 'right' or somehow 'fair'. Knight argues that existing imbalances of power act to constrain efficiency, as well as contributing to the manifest 'unfairness' of market outcomes; monopolisation of access to market knowledge illustrates the unfairness of imperfectly competitive outcomes. In Knight's opinion, therefore, government cannot avoid its responsibility to act in the best interest of all its citizens by asserting that market outcomes are always 'right'; the invisible hand of the large firm now controls access to market knowledge and, thereby, snatches away what was once a set of fair outcomes. Instead, governments are forced to make a normative judgement about the distribution of economic wealth, so as to discharge their responsibilities in an appropriate manner. However, this judgement should not be made lightly; it should be the subject of prudent consideration. Our policy proposal is an example of such a judgement.

The Efficiency Problem We argue that the existing industrial structure represents a generally inefficient use of resources. Specifically, we argue the economic resource of market knowledge is inefficiently used by the existing industrial structure. Because uncertainty-control costs are reduced with increased market share, we argue that the most efficient user of market knowledge is a firm who dominates an entire industry. Aimed with a monopoly position, the monopolist has the best possible access to market knowledge; it has the lowest uncertainty-control costs. In other words, the present industrial structure is inefficient because it is comprised of marginal (small) firms who lack preferential access to market knowledge; the marginal (small) firm will always have a higher cost of production than the large firm. The existence of the marginal (small) firm ensures that the large firm earns economic rent. While the most efficient use of market knowledge would entail the elimination of all the marginal (small) firms from the industry, we argue that such an outcome is contrary to the policy framework described in Chapter Two. In other words, governments are faced with the problem of how to increase economic efficiency, while adhering to the goal of attaining economic freedom with a satisfactory balance of economic power.

Having outlined the broad nature of the efficiency problem, we will now proceed with a more detailed analysis.[40] We depict the average cost curve of the marginal (small) firm as ACs in the diagram below, whereas

ACL corresponds to the average cost curve of the large firm. Similarly, we depict the marginal cost curve of the marginal (small) firm as MCs, whereas MCL corresponds to the marginal cost curves of the large firm.

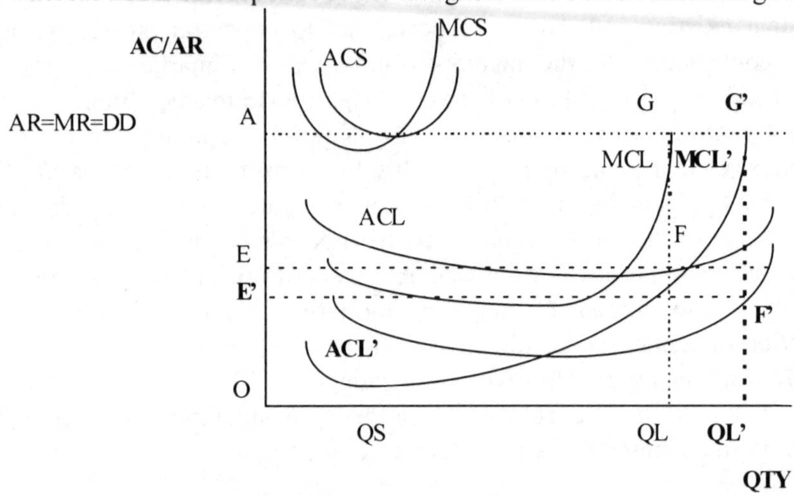

Figure 5.2 Normal and Abnormal Profit in Knight's Analysis of Imperfect Competition

In the above diagram the large firm produces an output equal to QL because this output equates the marginal cost of production to the marginal cost of production; it receives an amount of economic rent represented by the rectangle AGFE. In contrast, the marginal (small) firm produces an output equal to Qs, because this output equates the marginal cost of production with the marginal revenue of production. Here, the marginal (small) firm only makes a normal level of profit because price exactly equates the average cost of production.[41] Industrial output equals the sum of the outputs of all marginal (small) firms as well as the sum of the output which is produced by large firms.

Because the marginal (small) firm lacks preferential access to market knowledge, it fails to efficiently employ market knowledge in the reduction of uncertainty-control costs; this is reflected by the high level of average total costs (ACs) which face the marginal (small) firm. We propose that by progressively eliminating the firm with the highest ATC in the industry, we will increase the total efficiency of the industry. We could commence such a process of elimination by having the government regulate the industry price. By regulating industry price, so that price falls from OA to OE, we will eliminate the marginal (small) firm from the industry. Market share, held by those firms who are eliminated, would be transferred to the remaining firms in the industry. By increasing the market share of the large firm, we decrease its uncertainty-control costs so that the average cost curve falls to ACL'. In addition, industry output increases from QL to QL'.[42] This means that by regulating industry price, so that industry price equates the marginal cost of production, the government can deliver the benefits of increased efficiency to consumers. These benefits are, higher industry output and lower industry price. However, we argue that these benefits are not desirable, as far as Frank Knight is concerned.

Knight argues that the efficiency benefits will come at the cost of lower economic freedom, and a higher imbalance of economic power. As we show in Chapter Two, Knight argues that the concentration of economic power tends to constrain the activities of those who lack such power. In terms of competition between firms, this means that substantive economic freedom can only be enjoyed if all firms can pose a competitive threat to all other firms in the industry. If an entire industry is to be dominated by one firm, then this firm would be sheltered from competitive threat.[43] Such shelter will reduce long-run economic progress. Concentration of industries, therefore, smothers the mechanism of competitive challenge which delivers long-run benefits to the free-market system. As Knight explains, the free-market system is at risk of breaking down;

> ... in failing to solve the problems which have arisen naturally out of progress, especially the cumulative tendency toward inequality [of economic power] [brackets added] (Knight 1935c, 310-1; Knight 1921a, 119-21; Knight 1947a, 9-47).

Orthodox theory does not address the distribution problem, which Knight outlines, because it is only concerned with economic efficiency.[44] A policy proposal which enhances economic efficiency is, therefore, supported by orthodox economic theory. Furthermore, orthodox theory assumes that such policies will not reduce long-run economic progress because the large firm cannot capture - and exploit - access to market knowledge so as to maximise profit. Such an assumption rests on the premise that knowledge is perfect, and evenly distributed between firms.[45] Knight, however, argues that uncertainty dominates the activities of firms so that when firms attempt to maximise profit they actively seek to minimise the costs which uncertainty inflicts on them. This means that Knight cannot support this policy solution because the large firm will dominate the industry in question, and thereby reduce the level of competition in the industry.[46]

Conclusion

Knight's analytical contribution has not been regarded as being important for economic policy, especially welfare economics. This is because his theoretical analysis is not clearly understood; the commonly held opinion - that Knight establishes profit as being the reward for bearing uncertainty (Buchanan 1968, 425) - is incorrect. Specifically, under conditions of imperfect competition, we argue that abnormal (or super-normal) profit represents an economic rent which firms derive from access to market knowledge, as opposed to a form of compensation for bearing uncertainty. Imperfect competition, according to Knight (1921a), is centred on the existence of a diversity of (imperfect) market knowledge, rather than the existence of uncertainty. Accordingly, Knight's (1921a) theory of imperfect competition is centred around the competitive struggle to reduce uncertainty-control costs. However, this competitive struggle results in two very different policy problems.

First, we define the existence of a distribution problem, where the benefits of reduced uncertainty-control costs are shared only by non-marginal firms in the industry. In other words, the wider economic community fails to benefit from the economic rent which the large firm derives from preferential access to market knowledge. We consider two alternative methods of taxing away this economic rent. Initially, we consider a progressive rate of taxation, based on market share. However, this type of tax proposal requires us to make a set of much too strong assumptions, regarding the reaction of the marginal (small) firm to a reduction in the rate of taxation. We, therefore, consider a lump-sum tax which allows governments to transfer economic rent - derived from preferential access to market knowledge - to the areas of greatest social need. In addition, this form of tax does not inhibit economic efficiency; the market share of the large firm is unchanged. By more widely distributing these rents throughout society we satisfy Knight's policy targets, which are outlined in Chapter Two. In the final assessment, therefore, we support the proposal for a lump-sum tax.

Second, we address the efficiency problem. Here, we point out that aggregate output can be increased by eliminating all marginal (small) firms from the industry. Orthodox theory would tend to support this proposition, because the increase in output would enhance allocative efficiency. By weeding out all firms, except for the lowest cost firm, we can create a regulated monopoly where price is equal to the marginal cost of production. Such a regulated monopoly produces efficiency benefits, in terms of higher industry output, and lower industry price. However, we argue that such a solution is inconsistent with Knight's economic philosophy as described in Chapter Two above. In other words, the solution to the efficiency problem represents a difficulty for Knight, which is not recognised by orthodox theory. Such difficulty does not exist within orthodox theory, because it asserts that efficiency constitutes an exhaustive description of the economic problem.[47]

Appendix One

The Trade-off Between Equity and Efficiency

Our analysis illustrates that a trade-off exists between two objectives: equity (or distribution) and efficiency. On the one hand, we threaten the efficiency objective if we solely pursue the equity objective through increasing the taxation of large firms (relative to the marginal (small) firm). We represent this situation as point A on the diagram below, where the equity outcomes for the industry lead to greater equalisation of the equity outcomes for the entire economy. In addition, point A is associated with a deterioration in the efficiency outcomes for the economy as a whole. On the other hand, we threaten the equity objective if we were solely to pursue the efficiency objective by reducing the taxation on the large firm (relative to the marginal (small) firm). We represent this situation as point C' on the diagram below. If we were to do nothing, then we would change neither the efficiency nor equity of the industry in question. This situation is represented by point D on the below diagram. If we were to connect each of these points with a straight line, then we would obtain a schedule which describes the effects of marginal changes in the rate of taxation of large firms (relative to the marginal (small) firm). Here, incremental changes in the incremental taxation of the large firm (relative to the marginal (small) firm) alter the equity and efficiency of the industry to an equal degree. This implies that, for example, we cannot increase both efficiency and equity at the same time. We disagree.

Instead, we argue that a moderate increase in the taxation of the large firm (relative to the marginal (small) firm) can increase both efficiency and the equity of the industry. We describe this by the curvilinear relationship between point D and E in the below diagram. This outcome occurs because the differential taxation of firms would provide the marginal (small) firm with a degree of compensation for its lack of access to market knowledge. Such compensation will encourage small firms to more efficiently use existing resources, so as to increase market share and thereby secure lower uncertainty-control costs. In addition, some gains can be expected from innovation, as many small firms experiment with many more combinations of resource utilisation than the large firm would typically experiment with during the normal course of any business cycle. As a result of these results we can expect increases in both the equity, and efficiency, of the industry up to a level of taxation described by point E'. However, if the large firm is taxed any more (relative to the marginal (small) firm) than E', then the efficiency of the industry will deteriorate rapidly, and this will lead to a deterioration in the efficiency of the economy as a whole. This is because efficient users of market knowledge (large firms) are being substituted by less efficient users (small firms). In other words, an immoderate level of extra tax on the large firm (relative to the small firm) will cause rapid declines in economic efficiency. In contrast, a moderate increase in taxation of the large firm (relative to the marginal (small) firm) generates an economic environment where the marginal (small) firm competes on much the same footing as the large firm; gains in both equity and efficiency are then inevitable.

In the alternative, decreasing the taxation of the large firm (relative to the marginal (small) firm) will decrease equity, and reduce efficiency. Here, the large firm is substituted for the marginal (small) firm such that the marginal(small) firm is discouraged from efficiently utilising resources, since the large firm can easily increase market share as a result of taxation gains. In addition, the reduction in the number of firms in the industry will discourage innovation, as less and less firms will be combining resources in less combinations than before the tax regime was altered. I describe this by the curvilinear relationship between D and C' in the below diagram.

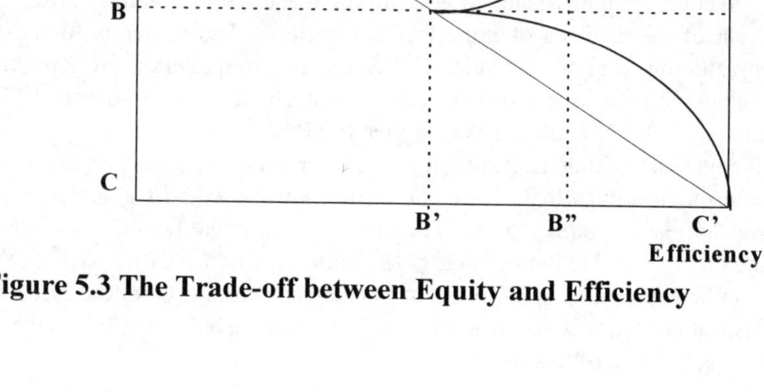

Figure 5.3 The Trade-off between Equity and Efficiency

Notes

1 In contrast, Knight delivers an analysis of imperfect competition which focuses on the ability of the firm to reduce the cost of production, rather than products. In this analysis only the marginal (small) firm sells products at a price which equates with the marginal cost of production. In other words, the marginal (small) firm receives normal profits, whereas the large firm receives abnormal (or super-normal) profit (Chamberlin 1933, 5, 51-4). Although Knight recognises that products are not perfect substitutes, his main emphasis is on the differentiated costs of production.

2 Although Harrod (1934) shows that firms can operate at the minimum point of the LRAC. Here, the marginal revenue (MR) curve *happens* to pass through the minimum of the LRAC. In this situation, profit will be abnormal. In other words, Harrod (1934) shows that long-run equilibrium, in the situation of a downward sloping demand curve, can exist in two main forms. First, it can have less than ideal output, with normal profit. Second, it can have ideal output with abnormal (or super-normal) profit. Refer to Chapter Four, section 4.2.5, for a discussion of this situation.

3 Advertising is an example of such a technique.

4 "Ideal" is used here in the sense of producing output on a scale which minimises average costs.

5 We argue that Knight's writing style is 'deliberately' obscure for two main reasons: (i) Knight's concern with the preservation of the free-market system, and (ii) Knight's desire to educate his students. As we shall see later, uncertainty essentially alters the position of the economic actor from the all-seeing rationalist to the prisoner of a constrained sociological environment. Any messages about economic reform have to be disguised from the majority of economic actors so that they might not be misused - thereby jeopardising the existence of the free-market system. Accordingly, economic reformers are the subject of an intense distrust (Knight 1951b, 29). Second, Knight wishes to educate his readers by providing most, but not all, of his analysis of imperfect competition. The reader is forced to complete the analysis for himself. Such an interpretation of Knight's teaching methods is consistent with almost all literature (Gordon 1974; Patinkin 1973a, 789; Shils 1981; Stigler 1973).

6 This style of writing is common with other great writers. For example, Montesquieu argues that, "One should not always exhaust a subject, and leave the reader nothing to do. The aim is to not make people read but to make them think " (Montesquieu 1949, Book 11, Chapter 20).

7 We outline this philosophic position in Chapter Two. Furthermore, such an industrial structure is inconsistent with Joan Robinson's (1933a) analysis. See Chapter Five of this work.

8 See Chapter Two.

9 Another misleading representation of Knight is that he is a critic, who does not provide any valid alternative to the issues which he chooses to criticise. For example, Emmett (1989) argues that Knight's work is not directed at providing a cohesive alternative to orthodox theory. Rather, Emmett (1989) argues, Knight strives to illustrate "the necessary limitations of any system of thought: including economic theory" (Emmett 1989, 1). By illustrating the limitations of economic theory Knight is shown to develop a series of important questions, which lead to further theoretical debate (Emmett 1989, 2; Wick 1973; Patinkin 1973a). Hammond (1990) develops Emmett's argument (1989) by contending that Knight is mainly a critic of economic methodology, particularly positivistic methodology (Hammond 1990, 1; Buchanan 1968). While these arguments possess some validity, they tend to over-emphasise this aspect of Knight's contribution without paying adequate attention to the coherent alternative which Knight intimates. This misunderstanding of Knight is partly the result of Knight's discursive writing style (Patinkin 1973a).

10 We agree that Knight distrusts economic reformers. However, we argue that such distrust is reflected more in Knight's efforts to conceal his reform proposals from reformers themselves, rather than a rejection of government intervention per se (See Chapter Six). As Patinkin (1973a) notes, Knight's writing style is discursive; we argue that, in some respects, it is 'intentionally' so. Knight writes to address the thoughtful reader, rather than the romantic reformer. Indeed, Knight is very much aware of the damage which could be inflicted on the free-market system by wanton reformers (Knight 1951b, 29; Patikin 1973a, 787-807).

11 Knight (1951b) illustrates this conclusion with reference to monopoly regulation, where he argues that the granting of patent rights is an example of good government policy. However, Knight argues that the granting of patent rights can increase the imbalance of economic power, and that such imbalance is bad for the free-market system. As a result, policy makers must seek to, "... differentiate between the good and the bad ... [so as to] make and enforce regulations to secure the best possible balance [between the good and the bad] [brackets added] (Knight 1951b, 294).

12 The authors maintain that Knightian uncertainty emanates from moral hazard, or the non-existence of insurance markets for the calculation of insurance premia (Le Roy and Singell 1987, 405). Barzel (1986) makes the point that, "... because of moral hazard, some risks, such as developing a new line of business, are prohibitively costly to insure" (Barzel 1986, 118).

13 In addition, Le Roy and Singell (1987) are not alone in this misunderstanding of Knight (1921a). For example, Buchanan (1968) argues that, "Knight explained profit as the result of uncertainty"

(Buchanan 1968, 425). Similarly, we contend that this interpretation of Knight (1921a) is incorrect because abnormal (or super-normal) profit accrues only to those non-marginal firms who reduce uncertainty-control costs. Profit accrues to those who are in a position to escape from high uncertainty-control costs, not to those who bear uncertainty.

14 As Chamberlin (1933) notes, Knight (1921a) does recognise product differentiation (Chamberlin 1933, 5; Knight 1921a, 193). In particular, Knight notes that the distinction between pure monopoly and perfect competition is made questionable because of the existence of product differentiation. We argue that Knight does not feature product differentiation as the key explanatory variable in his analysis of imperfect competition. Rather, he recognises product differentiation so as to question existing analyses of competition, thereby establishing a rationale for a new analysis of imperfect competition.

15 The marginal (small) firm just covers its uncertainty-control cost along with the other costs of production. Normal profit, rather than abnormal (or super-normal) profit, compensates the marginal (small) firm for facing high uncertainty-control costs.

16 For example, Knight (1921a) argues that, "... a drastic program of taxation for securing a greater degree of economic equality ...", is a possible response to the competitive imbalances which exist in imperfect competition (Knight 1921a, 194). Other authors have noted this gap in Knight's work. For example, Stigler (1987) remarks that Knight's treatment of how "the use of combination ... to reduce uncertainty ..." lacks a substantive structure (Stigler 1987, 55-9).

17 See, for example Galbraith (Galbraith 1952, 42-5).

18 Knight's understanding of the moral basis of the social sciences is extensive, considering his translation of Max Weber's *General Economic History* (Knight 1950a). The importance of Weber to the development of the social sciences cannot be overestimated, as Bloom (1987) remarks, "... with the possible exception of Weber and Freud, there are no social science books that can be said to be classic" (Bloom 1987, 345). Given such knowledge of Weber, we argue that Knight is well equipped to comment on the appropriateness of a moral dimension to economic theory. Similarly, Stigler remarks, "... he [Knight] was unusually well read and perceptive in his rare appearances as an economic historian" [brackets added] (Stigler 1987, 57).

19 Patinkin (1973a) trenchantly describes this aspect of Knight in the second part of his essay on Knight. Here, in the section entitled "Knight the Radical Economist - and the Conservative" Patinkin notes the apparent contradiction in Knight's work: while presenting a radical critique of the free-market system Knight apparently refrains from offering an equally

radical reform agenda (Patinkin 1973a, 798 -807). We argue that, while Knight is aware of the problems associated with radical change of the free-market system, a series of proposed reforms are embedded within the structure of Knight's work. In other words, Knight's proposals for reform exist, however they are intentionally difficult to access. Such an assessment of Knight's writing style is consistent with his lecturing style. As Patinkin (1973a) notes, Knight often obscures crucial points by turning them into, "... brief and cryptic summaries of views ..." which Knight develops elsewhere (Patinkin 1973a, 789). In this respect, we find a parallel with Pangle's (1973) interpretation of Montesquieu. As Pangle notes;

> ... the more fundamental rhetorical intention is that which is divined by those who call Montesquieu's [and that of Knight] style epigrammatic. This characterisation is not unjust, for the style often seems to be a kind of imitation of Latin writers whom Montesquieu found most beautiful. An epigram is graceful, brief, memorable, and clear, yet it summarises in a paradoxical or thought-provoking manner a whole range of reflections. In reading Montesquieu [and Knight], one experiences a similar effect, repeated many times ... what begins as light paradox in a single passage turns into a deeper puzzle of obscure transitions and connections. But the puzzles are so presented as to invite attempts at solution [brackets added] (Pangle 1973, 17).

20 As we describe in Chapter Two, uncertainty effectively imprisons the economic actor in a certain sociological environment in such a way that many economic actors are desperate to escape from this environment. Whereas Knight characterises the economic actor as the prisoner of his environment, orthodox theory characterises the economic actor as the master of his environment: these two characterisations are at polar extremes. Each characterisation demands a different mode of writing.

21 In this respect, Knight's description of the delicate intricacies of the social welfare function, combined with his awareness of the rashness of economic actors, delivers what Allyn Young calls "social wisdom" to the debate on policy issues (Young 1927b, 25; Knight 1943a, 93).

22 Apart from this inherent obligation to make his teachings difficult to access, the existing methodology of interpretation further clouds the understanding of Knight. Such a methodology argues that most of his work is irrelevant to economic theory. Indeed, the American Economics Association contributes to this confusion in its obituary to Knight (American Economics Association 1973). Here, the American Economics Association presumes that from the start of the 1930s Knight's, "... main interests began to shift from economic theory to social philosophy"

(American Economics Association 1973, 1048). Similarly, Stigler subdivides his biography of Knight into two sections: economics and philosophy (Stigler 1987, 55-9).

23 Our discussion in Chapter Four illustrates that enlarged samples of market information allow firms to reduce uncertainty-control cost. If an industry is characterised by firms of divergent size, then we argue that a divergence in uncertainty-control cost will characterise that industry. In this way, expansion of the scale of the firm will solve what Knight calls "the organisational problem" (Knight 1921a, 253). For Knight, the organisational problem is generally one of finding methods of controlling uncertainty, or the costs which flow from uncertainty (Knight 1921a, 233-64). In other words, by seizing market share the large firm is able to freely exploit the economic resource of market knowledge.

24 An alternative way of explaining the purchase price of market knowledge is that companies expend capital in the search for market share. Here, the firm either uses its own resources, or borrows, to expand market share. However, Knight does not clearly discern by which means a firm acquires market share. For example, Knight mentions this issue only in passing, along with a discussion of the nature of perpetual property rights (Knight 1921a, 372-3). We argue that debt funded (or equity-funded) expansion of market share would increase the costs of the firm, so as to offset the benefits of low uncertainty-control costs. We argue that pure luck and differential talent are major sources of large market shares.

25 While the large firm enjoys a perpetual stream of low uncertainty-control costs, the large firm incurs some cost in terms of maintaining its dominant market share. For example, advertising is such a cost. However, if all products in the industry are assumed to be roughly homogeneous then the possible scope of advertising must be restricted. Advertising must, therefore, be restricted to characteristics which are exogenous to the product. For example, firms can advertise product availability, rather than differences in the product. Alternatively, we can assume that if differences in the product are advertised, that these differences are empty forms of cajolery.

26 We envisage that a continuum exists between the marginal (small) firm and the large firm. This means that the medium size firm has lower uncertainty-control costs than the marginal (small) firm, yet higher uncertainty-control costs than the large firm.

27 A possible third category also exists, which we call access to government knowledge. We argue that as the size of the firm grows, relative to the industry, the knowledge of possible changes to government policy also increases. This occurs because the larger firms represent a segment of the industry which is less costly to consult than an array of smaller firms.

Governments will, therefore, consult with the large firm when considering possible changes in government policy, in preference to the marginal (small) firm. Even if the marginal (small) firm is aware of forthcoming changes in government policy, it does not have the level of abnormal (or super-normal) profit which is required to fund expenditure for research into the implications of alterations in government policy. This means that larger firms in the industry will better anticipate changes in government policy, when compared to smaller firms in the industry. Furthermore, the large firm has a degree of "political leverage", which allows them to direct - as well as follow - government policy.

28 The sample of data, used by the marginal (small) firm, is derived from its limited market share of input (and output) markets. We assume that all firms are price takers in output. The supply function facing the marginal (small) firm is unstable in terms of both the quantity and price of inputs.

29 In addition, we argue that the marginal (small) firm has a more volatile level of stocks, when compared to the large firm. Such volatility is the result of errors which are made by the marginal (small) firm, when estimating supply conditions. Because a relatively large amount of the marginal (small) firm's resources is diverted away from directly productive activities, to the more ancillary task of estimating the appropriate level of stock, such volatility is costly.

30 The efficiency of this compensation calculation depends on the competitiveness of the lending market. If the degree of competition is low, then lenders will be over-compensated for defaults on all loans. This is because the amount of interest, which is charged on borrowed funds, will exceed the actual amount of defaults the total loan portfolio incurs. Alternatively, if the degree of competition is high, then lenders will tend to be under-compensated for defaults on all loans. Here, the amount of interest, which the lender will charge on borrowed funds, will fall short of the actual amount of default which the loan portfolio incurs. In other words, the interest rate differential will provide a reliable indicator of profit if the lending market is characterised by an adequate degree of competition.

31 By assuming that all products are homogeneous we temporarily ignore Knight's recognition of product heterogeneity (Chamberlin 1933, 5; Knight 1921a, 193). We do not wish to misrepresent Knight on this point. Indeed, we argue that such an assumption is justified because it allows us to illustrate Knight's analysis of uncertainty in a way which highlights his peculiar interest in the cost function of the firm.

32 The dotted line, to the right of point B, therefore, represents a set of potential entrants to the industry. We can extend the cost curve, per unit of output, past point B so as to represent those firms that could operate in the industry if industry price is higher than at present.

33 In contrast, the marginal firm receives normal profit, because price equates average cost.

34 As an aside, we propose that abnormal (or super-normal) profits may condition the large firm to become a profit satisficer. Here, we note the work of Herbert Simons (1948). We argue that such a proposition is a logical extension of Knight's views on sociological conditioning. However, we argue that a full logical explanation of this proposition is beyond the scope of this discourse.

35 Lump-sum taxation is not supposed to effect the level of output of the firm (because it does not effect the marginal cost of the firm).

36 Further consideration is given to this form of taxation in Appendix One of Chapter Five

37 This amount of tax is equal to the area AGEF in the diagram which is contained in Chapter Five (figure 5.2). This form of intermittent taxation can be contrasted with the continuous reductions in net-earnings which a large firm would incur from a progressive system of corporate taxation. We argue that such a continuous reduction in earnings will reduce the market share of the large firm, and thereby erode the economic value of market knowledge. While a sound theoretical argument can be mounted for the imposition of such a lump-sum tax, several practical difficulties exist. First, large companies may seek to avoid such tax by dismantling themselves into a series of smaller firms. Second, the estimation of economic rent, which is derived from preferential access to market knowledge, is an inexact procedure.

38 Here we refer to 'allocative efficiency' as defined in orthodox economic theory.

39 Furthermore, we propose that Knight assigns the property rights, which are associated with access to market knowledge, to society as a whole (where the government acts as the agent for society). We base this proposition on two reasons. First, we argue that Knight is not averse to government intervention. Second, we argue that such a proposition is a logical extension of Knight's discussion of property rights (Knight 1921a, 1924). However, we argue that a full logical explanation of this proposition is beyond the scope of this discourse.

40 Here, we specify a set of assumptions which supplement those specified in the above section (which deals with the distribution problem). First, we assume that the industry can be stratified into two groups of firms: large, and marginal (small). The large firm enjoys the benefits of lower uncertainty-control costs, while the marginal (small) firm experiences difficulties in accessing market knowledge and, therefore, it faces high uncertainty-control costs. Second, we assume that all firms attempt to maximise profit and, therefore, produce a level of output which equates

marginal revenue with the marginal cost of production. Since all firms are price takers, the marginal revenue curve will correspond to the average revenue curve (or demand curve).

41 We can also express the amount of economic rent, which is derived from preferential access to market knowledge by the following formula: ER = (P-ATC)* Q. Where: P = Price, ATC = Average Total Cost, Q = Quantity of Production, and ER = Economic Rent (derived from access to market knowledge). While this formula reflects the standard textbook definition of economic rent, we augment it by arguing that, in our abstract model of imperfect competition, all the costs of firms, except for uncertainty-control costs, are identical. Here, we argue that ATC can be represented by the following formula: ATC= (FC+VC+UCC). Where: FC= Fixed Cost, VC = Variable Cost, and UCC = Uncertainty-Control Costs. Since both FC and VC are identical for all firms, ATC can be represented by the following formula: ATC = UCC. This understanding of the firms cost, therefore, alters the above-mentioned definition of economic rent. Here, we argue that economic rent can be represented by the following formula: ER = (P-UCC)*Q.

42 Such an expansion of industrial output is generated by the ability of one firm to more efficiently reduce uncertainty-control costs than a set of smaller firms.

43 In this extreme situation, the single monopolist will not be a price taker. Consequently, price (P) will be greater than marginal cost (MC), so that another efficiency problem may eventuate. This is because, where P>MC, output will be restricted to a lower level, than is feasible when P=MC.

44 Economic efficiency, as Pareto (1910, 1971) defines it in orthodox economic theory.

45 Exploitation of access to market knowledge can reduce economic progress because the large firm can effectively stifle all competition, due to the fact that the large firm has the lowest cost of production. By periodically reducing price, the large firm can wipe out the marginal (small) firm (which will fail if it sells goods at a price which is lower than its cost of production). Over time, the market will become less competitive and economic progress will slow. However, we argue that the large firm normally restrains itself from such predatory activities out of self-interest; the marginal (small) firms ensure the existence of economic rent because they set industry price at a higher level than the average cost of the large firm.

46 Knight's analysis indicates economic actors, or groups of economic actors, can shield themselves from the costs which uncertainty inflicts by holding market power. If consumption and production take place in a world saturated by uncertainty, and if economic power effectively shields its

holders from the costs which emanate from uncertainty, then Knight's analysis suggests that the allocation of resources will tend to be distorted. This will occur because economic agents operate with unequal costs, since markets fail to exist for the pricing of uncertainty-control costs. In this case, the distribution of economic resources will reflect the preferences of those who enjoy shelter from uncertainty, rather than the relative capacity of economic actors to manage economic resources. In other words, once economic power is created it tends to distort the ongoing creation of economic power and the ongoing distribution of economic resources. Governments have an essential role to play in terms of unbiasedly moderating the effects of this source of market failure. If we were to apply this idea to global trade policy then we would first have to think of large groupings of economic agents, namely countries, as equivalent to the competing firms in Chamberlin's analysis. Here, Chamberlin would argue that a stable equilibrium would occur as countries, who produced different products competed under conditions of uniform uncertainty. In contrast, Knight's analysis suggest that market power and uncertainty-control costs are linked so that small countries face high uncertainty-control costs when they engage in global trade, compared to more powerful countries. In the long-run it is reasonable to conclude that differential exposure to uncertainty-control costs will lead to a global misallocation of resources. In a perfect world a regulator of global trade would provide a mechanism for equilibrating uncertainty-control costs between countries, so as to avoid distortions in resource allocation. In the absence of such a mechanism it appears that government has a role to play in terms of moderating these differentials.

47 Third, I considered an application of Knight's analysis to international trade. We could solve the efficiency problem which exists in international trade by ensuring that the largest counties produced all the goods for the international community. However, such a solution conflicts with Knight's social welfare function described by Knight.

6 Conclusion

This work is primarily concerned with Knight's conception of imperfect competition and economic welfare: both of these issues are theoretically related through the presence of uncertainty. Knight conceives of imperfect competition as being centred around the acquisition of the most cost-efficient hedge against the costs which uncertainty can impose on the firm. If a firm can acquire such a hedge, then it will reduce the cost of production and enjoy abnormal (or super-normal) profit. While some firms are successful in their attempts to attain this hedge, most are not; large variations in profit margins, therefore, exist within the imperfectly competitive industry over the long-run. Such variations are inconsistent with the maximisation of the 'social welfare function'; a new conception of the 'social welfare function' is, therefore, outlined by Knight. This conception of the 'social welfare function' has long been ignored by economists because it has been - and remains - classified as 'social philosophy'.

We challenge this classification. Indeed, our driving motive is to dispute the view which sees Knight 'the philosopher' and Knight 'the economist' as two separate beings. To a large extent, this view has distorted the understanding of Knight: economists now attempt to decipher Knight's teaching by looking at the separate elements of the Knightian corpus as if they were independent of one another. Such a view of Knight reflects the view of the world which is accepted by orthodox economic theory: by maximising allocative efficiency the science of economics makes moral considerations largely obsolete. Knight's contribution, if it is treated as two separate parts, cannot challenge this view of the world. On the one hand, we are unable to interpret the outcomes of his analysis of imperfect competition if we fail to understand his conception of the 'social welfare function'. On the other hand, we cannot apply Knight's 'social welfare function' if we fail to understand his analysis of imperfect competition; both elements are dependent on each other. Recognition of this dependent relationship has been ignored mainly because it directly challenges the view of the world which is currently held by orthodox economic theory. Seen in this context, we can understand why inquiry into Knight's theory was either non-existent, or was marginalised.

The analysis of imperfect competition is selected as the vehicle by which we seek to demonstrate that Knight's scholarly *oeuvre* must be treated as an integrated whole: each part is indispensable to the understanding of the other. We contend that our interpretation can rekindle intellectual interest in Knight's work. By examining the interrelationships between the separate elements of the Knightian corpus, we reveal a veritable treasure trove of economic reasoning, which centres on the coherent integration of uncertainty into economic theory. Uncertainty forces Knight to rethink the orthodox conception of the 'social welfare function' as well as the analysis of imperfect competition. Consequently, without a clear understanding of Knight's 'social welfare function' we cannot obtain an adequate interpretation of his analysis of imperfect competition. We conclude that an adequate interpretation of Knight requires an intimate knowledge of all the various elements of his entire work, together with a clear understanding of how each element relates to all other elements. Otherwise, we are lost. A parallel exists with Montesquieu; Taine (1976) describes Montesquieu's writings with much the same mixture of respect and gratitude as we have for Knight. The following passage, where Taine (1976) refers to Montesquieu, can be readily applied to Knight.

> He [Montesquieu] always seems to be addressing a select circle of people with acute minds, and in such a way as to render them at every moment conscious of their acuteness. No flattery is more delicate; we feel grateful to him for making us satisfied with our intelligence. We must possess some intelligence to be able to read him, for he deliberately curtails developments and omits transitions; we are required to supply these and comprehend his hidden meanings. He is rigorously systematic but the system is concealed, his concise complete sentences succeeding one after the other separately, like so many precious coffers or caskets ... Open them and each contains a treasure; here is placed in narrow compass a rich store of reflections, of emotions of discoveries, our enjoyment being the more intense because we can easily retain all this for a moment in the palm of our hand ... he thinks in summaries; ... the summary itself often bears the air of an enigma, of which the charm is twofold; we have the pleasure of comprehension accompanying the satisfaction of divinity [brackets added] (Taine 1976, 260).

Thus, we do not regard Knight's analysis as a timely series of treatises on the events of the moment, or a running commentary on the "changing ideological context" (Emmett 1989). Indeed, most authors agree that Knight's work is free of "intellectual fashion", or "gadgetry" (Schultz 1973; Stigler 1973). Instead, Knight delivers a reasoned account of why uncertainty transforms - rather than supplements - the axiomatic premises of orthodox theory. Because firms share different burdens from uncertainty, Knight concludes the outcomes of imperfect competition reflect the relative power imbalances in the imperfectly competitive industry: these outcomes are fundamentally unfair. Moreover, if we generalise this conclusion to the operation of all markets, then we can argue that unconstrained self-interest will not always lead to outcomes which are fair, or which are beneficial for society as a whole. In this way, the operation of the 'invisible hand' is, therefore, questioned by Knight's analysis of imperfect competition. Such scepticism strikes at the heart of the orthodox notion of perfect competition: instead of 'popularising' perfect competition (Stigler 1957, 11) Knight establishes an alternative analysis of competition. Critical to this alternative analysis is Knight's conception of economic welfare, which drives his analysis of imperfect competition. At the core of his notion of economic welfare is the premise that economic welfare must not be identified with aggregate (ie. allocative) economic efficiency. Rather, welfare must be seen as the sum of economic freedom, the balance of economic power, and economic efficiency.

Furthermore, these three dimensions of socio-economic welfare must not be viewed in isolation to one another; they must be treated in unison. Welfare cannot be advanced by exclusively focusing on any one of these elements. Knight, therefore, rejects the standard ideal of allocative efficiency with economic welfare. As we discuss in Chapter Two, orthodox theory assumes that all economic actors continually share the same perfect information so that no allowance for (differential) environmental conditioning exists; perfect knowledge generates a homogeneous 'economic character', which allows economic agents to operate as perfectly rational beings (Knight 1943c, 117-8). In contrast, Knight argues that economic 'character' is fashioned within the confines of separate sociological environments. The inhabitants of these environments do not have access to information which might lead them to act in a more rational manner. Instead, these economic actors develop habits which Knight summarises in terms of economic 'character'. In this way, uncertainty contributes to the creation of an economic 'character' which tends to perpetuate poverty (Knight 1921a, 233-63; Knight 1943a, 115). Viner (1958) astutely expresses this idea where he observes that the poor in all societies are;

> ... breeding poverty, bequeathing it to the children, and thus cutting-off their access to health, to knowledge, to reasonable education, and so forth (Viner 1958, 134).

Accordingly, Knight argues that increasing allocative efficiency will not - necessarily - increase the welfare of those who are imbued with the economic 'character' of the poor. This means that policies which aim to solely increase economic efficiency are not consistent with the maximisation of welfare: all three elements of socio-economic welfare are equally important. Indeed, Knight's awareness of how uncertainty often hinders the development of a purely rational economic 'character', renders the orthodox goal of economic efficiency somewhat obsolete. Uncertainty not only influences the outcomes of imperfect competition, but it shapes the economic 'character' of individual economic actors. Economists, therefore, should supplement the search for allocative efficiency with an attempt to understand the economic 'character' which tends to perpetuate poverty.

Once imperfect competition is analysed against the backdrop of this particular definition of economic welfare, a new light is shed not only on Knight's discourse on perfect and imperfect competition, and the scope for remedial policy, but also on what precisely he had in mind when he draws a link between uncertainty and profit. Uncertainty is at the root of the ability to earn abnormal (or super-normal) profit but it is not a reward for taking on a large burden from uncertainty. We show that the marginal (small) firm faces the largest burden from uncertainty, yet only receives normal profit in the long-run. In contrast, the large firm faces the smallest burden from uncertainty, yet receives abnormal (or super-normal) profit. We conclude, therefore, that abnormal (or super-normal) profit represents a windfall for the firm which succeeds in minimising the weight of this burden by seizing the lion's share of the market. In capturing such market share the large firm effectively lays claim to a unique vantage point which, as the thesis argues at some length, endows the firm with a solid knowledge base. Such information reduces the level of costs which uncertainty may inflict on the large firm; it arms the large firm so that it can potently 'use force' (Machiavelli 1513, 24), or so that it applies resources in a more cost-effective manner than the marginal (small) firm.

Placing Knight in the broader historical context of economic thought, the thesis outlines a line of influence which runs from J.B. and J.M. Clark, A. Young, I. Fisher, and F.B. Hawley, to Knight. While drawing on a range of ideas put forward by these scholars, Knight transforms each of them fairly radically. From J.B Clark Knight adopts the notion of profit as being the analytical focus of his work, yet he turns Clark's analysis on it's head by rejecting the notion of 'friction'. Fisher and Hawley apply an interdisciplinary approach which Knight adopts, however Knight argues that profit is not related to the exertion or 'irksomeness' which is involved with facing uncertainty. Similarly, Knight incorporates Young's interest in increasing returns, yet argues that such returns are mainly derived from the firm's access to the stock of available market knowledge instead of 'roundabout' methods of production. Finally, Knight utilises J.M. Clark's analysis of overhead cost, however he modifies the explanation of how a firm derives economies of scale. Here, Knight argues that overhead costs fall as the scale of the firm increases because the large firm has better access to the stock of available knowledge.

While Knight transforms each of these influences, we can say that Knight's conceptualisation of the 'social welfare function' is consistent with the moral vision of J.B. Clark, who (especially in his earlier writings) was striving to create policies which would preserve a large degree of economic opportunity for all. Ideally, for Clark, competition had to be both efficient, and 'fair': 'unfair' competition is just as undesirable to Clark as inefficient competition.

Knight's perspective on imperfect competition has to be juxtaposed with the canonised perspective of J. Robinson and E.H. Chamberlin. The starting point of Knight, as compared to J. Robinson and E.H. Chamberlin, is different: Knight's analysis is intimately linked to his broader conception of economic welfare, whereas theirs is inspired by the standard identification of allocative efficiency with economic welfare. Imperfect access to the stock of available knowledge renders the achievement of allocative efficiency problematic because the marginal (small) firm faces a significant barrier to such access. Because the marginal (small) firm is less efficient than the large firm, its elimination will augment allocative efficiency. However, the consequent rise in the imbalance of economic power would contradict Knight's conception of the 'social welfare function' where economic efficiency is but one of the criteria employed for assessing the level of socio-economic welfare. Instead, Knight's framework suggests that the marginal (small) firm should be compensated - in some way - for its lack of access to market knowledge. In addition, the analytical core of each analysis of imperfect competition vary greatly. Whereas the analyses of J. Robinson and E.H. Chamberlin centre on product differentiation, essentially assuming trivial cost differentiation across firms, Knight - we have argued - centres his analysis on cost differentiation as the analytical mainspring of imperfect competition. As we explain in the thesis, this means that the large firm receives abnormal (or super-normal) profit in the long-run, not only in the short to medium term. Such profit indicates the existence of an equity problem, which is not identified by Chamberlin or Robinson.

As an epilogue, the thesis briefly puts forward a policy proposal, which although not advanced by Frank Knight himself, can nevertheless be put forward by drawing on some of Knight's ideas. Our discussion in Chapter Five shows how the large firm effectively "crowds out" access to market knowledge, which is the source of abnormal (or super-normal) profit in Knight's analysis of imperfect competition (Young 1927a, 97). This analysis illustrates Knight's conception of the 'social welfare function' where the large firm increases the cumulative tendency toward the imbalance of economic power by monopolising access to market knowledge (Knight 1943a, 115-6). If this tendency is left unchecked, then Knight fears that, "... the so called 'class structure' of society ..." will re-emerge (Knight 1943a, 115-6). As Knight warns throughout his work, such a class structure is the precursor to significant social tensions within the wider community; something which other authors have warned of at previous junctures in the history of democratic society. For example, Tocqueville identifies such tensions in French society before the revolution of 1848 (Stone and Mennell 1982, 11). We argue that Knight's warnings about the social repercussions, which are associated with the cumulative increase in the imbalance of economic power, parallel the sentiments of Tocqueville. In addressing the Chamber of Deputies, only a month before the French Revolution, a distressed Tocqueville warns that the economic discontent among the French people is such as to suggest that a revolution was imminent; he warns that, "... we are sleeping on a volcano ..." (Stone and Mennell 1982, 11).

While our policy proposal goes some way to alleviating the social tensions which threaten the free-market mechanism of exchange, much more work is required so as to develop a more cohesive approach to the problems presented by Knight's analysis of imperfect competition. Hopefully, this thesis may inspire the commencement of such work.

Knight's contribution has not yet received the attention it deserves. While enriching our understanding of the 'economic', Knight opens the window into a subject which economic analysis remains silent: the vital links between the 'economic' and 'moral' domains of our social existence. By examining these links we are able to shed a new light on the great intellectual challenge which Knight presents; a challenge which has never been fully understood. Our study of Knight goes some way to explaining what a generation of economic theorists saw as the enigma of Knight (Patinkin 1973a). Knight's remarkable expedition into the depths of economic theory is not a frivolous exercise in the de-construction, and re-construction, of intellectual systems. Rather, it is an earnest attempt to rethink the basic premises of economic theory, so as to ensure that the free-market system of exchange remains the dominant mechanism of exchange.

Knight's analysis of imperfect competition shows us that unrestrained self-interest cannot maximise the value of the aggregate 'social welfare function'. By monopolising the vantage point which is required for hedging against the costs imposed by uncertainty the large firm ensures that it receives abnormal (or super-normal) profit, while all other firms receive normal profit. In other words, Knight suggests that unequal exposure to uncertainty undermines the orthodox conception of welfare such that the 'invisible hand' cannot be relied upon to deliver the public good. Knight cogently argues that the 'invisible hand' bestows advantages on the large firm, which places its own interests before those of all others. By seeking to moderate monopolisation we do not claim to have paved the road to a perfectly just system of reward for labour. Rather, we argue that this form of regulation will ensure that the free-market will continue as a mechanism for the exchange of goods and services. While this is not a lofty goal, Knight enables us to see just how difficult it is to achieve. Indeed, it demands our complete attention, so that we might salvage the system of exchange which is responsible for the safe delivery of an unprecedented prosperity. We suggest that a prudent modification to this system is required: the system should provide some compensation for those who lack access to market knowledge. Refusal to adopt this modification is just as hazardous as to rashly undertake the task of reform.

Bibliography

Albon, R. (1989), 'Alfred Marshall and the Consumers' Loss from the British Post Office Monopoly', *History of Political Economy*, vol. 21, p. 4.

Alchian, A.A. and Demsetz, H. (1972), 'Production, Information Costs, and Economic Organisation', *American Economic Review,* pp. 777-95.

Allen, W.A. (1980), 'Irving Fisher, F.D.R, and the Great Depression', *History of Political Economy,* pp. 561-87.

American Economics Association (1973), 'In Memoriam: Frank H. Knight, 1885-1972', *American Economic Review,* vol. 63, pp. 1047-8.

Anderson, G. M., D., Levy M., and Tollison, R. D. (1989), 'The Half Life of Dead Economists', *Canadian Journal of Economics,* vol. 22, pp. 174-83.

Archibald, G.C. (1961), 'Chamberlin Versus Chicago', *Review of Economic Studies,* Oct.

Arrow, K.J. (1948), 'Social Choice and Justice' in *Collected Papers of K.J. Arrow,* Blackwell, Oxford.

____ (1970), 'Alternative Approaches to the Theory of Choice in Risk-Taking Situations', in *Essays in the Theory of Risk-Bearing,* North Holland, Amsterdam.

Ault, R.W. and Ekelund, R.B. Jr. (1988), 'Habits in Economic Analysis: Veblen and the Neoclassicals', *History of Political Economy,* vol. 20, p. 3.

Bain, J.S. (1967), 'Chamberlin's Impact On Micro-economic Theory', in R.E. Kuenne (ed), *Monopolistic Competition Theory: Studies in Impact*, John Wiley, New York.

Bannister, R.C. (1987), *Sociology and Scientism: The American Quest for Objectivity, 1880-1940,* University of North Carolina Press, Chapel Hill.

Barber, W.J. (1985), 'From New Era to New Deal: Herbert Hoover, the Economists, and American Economic Policy 1921-1933', in *Historical Perspectives on Modern Economics*, Cambridge University Press, Cambridge.

Barone, E. (1935), 'The Ministry of Production in the Collectivist State', in F.A Von Hayek (ed), *Collectivist Economic Planning*, George Rootledge & Sons, London.
Barzel, Y. (1986), 'Knight's Moral Hazard Theory of Organisation', *Economic Inquiry,* vol. 25, pp. 117-20.
Baumol, W.J, Panzar, J.C, and Willing, R.D. (1982), *Contestable Markets and The Theory of Industry Structure,* Harcourt Brace Jovanovich Inc, New York.
Berlin, I (1987), *Four Essays on Liberty*, Oxford University Press, London.
Bharadwaj, K. (1972), 'Marshall on Pigou's Wealth and Welfare', *Economica,* vol. 39, Feb.
____ (1991), 'History versus Equilibrium', in H.R. Rima (ed), *The Joan Robinson Legacy*, M.E. Sharpe Inc, New York.
Blaug, M. (1962), Eco*nomic Theory in Retrospect*, 3rd edn, Cambridge University Press, London.
____ (1982), *The Methodology of Positive Economics*, St.Martins Press, New York.
____ (1992), *Frank Knight (1885-1972), Henry Simons (1899-1946) and Joseph Schumpeter (1883-1950),* Edward Elgar Publishing, London.
Blitch, C.P. (1973), 'The Genesis of Chamberlinian Monopolistic Competition Theory: Addendum', *History of Political Economy,* vol. 17, pp. 396-400.
____ (1983a), 'Allyn A. Young, A Curious Case of Professional Neglect', *History of Political Economy,* vol. 15, p. 1.
____ (1983b), 'Allyn Young on Increasing Returns', *Journal of Post Keynesian Economics,* vol. 5, p. 3.
Bloom, A. (1987), *The Closing of the American Mind*, Penguin, New York.
____ (1990), 'Epilogue', in J.H. Nichols Jr. (ed), *From Political Economy, and Back?,* Institute for Contemporary Studies, San Fransisco.
____ (1993), *Love and Friendship*, Simon and Schuster, New York.
Bohm-Bawerk, E.Von (1923), *Capital and Interest*, Libertarian Press, South Holland.
Bowley, A.W. (1924), *The Mathematical Groundwork of Economics*, Clarendon Press, Oxford.
Breit, W. and Ransom, R.L. (1982), *The Academic Scribblers*, Dryden, Chicago.
Bronfenbrenner, M. (1962), 'Observations on The Chicago School(s)', *Journal of Political Economy,* vol. 70, pp. 72-6.

Buchanan, J. M. (1968), 'Frank H. Knight', in D. Sills (ed), *International Encyclopaedia of the Social Sciences*, Macmillan, New York, vol. 3, pp. 424-8.

Buechner, M. N. (1976), 'Frank Knight on Capital as the Only Factor of Production', *Journal of Economic Issues*, vol. 10, no.3, Sep, pp. 598-617.

Burns, A.M. (1924), *The Decline of Competition*, McGraw-Hill, New York.

Burstein, J. (1991), 'History Versus Equilibrium: Joan Robinson and Time in Economics', in H.R. Rima (ed), *The Joan Robinson Legacy*, M.E.Sharpe Inc, New York.

Caldwell, B.J. (1982), *Beyond Positivism: Economic Methodology in the Twentieth Century*, Allen and Unwin, London.

Carey, G.V. (1976), *Mind The Stop: A Brief Guide to Punctuation*, Penguin, London.

Carver, T.N. (1911), *The Distribution of Wealth*, The Macmillan Company, New York.

Chamberlin, E.H. (1932), Discussion of Knight, F.H., 'New Frontiers in Economic Thought, Immutable Law in Economics: Its Reality and Limitations', *American Economic Review*, pp. 139-42.

____ (1933), *The Theory of Monopolistic Competition*, Cambridge, Harvard University Press, (1983 edn).

____ (1946), 'Discussion', *American Economic Review,* vol. 36, p. 2 (Proceedings).

____ (1951a), 'The Impact of Recent Monopoly Theory on The Schumpeterian System', in S.E. Harris (ed), *Schumpeter: Social Scientist*, Harvard University Press, Cambridge.

____ (1951b), 'The Theory of Monopolistic Competition Revisited', *Economica,* vol. 18, Nov.

____ (1951c), 'Monopolistic Competition Revisited', *Economica,* Nov.

____ (1957), *Toward A More General Theory of Value*, The University Press, Oxford.

Clapham, J.H. (1922a), 'Of Empty Economic Boxes', *Economic Journal,* vol. 32, Sep.

____ (1922b), 'The Economic Boxes: A Rejoinder', *Economic Journal,* vol. 32, Dec.

Clark, J.B. (1886), *The Philosophy of Wealth*, Augustus M. Kelly Publishers, New York, 1961 edn.

____ (1899), *The Distribution of Wealth,* MacMillan, New York.

____ (1904), *The Problem of Monopoly*, Columbia University Press, New York.

____ (1907), *Essentials of Economic Theory, as Applied to Modern Problems of Industrial and Public Policy*, Augustus M. Kelly Publishers, New York., 1927 edn.

Clark, J.B. and Clark J.M. (1912), *The Control of Trusts*, Augustus M. Kelly Publishers, New York, 1971 edn.

Clark, J.M. (1917), 'Economic and Modern Psychology II- Constructive Statement: Outline of The Theory of Economic Guidance', *Journal of Political Economy*, pp. 137-66.

____ (1918), 'Economics and Modern Psychology, Parts I and II', *Journal of Political Economy,* vol. 26, pp. 1-30; pp. 136-66.

____ (1923), *Studies in the Economics of Overhead Costs,* University of Chicago Press, Chicago.

____ (1925), *Social Control of Business,* The University of Chicago Press, Chicago.

____ (1927), 'The Relation Between Statics and Dynamics', in *Economic Essays Contributed in Honour of J.B. Clark*, The Macmillan Company, New York.

____ (1936), 'Past Accomplishments and Present Prospects of American Economists', *The American Economic Review,* vol. 26 no.1, pp. 1-11.

____ (1940), 'Toward A Concept of Workable Competition', The *American Economic Review,* vol. 30, p. 2.

____ (1948), *Alternative To Serfdom*, Basil Blackwell, Oxford.

____ (1955), 'Competition: Static Models and Dynamic Aspects', *American Economic Review,* May.

____ (1961), *Competition as A Dynamic Process*, The Brookings Institution, Washington.

Clemens, E.W. (1951), 'Price Discrimination and The Multi-Product Firm', *Review, of Economic Studies,* vol. 19, p. 1.

Coase, R.H. (1937), 'The Nature of The Firm', *Economica*, vol. 4, pp. 386-405.

Coats, A.W. (1963), 'The Origins of the Chicago School(s)' *Journal of Political Economy,* vol. 71, Aug.

Cournot, A. (1938), *Recherches Sur Les Principles Mathematiques De La Theortic Des Richness*, trans. N.Bacon, London.

Crockett, J.A. Jr. (1980), 'Irving Fisher on the Financial Economics of Uncertainty', *History of Political Economy,* pp. 65-82.

Davis (1968), 'Chicago Economists, Deficit Budgets, and the Early 1930s', *American Economic Review*, vol. 58, Part 1, Jun, pp. 476-82.

Dewey, D. (1958), *Monopoly in Law and Economics*, Rand and McNally and Co, Chicago.

____ (1987), '*The Uncertain Place of Frank Knight in Chicago Economics'*, Paper presented at a joint session of the American Economics Association and the History of Economics Society, Chicago, 30 Dec 1987.

____ (1990), 'Frank Knight Before Cornell: Some Light on the Dark Years', Research in *The History of Economic Thought and Methodology*, vol. 8.

Dorfman, J.(1949), *The Economic Mind in American Civilisation,* Vol. 3-5, Viking Press, New York.

____ (1955), 'The Role of The German Historical School in American Economic Thought', *American Economic Review,* pp. 17-28.

____ (1970), J.B. and J.M. Clark on Monopoly and Competition, in J.M. and J.B. Clark, *The Control of Trusts*, Augustus M. Kelly, New York.

Ekelund, R.B.Jr. and Herbert, R.F. (1975), *A History of Economic Theory and Method*, McGraw Hill, New York.

Emmett, R.B. (1989), *Rationality and Organisation in a Changing World: the Therapeutic Quality of Frank H. Knight's Risk Uncertainty and Profit'*, Proceedings, Vol. 2, History of Economics Society, University of Richmond Press, Richmond.

____ (1992), 'Frank H. Knight on the Conflict of Values in Economic Life', in W. J. Samuels (ed), *Research in the History of Economic Thought and Methodology*, vol. 9.

____ (1994), 'Frank Knight: Economics vs. Religion', in H.G. Brennan and A.M.C. Waterman (eds), *Recent Economic Thought*, Kluwer Academic Press.

____ (1995), 'Maximizers vs. Good Sports: Frank Knight's Curious Understanding of Exchange Behaviour', *History of Political Economy,* Sup.

Feiwel, G.R. (1991), 'Joan Robinson Inside and Outside the Seam', in G.R Feiwel (ed), *Joan Robinson and Modern Economic Theory*, Macmillan Press, London.

Fellner, W. (1949), *Competition Among the Few - Oligopoly and Similar Market Structures*, Augustus M. Kelly, New York.

____ (1967), 'The Adaptability and Lasting Significance of The Chamberlinian Contribution', in R.E. Kuenne (ed), *Monopolistic Competition Theory: Studies in Impact*, John Wiley, New York.
Fetter, F.A. (1916), *Economics*, Century Books, New York.
Fisher, I. (1892), *Mathematical Investigations in the Theory of Value and Prices*, Yale University Press, New Haven.
____ (1906),*The Nature of Capital and Income*, Yale University Press, New Haven.
Fisher, I.N. (1956), *My Father Irving Fisher*, Comet Press, New York.
Friedman, M. (1962), *Capitalism and Freedom*, University of Chicago Press, Chicago.
____ (1972), 'Comments on the Critics', *Journal of Political Economy,* vol. 80, Jul-Dec.
Furner, M.O. (1975), *Advocacy & Objectivity: A Crisis in the Professionalisation of American Social Science, 1865-1905*, University Press of Kentucky, Lexington.
Galbraith, J.K. (1952), *American Capitalism: The Concept of Countervailing Power*, Houghton Mifflin, Boston.
____ (1956), *The Affluent Society*, Penguin, New York.
____ (1967), 'The New Industrial State', in E. Mansfield (ed), *Monopoly Power And Economic Performance - The Problem of Industrial Concentration*, W.W.Norton, New York, 1974 edn.
Gilchrist, J.K and Stigler, G. (1972), A Guide to the Knight Papers, *Joseph Regenstein Library*, University of Chicago, Chicago.
Gildin, H. (1983), *Rousseau's Social Contract: The Design of the Argument*, University of Chicago Press, Chicago.
Gill, F. (1984), 'The Costs of Adjustment and the Invisible Hand; with Special Reference to the Labour Market', *Economie Appliquee*, vol. 3-4, pp. 523-41.
____ (1992), 'Inequality and the Wheel of Fortune: Systematic Causes of Economic Depravation', *Social Policy Research Centre Reports and Proceedings*, 97, Feb.
Golffing, F. (1961), Review of Knight F.H., 'Intelligence and Democratic Action', *Ethics*, vol. LXXI, pp. 224-6.
Gonce, R. A. (1972), 'Frank H. Knight on Social Control and the Scope and Method of Economics', *Southern Economic Journal* vol. 38, pp. 547-58.
Gordon, K. (1955), 'Discussion', *American Economic Review,* May.

Gordon, S. (1974), 'Frank Knight and the Tradition of Liberalism', *Journal of Political Economy,* vol. 82, pp. 571-7.

Gower, E. (1987), *The Complete Plain Words*, Penguin, London.

Groenewegen, P.D. (1988), 'Alfred Marshall and the Establishment of the Cambridge Economic Tripos', *History of Political Economy,* vol. 20, p. 4.

____ (1990), 'Marshall and Hegel', *Economie Appliquee*, no.1, pp. 63-84.

Guillebaud, C.W. (1942), 'The Evolution of Marshall's Principles of Economics', *The Economic Journal,* vol. 52, Dec.

Graham, F.D. (1947), Review of Knight, F.H., 'Freedom and Reform', *American Economic Review*, Dec, pp. 938-43.

Hahn, F.H. (1980), Monetarism and Economic Theory, *Economica*.

Hammond, J.D. (1990), *'Frank Knight's Anti-Positivism',* Proceedings Vol. II, History of Economics Society, University of Richmond Press, Richmond.

Harris, S.E. (ed) (1951), *Schumpeter, Social Scientist*, Harvard University Press, Cambridge.

Harrod, R.F. (1931), 'The Law of Decreasing Costs', *Economic Journal,* vol. XLI, pp. 566-76.

____ (1934), 'Doctrines of Imperfect Competition', *Quarterly Journal of Economics,* vol. XLVIII, pp. 442-70.

____ (1967), 'Increasing Returns', in R.E. Kuenne (ed), *Monopolistic Competition Theory: Studies in Impact*, John Wiley, New York.

Hart, N. (1989), *Economic Theory and Returns To Scale: A Study of Controversies in Marshallian Economics*, Unpublished Master of Economics Thesis, University of Sydney, Sydney.

Hawley, F.B. (1901), 'Reply to Final Objectives to the Risk Theory of Profit', *The Quarterly Journal of Economics,* vol. 15, pp. 603-20.

Hawthorn, G. (1987), *Enlightenment and Despair: A History of Social Theory*, Cambridge University Press, Cambridge.

Hayek, F. (1944), *The Road to Serfdom*, University of Chicago Press Chicago.

____ (1948), *Individualism and Economic Order*, University of Chicago Press, Chicago.

____ (1960), *The Constitution of Liberty*, University of Chicago Press, Chicago.

Hegel, G.W.F. (1899), *Philosophy of History*, trans. J.Sibree, Dover Publications, New York, 1956 edn.

Henry, J.F. (1982), 'The Transformation of John Bates Clark: An Essay in Interpretation', *History of Political Economy,* vol. 14, p. 2.

____ (1983),'John Bates Clark and the Marginal Product: An Historical Inquiry into the Origins of Value-free Economic Theory', *History of Political Economy,* vol. 15, p. 3.

Herskovits, M.J. (1941), 'Economics and Anthropology: A Rejoinder', *Journal of Political Economy*, Apr, pp. 269-78.

Hildebrand, G.H. (1955), 'Discussion: The Role of The German Historical School in American Economic Thought', American *Economic Review,* 34-7.

Hirsh, A. and Hirsh, E. (1980), 'The Heterodox Methodology of Two Chicago Economists', in W.J. Samuels (ed), *The Methodology of Economic Thought*, Transaction Books, New Brunswick.

Hollander, J.H. (1927), *The Economic Essays Contributed in Honour of John Bates Clark*, The Macmillan Company, New York.

Horsburgh, H.J.N. (1958), 'Philosophers Against Metaphor', *Philosophical Quarterly,* vol. 32, pp. 231-45.

Hoselitz, B.F. (1957), Review of Knight F.H., 'On the History and Method of Economics', *American Journal of Sociology,* Jul, pp. 113-4.

Howey, R.S. (1983), 'Frank Hyneman Knight and The History of Economic Thought', *Research in the History of Economic Thought and Methodology,* vol. 1.

Hutchison, T.W. (1941), 'The Significance and Basic Postulates of Economic Theory: A Reply to Professor Knight', *Journal of Political Economy*, Oct, pp. 732-50.

____ (1952), *A Review of Economic Doctrines 1870-1929*, Oxford University Press, Oxford.

Jaffe, W. (1955),'Discussion: The Role of The German Historical School in American Economic Thought', *American Economic Review,* pp. 37-9.

____ (1975), 'Leon Walras, An Economic Adviser Manque', *Economic Journal,* vol. 85.

Jalladeau, J. (1975), 'The Methodological Conversion of John Bates Clark', History *of Political Economy,* vol. 7.

Johnson, A.S. (1952), *Pioneer's Progress*, The Viking Press, New York.

Kahn, R.F. (1935), 'Some Notes on Ideal Output', *Economic Journal* vol. XLV.

Kaldor, N. (1925), 'The Irrelevance of Equilibrium Economics', *The Economic Journal*, Dec, pp. 1237-52.

____ (1938), 'Professor Chamberlin on Monopolistic and Imperfect Competition', *Quarterly Journal of Economics,* vol. LII.

____ (1961), 'Increasing Returns and Technical Progress, A Comment on Professor Hick's Article', *Oxford Economic Papers*, vol. 13, Feb.

Kasper, S.D. (n.d.), '*Frank Knight's Case for Laissez-faire*: Proceedings', History of Economics Society, vol. 2, University of Richmond Press, Richmond.

Kay, J. (1993), *Foundations of Corporate Success: How Business Strategies Add Value*, Oxford University Press, Oxford.

Kern, W.S. (1985), 'Frank Knight on Preachers and Economic Policy', *Papers: History of Economics Society- Annual Meeting*, vol 2, May 20-22, 1985, George Mason University, in *American Journal of Economics and Sociology* (1988), vol. 47, no.1, Jan, pp. 61-9.

____ (1987), 'Frank Knight's Three Commandments', *History of Political Economy,* vol. 19, p. 4.

Keynes, J.M. (1937), 'The General Theory of Employment', *Quarterly Journal of Economics,* vol. 51, pp. 209-23.

Kirzner, I.M. (1973), *Competition and Entrepreneurship*, University of Chicago Press, Chicago.

Knight, F.H. (1913), *Gerhart Hauptmann*, unpublished M.A. thesis: University of Tennessee.

____(1915a),'Thirteenth Census Report on Occupations', *American Economic Review,* vol. 15

____ (1915b), 'Mechanical Devices in European Statistical Work', *American Statistical Association Publication,* vol. 14, pp. 596-9.

____ (1915c), 'A Correction', *American Statistical Association Publication,* vol. 14, p. 700.

____ (1916a), 'Neglected Factors in the Problem of Normal Interest', *Quarterly Journal of Economics,* Feb.

____ (1916b), *A Theory of Business Profit*, PhD thesis, Cornell University.

____ (1916c), 'Neglected Factors in the Problem of Normal Interest', Quarterly Journal of Economics, vol. 30, pp. 279-310.

____ (1917), 'The Concept of Normal Price in Value and Distribution', *Quarterly Journal of Economics,* vol. 32, pp. 66-100.

____ (1919a), Review of Russell, B., 'Proposed Roads to Freedom: Socialism, Anarchism and Sydicalism', *American Journal of Sociology,* vol. 25, pp. 227-8.

____ (1919b), Review of Woolf, L.S., 'Co-operation and the Future of Industry', *Journal of Political Economy,* vol. 27, pp. 805-6.

____ (1919c), 'to Minerva Knight', 29 Jul 1919 Knight Shelbourne Family Papers, held by Laura Safir, Kensington, California, in D. Dewey, *The Uncertain Place of Frank Knight in Chicago Economics*, Paper presented at a joint session of the American Economics Association and the History of Economics Society, 30 Dec 1987, Chicago.

____ (1919d), Review of Charriault, H. and Hacault, R., 'La Liquidation Financiere', *Journal of Political Economy,* vol. 27, pp. 611-3.

____ (1919e), Review of Hetherington H.JW. and Muirhead J.H., 'Social Purpose', *Journal of Political Economy,* vol. 27, pp. 898-900.

____ (1919f), Review of J.S. Mackenzie, 'Outlines of Social Philosophy', *Journal of Political Economy,* vol. 27, pp. 898-900.

____ (1920a), '*Social Organisation: A Survey of its Problems and Forms from the Standpoint of the Present Crisis',* B31, F6-7, F. H. Knight Papers, Special Collections, *Joseph Regenstein Library*, University of Chicago, Chicago.

____ (1920b), Review of Veblen. T., 'The Place of Science in Modern Civilisation', *Journal of Political Economy,* vol. 28, pp. 518-20.

____ (1920c), '*Economics 1920's'* (n.d.). (Unpublished material in boxes 8 and 9 of Knight's papers that have been catalogued by G. Gilchrist under George Stigler's direction).

____ (1921a), *Risk, Uncertainty, and Profit*, Houghton Mifflin, New York, 1985 edn.

____ (1921b) et al, 'Discussion of Traditional Economic Theory', *American Economic Review,* vol. 11 (Supplement), Mar, pp. 143-47.

____ (1921c), 'Cost of Production over Long and Short Periods', *Journal of Political Economy,* vol. 29, Apr, pp. 304-35.

____ (1921d), Review of Cassel, G., 'Theoretische Sozialoekonomie', by G. Cassel, *Quarterly Journal of Economics,* vol. 36, pp. 145-53.

____ (1921e), 'Traditional Economic Theory', *American Economic Review,* pp. 143-6.

____ (1922a), 'The Relation between Economics and Ethics', *American Economic Review,* vol. 12 (Supplement), Mar, pp. 192-3.

____ (1922b), 'Ethics and the Economic Interpretation', *Quarterly Journal of Economics,* vol. 36, May, pp. 451-81.

____ (1922c), 'On the Other Hand', *Signboard,* Issued Monthly by Gamma Epsilon Pi, May, pp. 1-4.

____ (1922d), Review of Fray, C.R., 'Co-operation at Home and Abroad', *Journal of Political Economy,* vol. 30, pp. 582-5.

____ (1922e), Review of Muir, R., 'Liberalism and Industry', *Journal of Political Economy,* vol. 30, pp. 582-5.

____ (1922f), Review of Pasolsky, l., 'The Economics of Communism', *Journal of Political Economy,* vol. 30, pp. 582-5.

____ (1923a), 'Discussion of Economic Theory and Practice', *American Economic Review,* vol. 8 (Supplement), Mar, pp. 105-7.

____ (1923b), 'Business Management: Science or Art?', *The Journal of Business*, State University of Iowa, Mar, pp. 5-9.

____ (1923c), Review of Bourke, O.F., 'A Critique of Economics', *American Economic Review,* vol. 8, pp. 286-8.

____ (1923d), 'Some Books on Fundamentals': Review of Henderson H.D., 'Supply and Demand'; Review of Pigou A.C., 'The Economics of Welfare'; Review of Edie, L.D., 'Principles of New Economics'; Review of Johnson, A.S., 'Introduction to Economics (revised)''; *Journal of Political Economy,* vol. 31, Jun, pp. 342-59.

____ (1923e), 'The Ethics of Competition', *Quarterly Journal of Economics,* vol. 37, Aug, pp. 579-624.

____ (1924a), 'Some Fallacies The Interpretation of Social Cost', in M. Friedman, H.Jones, and G.Stigler (eds), *The Ethics of Competition*, George Allen and Unwin, London. See also, *Quarterly Journal of Economics*, vol. 38, Aug, pp. 582-606.

____ (1924b), 'The Limitations of Scientific Method in Economics', in R.G. Tugwell (ed), *The Trend of Economics*, pp. 229-67.

____ (1924c), Review of Hedrick,W.O., 'The Economics of Food Supply', *Journal of Social Forces,* vol. 2, p. 757.

____ (1924d), Review of Marriot, J.A.R., 'Economics and Ethics' J.A.R. Marriot, *Journal of Social Forces*, vol. 2, p. 757.

____ (1924e), Review of Atkins D., 'The Economics of Freedom', *American Economic Review,* vol. 14, pp. 718-9.

____ (1925a), Review of Small, A.W., 'Origins of Sociology', *American Economic Review,* Dec.

____ (1925b), Letter to Jacob Viner, September 9, 1925, *Viner Papers*, Princeton University.

____ (1925c), Review of Franklin, F., 'Plain Talks of Economics', *Journal of Social Forces,* vol. 3, pp. 353-4.

____ (1925d), 'On Decreasing Cost and Comparative Cost - a Rejoinder', *Quarterly Journal of Economics,* vol. 34, Feb, pp. 331-3.

____ (1925e), Review of McDougall, W., 'Ethics and Some Modern World Problems', *Political Science Quarterly,* vol. xl, pp. 138-40.

____ (1925f), 'Economic Psychology and the Value Problem', *Quarterly Journal of Economics,* vol. 34, May, pp. 372-409.

____ (1925g), Review of Carver, T.N., 'The Economy of Human Energy', *Journal of Social Forces,* vol. 3, pp. 777-8.

____ (1925h), Review of Harris, F.S., 'Scientific Research and Human Welfare', *Journal of Social Forces,* vol. 3, p. 778.

____ (1925i), 'A 'Scientific' Observation Regarding Socialism', *The Iowa Liberal*, May, pp. 5-6.

____ (1925j), 'Fact and Metaphysics in Economic Psychology', *American Economic Review,* vol. 15, Jun, pp. 247-66.

____ (1925k), Review of Scovell, C.H., 'Interest as a Cost', *Journal of Political Economy,* vol. 33, pp. 468-70.

____ (1925l), 'A Note on Professor Clark's Illustration of Marginal Productivity', *Journal of Political Economy,* vol. 33, Oct, pp. 550-62.

____ (1925m), Review of Ashley, Sir, William J., 'The Christian Outlook', *Political Science Quarterly,* vol. xl, pp. 624-6.

____ (1925n), Review of Small, A.W., 'Origins of Sociology', *American Economic Review,* vol. 15, pp. 724-7.

____ (1925o), Review of Ashley, W.T., 'Being the Sermons of an Economist', *Joseph Regenstein Library*, University of Chicago, 3,39,11.

____ (1925p), 'Rejoinder: A Note on Professor Clark's Illustration of Marginal Productivity', *Journal of Political Economy*, vol. 33, Oct, p. 25.

____ (1926a), Review of Pigou, A.C., 'Economics at Its Best: A Review of The Economics of Welfare (2nd edn)', *American Economic Review,* vol. 16, Mar, pp. 51-8.

____ (1926b), Review of Foster W.T. and Catchings W., 'Profits', *Political Science Quarterly,* vol. xli, pp. 468-71.

____ (1926c), *General Economic History*, trans of Weber, M., George Allen and Unwin, New York.

____ (1927a), Review of Hoyt, E.E., 'Primitive Trade: Its Psychology and Economics', *American Economic Review,* vol. 17, pp. 73-4.

____ et al (1927b), 'Discussion of Interest Theory and Price Movements', *American Economic Review,* 17 (Supplement), Mar, pp. 120-1.

____ (1927c), Review of Boucke F.F., 'Principles of Economics', *Journal of Political Economy,* vol. 35, pp. 315-7.

____ (1927d), Review of Soddy, F., 'Wealth, Virtual Wealth and Debt. The Solution to the Economic Paradox', in *The Saturday Review of Literature*, April 16, p. 732.

____ (1927e), Review of Atkins, D., 'The Measurements of Economic Value', *Journal of Political Economy,* vol. 35, pp. 552-7.

____ (1927f), Review of Weatherly U.G., 'Social Progress', *American Economic Review,* vol. 17, pp. 487-8.

____ (1927g), Review of Hayes, E.C. (ed), 'Recent Developments in the Social Sciences', *American Economic Review,* vol. 17, pp. 686-7.

____ (1927h), Review of Mayer, J., 'The Seven Seals of Science', *Journal of Political Economy,* vol. 17, pp. 688-9.

____ (1927i), 'Preface', in *General Economic History*, by M. Weber, trans. F.H. Knight, Greenberg, New York.

____ (1928a), 'Historical and Theoretical Issues in the Problem of Modern Capitalism', *Journal of Economic and Business History* vol. 1, Nov, pp. 119-36.

____ (1928b), Review of Ogburn and Goldenweiser (eds), 'The Social Sciences and Their Interrelations', *American Economic Review,* vol. 28, pp. 82-3.

____ (1928c), Review of Dawson E. et al, 'Teaching the Social Sciences', *American Economic Review,* vol. 28, p. 84.

____ (1928d), 'A Suggestion for Simplifying the Statement of the General Theory of Price', *Journal of Political Economy,* vol. 36, Jun, pp. 353-70.

____ (1928e), Review of Bousquet, G.H., 'Essai sur l'evolution de la pensee economique', *American Economic Review,* vol. 28, pp. 278-9.

____ (1928f), 'Homan's Contemporary Economic Thought', *Quarterly Journal of Economics,* Nov, pp. 132-41.

____ (1928g), Review, 'Oppenheimers Theorie der Reinen Und Politischen Oekonomie', *Joseph Regenstein Library,* University of Chicago, Chicago, 3,39,8.

____ et al (1928h), Discussion, 'The Theory of Economic Dynamics as Related to Industrial Instability', *American Economic Review*, vol. 20, Mar, pp. 30-9.

____ (1929a), 'Discussion on Economic History', *American Economic Review,* Mar.

____ (1929b), 'Freedom as Fact and Criterion', *The International Journal of Ethics,* vol. 34, pp. 129-47.

____ (1929c), 'Discussion of Economic History', *American Economic Review,* (Supplement), pp. 156-8.

____ (1929d), '*Beauty and Economics*', Manuscript of lecture given before Bureau of Personnel Administration, New York, March 28 1929. Mimeographed for private circulation.

____ (1929e), Review of See, H., 'Economic and Social Conditions in France during the Eighteenth Century', *Journal of Political Economy,* vol. 37, pp. 235-36.

____ (1929f), 'Absolutism, or - Absolutism!', *The New Humanist,* vol. 2, no. 2, pp. 1-3.

____ (1929g), Review of Florence, P.S., 'Economics and Human Behaviour - A Reply to Social Psychologists', *Journal of Political Economy,* 37, pp. 363-4.

____ (1929h), Review of Guyot, Y., 'La science economique: ses lois inductives', *Journal of the American Statistical Association,* vol. 24, pp. 345-6.

____ (1929i), Notes on Economic Theory, *Joseph Regenstein Library,* University of Chicago, 1,1,15.

____ (1929j), Review of Sven, A., 'Uncertainty-bearing and the Income Tax', *Joseph Regenstein Library*, University of Chicago, 3,39,8.

____ (1930a), 'Absentee Ownership', *Encyclopaedia of the Social Sciences 1*, pp. 376-8.

____ (1930b), 'Abstinence', *Encyclopaedia of the Social Sciences* 1, pp. 376-8.

____ (1930c), Review of Taylor, H., 'Making Goods and Making Money', *Journal of Political Economy,* vol. 38, pp. 117-8.

____ (1930d), 'Fact and Interpretation in Economics', Graduate School of U.S. Department of Agriculture, *Special Lectures on Economics*, Feb-Mar.

____ (1930e), 'Discussion on The Theory of Economic Dynamics', *American Economic Review,* vol. 20, (Supplement), pp. 35-7.

____ (1930f), Review of Jenks, E., 'The Book of English Law', *Journal of Political Economy,* vol. 38, pp. 237-8.

____ (1930g), Review of Smith, M., 'The Development of European Law', *Journal of Political Economy,* vol. 38, pp. 23-38.

____ (1930h), Review of Ehrenberg, R. 'Capital and Finance in the Age of the Renaissance', *Journal of Political Economy,* vol. 38, pp. 361-4.

____ (1930i), Review of Lipson, E., 'The Economic History of England', Vol. 1, 5th edn, *American Economic Review,* vol. 20, p. 278.

____ (1930j), 'Statik und Dynamik - zur Frage der Mechanischen Analogie in den Wirtschaftswissenschaften, Zeitschrift fur Nationaloekonomie', 2, 1, Aug, 1-26, Mimeographed in English as *Statics and Dynamic,* for private circulation.

____ (1931a), Review of Spann, O., 'The History of Economics', *Journal of Political Economy,* vol. 39, pp. 258-60.

____ (1931b), 'Marginal Utility Economics', *Encyclopaedia of the Social Sciences*, New York.

____ (1931c), 'Relation of Utility Theory to Method in the Work of William Stanely Jevons and Others', in S. Rice (ed), *Methods in Social Science*, University of Chicago Press, Chicago, pp. 59-69.

____ (1931d), 'Professor Fisher's Interest Theory: A Case in Point', *Journal of Political Economy,* vol. 39, Apr, pp. 258-60.

____ (1931e), 'Davenport, Herbert Joseph', *Encyclopaedia of the Social Sciences,* vol. 5, pp. 8-9.

____ (1931f), 'Demand Curves - Theory', *Encyclopaedia of the Social Sciences,* vol. 5, pp. 69-72.

____ (1931g), 'Exchange', *Encyclopaedia of the Social Sciences,* vol. 5, pp. 666-9.

____ (1931h), Review of Dennison, H., 'Organisation Engineering', *American Journal of Sociology,* vol. 37, p. 316.

____ (1932a), Review of Suranyi-Unger, T., 'Economics in the Twentieth Century', *Journal of Political Economy,* vol. xl, pp. 708-10.

____ (1932b), Review of Grey, A., 'The Development of Economic Doctrine', *Journal of Political Economy,* Oct.

____ (1932c), 'Interest', in *The Encyclopaedia of the Social Sciences*, New York, vol. 5, p. 79.

____ (1932d), Review of Slichter, S.H., 'Modern Economic Society', *Journal of Political Economy,* vol. 40, pp. 433-76.

____ (1932e), 'Modern Economic Society Further Considered', *Journal of Political Economy,* vol. xl, pp. 814-27.

____ (1932f), 'New Frontiers in Economic Thought, Immutable Law in Economics: Its Reality And Limitations', *American Economic Review,* pp. 91-138.

____ (1932g), 'Social Economic Organisation, The Price System and the Economic Process, Demand and Supply Price, Distribution: The Pricing of Productive Services Individually', in *Second-Year Course in the Social Sciences (Social Sciences II): Syllabus and Selected readings*, Preliminary Edition, Chicago.

____ (1932h), 'Das Wertproblem in der Wirtschaftstheorie', in *Die Wirtschaftstheorie der Gegenwart*, 2, Vienna, pp. 52-72.
____ (1932i), Review of Chang, S.H.M., 'The Marxian Theory of the State', *Journal of Political Economy,* vol. xl, pp. 130-1.
____ (1932j), Review of Slichter, S.H., 'Modern Economic Society', *American Journal of Sociology,* vol. 38, pp. 130-2.
____ (1932k), Review of Dahlberg, A.O., 'Jobs, Machines, and Capitalism', *Journal of Political Economy,* vol. xl, p. 573.
____ (1932l), Review of Dennis, L., 'Is Capitalism Doomed?', *American Economic Review,* vol. 22, pp. 512-3.
____ (1932m), Review of Mises L. and Spiethoff A. (eds), 'Probleme der Wertlehre', *American Journal of Sociology*, vol. 38, pp. 471-2.
____ (1932n), Review, 'The Newer economics and the Control of Economic Activity', vol. 32, Aug, pp. 433-76.
____ (1932o), Comment on Slichter, S.H., 'Modern Economic Society Further Considered, a Comment on Mr. Slichter's Comment on the Issues', *Journal of Political Economy*, vol. 32, Dec, pp. 820-5.
____ (1933a), Review of Patterson, S.H., 'Readings in the History of Economic Thought', *Journal of Political Economy,* vol. xli, pp. 557-78.
____ (1933b), Review of Geiger, R.G., 'The Philosophy of Henry George', *International Journal of Ethics*, vol. xli, 687-90; see also *The International Journal of Ethics*, vol. xliv, pp. 162-5.
____ (1933c), *The Economic Organisation*, University of Chicago Press, Chicago, 1951 edn.
____ (1933d), 'The Case for Communism: From the Standpoint of an Ex-Liberal', in *The Dilemma of Liberalism*, Ann Arbor.
____ (1933e), Review of Hansen, A.H., 'Economic Stabilisation in an Unbalanced World', *Journal of Political Economy*, vol. xli, pp. 242-5.
____ (1933f), 'Pseudo-scientific Method in Economics', *Econometrica*, vol. 1, Oct, pp. 428-9.
____ (1933g), *Risk, Uncertainty, and Profit* (With a new Introductory Essay), London School of Economics and Political Science, Reprints of Scarce Tracts in Economics and Political Science, No. 16, London.
____ (1933h), 'Capitalistic Production, Time, and the Rate of Return', in *Economic Essays in Honour of Gustav Cassel*, London, pp. 327-42.
____ (1933i), '*The Dilemma of Liberalism*', Edward Brothers Inc., Michigan: Ann Arbor. Planotyped for private circulation, *Joseph Regenstein Library,* University of Chicago, 1, 2, 8.

____ (1933j), 'A Criticism of Professor Perry on The Arbitrary as Basis for Rational Morality', *The International Journal of Ethics,* vol. xlii, pp. 148-51.

____ (1933k), 'Can We Vote Ourselves out of the Fix We Are In?', *The Christian Century*, Feb, pp. 151-4.

____ (1933l), Review of Obolensky-Ossinsky V.V., Ronin S.L., Gayster, A., and Kroval, I.A., 'Social Economic Planning in the Union of Soviet Socialist Republics', *Journal of Political Economy,* vol. xli, pp. 131-2.

____ (1933m), Review of Clark, H.F., 'Economic Theory and Correct Occupational Distribution', by Clark, *Journal of Political Economy,* vol. xli, p. 260.

____ (1933n), Review of Soule, G., 'A Planned Society', *Journal of Political Economy,* vol. xli, pp. 421-3.

____ (1933o), Review of The International Industrial Relations Institute, 'World Social Economic Planning' *American Economic Review,* vol. 33, pp. 357-9.

____ (1933p), Review of Blaisdell, T.C. Jr, 'The Federal Trade Commission', *American Journal of Sociology,* vol. 39, pp. 133-4.

____ (1933q), Review of Boucke O.F., 'Laissez Faire and After', *American Journal of Sociology,* vol. 39, pp. 148-9.

____ (1933r), 'To Joseph Mayer on Pseudo-Scientific Method in Economics', *Econometrica*, vol. 1, pp. 428-9.

____ (1934a), 'The Common Sense of Political Economy, (Wicksteed Reprinted)', *Journal of Political Economy,* vol. 42, Oct, pp. 660-73.

____ (1934b), Review of Scott, W.A., 'The Development of Economics', *American Journal of Sociology,* vol. xl, pp. 413-14.

____ (1934c), 'Profit', Encyclopaedia of the Social Sciences, vol. 12, pp. 480-6.

____ (1934d), 'Modern Thought: Is it Anti-Intellectual?', *University of Chicago Magazine,* vol. 27 (1), Nov: 20-1, 23.

____ (1934e), 'Supply', *Encyclopaedia of the Social Sciences,* 14, pp. 370-4.

____ (1934f), 'Taylor, F.M', *Encyclopaedia of the Social Sciences,* vol. 12, pp. 541-2.

____ (1934g), Review of Robbins, L., 'The Nature and Significance of Economic Science', *Ethics,* Apr, pp. 358-61.

____ (1934h), Review of Souter, R.W., 'Prolegomena to Relativity Economics entitled The Nature of Economic Science in Some Recent Discussion', *American Economic Review,* vol. 24, pp. 225-38.

____ (1934i), 'Social Science and the Political Trend', *University of Toronto Quarterly*, vol. 3, pp. 407-27.
____ (1934j), 'The New Deal and Liberalism', in *Report of Midwest Conference on Industrial Relations*, School of Business, University of Chicago, Oct, pp. 35-44.
____ (1934k), 'Capital, Time, and the Interest Rate', *Economica*, vol. 34, Aug, pp. 257-86.
____ (1934l), '*The Development of Economic Institutions and Ideas*', Mimeographed for private circulation.
____ (1934m), 'The Nature of Economic Science in Some Recent Discussion', *American Economic Review*, Jun, pp. 225-38.
____ (1935a), Review of Dupuit, J., 'De L'utilite et de sa mesure', Torino, *Journal of Political Economy*, Feb.
____ (1935b), 'The Ricardian Theory of Production and Distribution', *Canadian Journal of Economics and Political Science*, Part I, Feb, pp. 3-25; Part II May, pp. 71-962, 1.
____ (1935c), *The Ethics of Competition and Other Essays*, M. Friedman, H. Jones, G. Stigler, and A. Wallis (eds), George Allen and Unwin, London.
____ (1935d), 'The Quantity Theory of Capital and the Rate of Interest, Part 1, and 2', *Journal Political Economy*, Aug-Oct.
____ (1935e), 'Intellectual Confusion on Morals and Ethics', *The International Journal of Ethics*, Jan, pp. 200-20.
____ (1935f), 'Value and Price', *Encyclopaedia of the Social Sciences*, 15.
____ (1935g), Review of Moll, B., 'Gerechtigkeit in der Wirtschaft', *Journal of Political Economy*, vol. xliii, pp. 113-6.
____ (1935h), Review of Souter, R.W., 'Prolegomena to Relativity Economics entitled The Nature of Economic Science in Some Recent Discussion', *American Economic Review*, vol. 24, pp. 225-38.
____ (1935i), 'Professor Hayek and the Theory of Interest', *Economic Journal*, vol. 45, Mar, pp. 77-94.
____ (1935j), Review of Mises, L. and Spiethoff, A. 'Probleme der Wertlehere, Teil II', *American Journal of Sociology*, vol. 39, May.
____ (1935k), 'Economic Rationality as a Social-Psychological Phenomena', *Bulletin of the Society for Social Research*, Dec.
____ (1935l), 'The Theory of Investment Once More: Mr. Boulding and the Austrians', *Quarterly Journal of Economics*, Nov.
____ (1935m), Review of Commons, J.R., 'Institutional Economics', *Columbia Law Review*, May, pp. 803-5.

____ (1935n), 'Professor Knight and 'The Period of Production'', *Journal of Political Economy*, vol. 43, Oct, pp. 625-7.

____ (1935o), 'A Final Word: 'Professor Knight and 'The Period of Production'', *Journal of Political Economy*, vol. 43, Dec, p. 35.

____ (1935p), 'The Theory of Investment Once More: Mr Boulding and the Austrians', *Quarterly Journal of Economics*, 50, Nov, pp. 36-67.

____ (1935q), Review, 'Barbara Wootton on Economic Planning', *Journal of Political Economy*, vol. 43, Dec, 809-14.

____ (1936a), 'Some Issues in The Economics of Stationary States', *The American Economic Review*, 26, Sep, pp. 393-411.

____ (1936b), 'The Quantity of Capital and the Rate of Interest, Part 1', Journal *of Political Economy,* Part I, Aug, 44, pp. 433-63; Part II, Oct 44, pp. 612-42.

____ (1936c), Review of The American Philosophical Society 'Symposium on the Totalitarian State from the Standpoints of History', by, *Joseph Regenstein Library*, University of Chicago, 3,39,8.

____ (1936d), 'The Ricardian Theory of Production and Distribution', *Canadian Journal of Economics and Political Science*, 1, Feb.

____ (1936e), 'The Place of marginal Economics in a Collectivist System', *American Economic Review*, (Supplement), 26, Mar, pp. 255-66.

____ (1937a), Review of Keynes J.M., 'Unemployment and Mr. Keynes's Revolution in Economic Theory', *Canadian Journal of Economics,* Feb, pp. 100-23.

____ (1937b), 'Note on Dr Lange's Interest Theory', *Review of Economic Studies*, vol. 4, Jun, pp. 223-30.

____ (1937c), Review of Wallace, H.A., 'Technology, Corporations, and the General Welfare',: University of North Carolina Press, Chapel Hill, *Joseph Regenstein Library,* University of Chicago, 1, III, 7.

____ (1938a), Review of Smith, A., 'An Inquiry into the Nature and Causes of the Wealth of Nations', *American Journal of Sociology*, Mar.

____ (1938b), Review of Wermel, M.T., 'The Evolution of the Classical Wage Theory', Columbia University Press, New York *Joseph Regenstein Library,* University of Chicago, 1, III, 8.

____ (1938c), Free Enterprise, Ideal and Real, Lectures Given at The London School of Economics, *Joseph Regenstein Library,* University of Chicago, 1, 20, 16-17.

____ (1938d), 'Ethics, Lectures Given at The London School of Economics', *Joseph Regenstein Library,* University of Chicago, 1, 20, 18-28.
____ (1938e), 'Collectivism as an Economic Problem', Lectures Given at The London School of Economics, *Joseph Regenstein Library,* University of Chicago, 1, 21, 1-8.
____ (1938f), 'The Problem of Group Action: Social Problem Solving', Lectures Given at The London School of Economics, *Joseph Regenstein Library,* University of Chicago, 1, 21, 9-15.
____ (1938g), 'On the Theory of Capital: In Reply to Mr. Kaldor', *Econometrica*, vol. 6, Jan, pp. 63-82.
____ (1938h), 'Two Economists on Socialism', *Journal of Political Economy*, vol. 46, Apr, pp. 241-50.
____ (1938i), 'Lippmann's The Good Society', *Journal of Political Economy*, Dec, 864-72.
____ (1939a), Review of Bowley, M., 'Nassau Senior: And Classical Economics', *Journal of Political Economy,* Feb.
____ (1939b), Review of Barnes, H.E. and Becker, H., 'Social Thought from Lore to Science', *Journal of Political Economy,* Jun.
____ (1939c), 'Letter to Richard H. Tawney 28 Apr, 1939', B62, F9, F. H. Knight Papers, *Special Collections. Joseph Regenstein Library*: University of Chicago.
____ (1939d), 'Imperfect Competition', *The Journal of Marketing,* vol. 3, pp. 360-6.
____ (1939e), 'Bertrand Russel on Power', *Ethics*, vol. 3, Apr, pp. 360-6.
____ (1939f), 'The Genesis and Character of the Modern Liberal Regime, The Breakdown of the Liberal System: Its Weaknesses-Reasons for Failure', in *Selected Readings for the Second-Year Course in the Study of Contemporary Society* (Social Science II), 8th edn, multilith, Chicago.
____ (1939g), Review of Wermel M.T., 'The Evolution of the Classical Wage Theory', *Joseph Regenstein Library,* University of Chicago, 1,3,8.
____ (1939h), Review of The American Philosophical Society, 'Symposium on the Totalitarian State from the Standpoints of History', *Joseph Regenstein Library*, University of Chicago, 3,39,8.
____ (1939i), 'Professor Fisher's Interest Theory: A Case in Point', *Journal of Political Economy*, vol. 39, Apr.

____ (1939j), 'Ethics and Economic Reform', *Economica*, Part I, 6, Feb, pp. 1-29; Part II, 6, Aug, pp. 296-321; Part III, 6, Nov, pp. 398-422.

____ (1940a), Review of Wermel, M.T., 'The Evolution of The Classical Wage Theory' *Journal of Political Economy,* Jun.

____ (1940b), Review of Herkovits, M.J., 'The Economic Life of Primitive Peoples', Knopf, New York, *Joseph Regenstein Library,* University of Chicago, 1, III, 5.

____ (1940c), 'Money, Interest, and Hicks', Quarterly Journal of Economics.

____ (1940d), 'Socialism: The Nature of the Problem', *Ethics*, 50.

____ (1940e), 'What is Truth in Economics', *Journal of Political Economy,* Feb, pp. 1-32.

____ (1940f), Review of Anshen, R.E., 'Freedom: Its Meaning', *Joseph Regenstein Library*, University of Chicago, 3,39, 9-10.

____ (1940g), 'Comment: Quantification', in L. Wirth, L. (ed), *Eleven Twenty-Six*, University of Chicago Press, Chicago pp. 167-70.

____ (1940h), 'Professor Parsons on Economic Motivation', *Canadian Journal of Economics*, vol. 6, Aug, pp. 460-5.

____ (1941a), 'A Rejoinder (to Hutchison, T.W.)', *Journal of Political Economy,* vol. 49, Oct, pp. 750-3.

____ (1941b), Review of Whittaker, E., 'A History of Economic Ideas', *Journal of Political Economy,* Aug.

____ (1941c), 'The Business Cycle, Interest, and Money: A Methodological Approach', *Review of Economics and Statistics*, 23, May, pp. 53-67.

____(1941d),'Social Science', *Ethics*, Jan.

____ (1941e), 'The Meaning of Democracy: Its Politico-Economic Structure and Ideals', *Journal of Negro Education*, Jul.

____ (1941f), 'Religion and Ethics in Modern Civilisation', *Journal of Liberal Religion.*

____ (1941g), 'The Role of the Individual in the Economic World of the Future', *Journal of Political Economy,* vol. 49, Dec, pp. 817-32.

____ (1941h), 'A Dialectic of Morals', *Joseph Regenstein Library,* University of Chicago, *3,39,7.*

____ (1941i), 'Professor Von Mises and the Theory of Capital', *Economica*, vol. 8, Nov, pp. 409-27.

____ (1941j), 'Anthropology and Economics', *Journal of Political Economy,* vol. 49, Apr, pp. 247-68.

____ (1941k), 'The Significance and Basic Postulates of Economic Theory', *Journal of Political Economy*, vol. 49, Oct, pp. 750-3.
____ (1942a), Review of Buck, P.W., 'The Politics of Mercantilism', *Journal of Political Economy,* Dec.
____ (1942b), Review of Kaulla, R., 'Theory of the Just Price', *Journal of Political Economy,* Dec.
____ (1942c), 'Profit and Entrepreneurial Functions', *Journal of Economic History*, (Supplement), vol. 2, Dec, pp. 126-32.
____ (1942d), 'Science, Philosophy, and Social Procedure', *Ethics*, 52.
____ (1942e), Review of G.P. Adams, W.R. Dennes, and S.P. Pepper (eds), 'Civilisation', *Joseph Regenstein Library*, University of Chicago, 3,39,6.
____ (1942f), Review of The American Economics Association, 'Readings in the Social Control of Industry', *Joseph Regenstein Library*, University of Chicago, 3, 39, 8.
____ (1943a), Review of Roll, E., 'A History of Economic Thought', *Journal of Political Economy,* Aug.
____ (1943b), Review of Ledermann, L., 'Sur Sismandi', *Journal of Political Economy,* Dec.
____ (1943c), 'The Meaning of Freedom and The Ideal of Freedom', in C.M.Perry (ed), *The Philosophy of American Democracy*, University of Chicago Press, Chicago.
____ (1944a), 'Realism and Relevance in the Theory of Demand', *Journal of Political Economy,* 52, Dec, pp. 289-318.
____ (1944b), 'Diminishing Returns from Investment', *Journal of Political Economy,* vol. 52, Mar, pp. 26-47.
____ (1944c), 'The Issue at the University of Chicago', June, *Joseph Regenstein Library,* University of Chicago, 1, 2, 14.
____ (1944d), 'Economics, 1939-44', an untitled and unpublished group of papers which were found bound together under the above title, *Joseph Regenstein Library,* University of Chicago, 1, 9-13.
____ (1944e), 'Economics, Political Science, and Education', *American Economic Review*, (Supplement), vol. 34, Mar, pp. 68-76.
____ (1944f) et al, 'Political Science, Political Economy, and Values', *American Economic Review*, (Supplement), vol. 34, Mar, pp. 48-57.
____ (1945a), Review of Stark, W., 'The Ideal Foundations of Economic Thought', *Journal of Political Economy,* Sep.
____ (1945b), *The Economic Order and Religion*, New York.

____ (1945c), 'Capital and Interest', *Encyclopaedia Britannica*, Encyclopaedia Britannica.

____ (1945d), Pacific University Lectures, 1945, *Joseph Regenstein Library*, University of Chicago, 1 24, 17-23.

____ (1946a), 'On Mr Bishop's Article: On the Theory of Demand', *Journal of Political Economy,* vol,54, Apr, pp. 170-6.

____ (1946b), 'Immutable Law in Economics: Its Reality and Limitations', *American Economic Review,* (Supplement), 36, May, pp. 93-111.

____ (1946c), 'Liberalism', *Encyclopaedia Britannica,* Encyclopaedia Britannica.

____ (1946d), 'The Sickness of Liberal Society', *Ethics*, 56.

____ (1946e), 'Capital and Interest', in W. Fellner and B.F Halley (eds), *Readings in the Theory of Income Distribution*, Philadelphia.

____ (1946f), 'Heimann's History of Doctrine and Current Issues', *Journal of Political Economy*, vol. 54, Aug, pp. 363-7.

____ (1946g), 'Freedom Under Planning', *Journal of Political Economy*, vol. 54, Oct, pp. 451-4.

____ (1947a), '*Freedom And Reform: Essays in Economics and Social Philosophy'*, H. Bonner, W.Grampp, M. Singer, and B. Weinberg (eds), Harper and Bros, New York.

____ (1947b), Review of Salin, E., 'Geschichte der Volkswirtschaftslehre', *Journal of Political Economy,* Feb.

____ (1947c), 'Salvation by Science: The Gospel According to Professor Lunberg', *Journal of Political Economy*, vol. 55, Dec, pp. 537-52.

____ (1948), 'Professor Heimann on Religion and Economics, *Journal of Political Economy*, vol. 56, Dec, pp. 480-97.

____ (1949a), 'Natural Law: Last Refuge of the Bigot', *Ethics*, vol. 59, 2, Jan.

____ (1949b), 'Truth and Relevance at Bay', *American Economic Review*, vol. 39, Dec, pp. 1273-6.

____ (1950a), *General Economic History*, trans. of M. Weber, Glencoe: Free Press.

____ (1950b), 'Introduction', *Principles of Economics*, C. Menger (ed), Glencoe.

____ (1950c), 'On Professor Parson's Article', *Journal of Farm Economics*, vol. 32, Feb, pp. 112-20.

____ (1950d), 'Economics and Social Policy in Democratic Society', *Journal of Political Economy,* vol. 58, Dec, pp. 513-22.

____ (1950e), 'The Rate of Interest and the Marginal Productivity of Capital', *Journal of Political Economy,* Aug.

____ (1950f), 'On Professor Parson's Article', *Journal of Farm Economics,* vol. 32, Feb, pp. 112-20.

____ (1951a), 'Economics', *Encyclopaedia Britannica,* Encyclopaedia Britannica.

____ (1951b), 'The Role of Principles in Economics and Politics', *American Economic Review,* Mar, vol. 41, pp. 1-29.

____ (1952a), 'Institutionalism and Empiricism in Economics', *American Economic Review,* (Supplement), 42, May, pp. 45-55.

____ (1952b), 'Economic Freedom and Social Responsibility', Emory University, Graduate School of Business and Economics, 7.

____ (1953a), 'Professor Tawney: Essayist and Christian Socialist', *Journal of Political Economy,* vol. 61, Oct, pp. 406-12.

____ (1953b), 'Is Group Choice Part of Economics', *Quarterly Journal of Economics,* Nov, vol. 67, pp. 605-9.

____ (1953c), 'Theory of Economic Policy and the History of Doctrine', *Ethics,* Jul, pp. 276-92.

____ (1953d), Pacific University Lectures, 1953-5, *Joseph Regenstein Library,* University of Chicago, 1,24, 24-9.

____ (1954a), 'An Appraisal of Economic Change: Discussion', *American Economic Review,* (Supplement), vol. 54, May, pp. 63-6.

____ (1954b), Review of Collins, M., 'The Judgement of History', Philosophical Library, New York, *Joseph Regenstein Library,* University of Chicago, 1, 3, 4.

____ (1954c), Review of Schumpeter, J.A., 'A History of Economic Analysis', *Joseph Regenstein Library,* University of Chicago, 1, 3, 6.

____ (1955a), Review of Schumpeter, J.A., 'Schumpeter's History of Economics', *Southern Economic Journal,* vol. 21, Jan, pp. 261-72.

____ (1955b), 'Structure and Operation of the Economic Order', *University of Arizona Bulletin,* vol. 1, pp. 31-67.

____ (1955c), 'Professor R.B. Perry on Value', *Journal of Political Economy,* vol. 63, Apr, pp. 162-73.

____ (1956a), *On the History and Method of Economics,* The University of Chicago Press, Chicago.

____ (1956b), 'On Authority', *Joseph Regenstein Library,* University of Chicago, 1,1,2-4.

____ (1956c), 'Value Theory for Economists', *American Economic Review,* vol. 46, Mar, pp. 142-50.

____ (1957a) et al, 'A New Look at Institutionalism', *American Economic Review*, vol. 47, May, pp. 13-27.

____ (1959), 'Social Economic Planning', *Canadian Journal of Economic and Politics*.

____ (1960a), *Intelligence and Democratic Action*. Lectures delivered at the Thomas Jefferson Centre for Studies in Political Economy University of Virginia Cambridge: Harvard University Press.

____ (1960b), 'I, Me, Myself, and My Duties', draft of a discussion of articles in Ethics, Jan 1960, *Joseph Regenstein Library*, University of Chicago, 1,16,19.

____ (1960c), 'Social Economic Policy', *Canadian Journal of Economics*, Feb, pp. 19-34.

____ (1961), 'Methodology in Economics', *Southern Economic Journal*, Jan, pp. 185-193; Apr, pp. 273-82.

____ (1963), 'Christian Ethics and Social Betterment', Pulpit Address, First Unitarian Church, Chicago, August 18, 1963. Xerox. *Joseph Regenstein Library*, University of Chicago, 1,4, 6.

____ (1964), 'Philosophy and History', *Journal of the History of Ideas*, Oct/Dec.

____ (1966a), 'Abstract Economics as Absolute Ethics', *Ethics*, vol. LXXVI 3, pp. 163-77.

____ (1966b), 'A Word of Explanation', a draft regarding the article entitled Abstract Economics as Absolute Ethics, April, *Joseph Regenstein Library*, University of Chicago,: I, 1,6.

____ (1966c), 'Economics', in J.B.Herendeen (ed), *Modern Political Economy: Ideas and Issues* University Park: Pensylvania State University.

____ (1967), 'Laissez Faire: Pro and Con', *Journal of Political Economy*, vol. 75, pp. 782-95.

____ (1968a), 'Free Society: Its Basic Nature and Problem', *Philosophical Review*, vol. 57 (1), Jan.

____ (1968b), 'Laissez Faire: Economic Freedom and Its Limits', *Mercurio*.

____ (1969), 'Some Fallacies in the Interpretation of Social Cost', in K.J. Arrow, and T.Scitovsky (eds), *Readings in Welfare Economics*, vol 12, Ontario: Irwin-Dorsey.

____ (1973a), 'Economic History', in *Dictionary of the History of Ideas: Studies of Selected Pivotal Ideas*, New York.

____ (1973b), 'Social Science and Social Action', an untitled and unpublished collection of draft essays which were to comprise an entire book, *Joseph Regenstein Library,* University of Chicago, 1,32-4.

____ (n.d.), *The Problem,* B55, F15, F. Knight Papers, Special Collections, *Joseph Regenstein Library*: University of Chicago.

Kolb, D. (1986), *The Critique of Pure Modernity: Hegel, Heidegger and After*, University of Chicago Press, Chicago.

Koutsoyiannis, A. (1985), *Theory of Econometrics,* Macmillan Publishers Ltd, London.

Lachmann, L.M. (1947), Review of Knight, F.H., 'Freedom and Reform', *Economica,* Nov, pp. 314-7.

Lawson, T. (1988), 'Probability and Uncertainty of Economic Analysis', Journal *Post-Keynesian Economics,* vol. 11.

Le Roy, S. F., and L. D. Singell, Jr. (1987), 'Knight on Risk and Uncertainty', *Journal of Political Economy,* vol. 95, Apr.

Leigh, A.H. (1974), 'Frank Knight as Economic Theorist', *Journal of Political Economy,* vol. 82.

Lerner, A.P. (1934), 'The Concept of Monopoly and the Measurement of Monopoly Power', *Review of Economic Studies* vol. 1.

Letiche, J.M. (1955), 'Discussion: The Role of The German Historical School in American Economic Thought', *American Economic Review,* pp. 29-34.

Levine, A.L. (1980), 'Increasing Returns, the Competitive Model and the Enigma that was Alfred Marshall', *Scottish Journal of Political Economy,* vol. 27, p. 3.

Levine, L. (1991), 'Joan Robinson: Journeys into Heterogeneity,' in H.R. Rima (ed), *The Joan Robinson Legacy,* M.E.Sharpe Inc, New York.

Levitt, T. (1976), 'Alfred Marshall - Relevance For Modern Economics', *Quarterly Journal of Economics*.

Lipsey, R. and Lancaster, K. (1956), 'The General Theory of Second Best', *Review of Economic Studies,* Dec.

Loasby, B.J. (1991), 'Joan Robinson's Wrong Turning', in H.R. Rima (ed), *The Joan Robinson Legacy,* M.E.Sharpe Inc, New York.

Lyons, G. M. (1969), *The Uneasy Partnership: Social Science and the Federal Government in the Twentieth Century,* Russell Sage Foundation, New York.

Lyotard, J.F. (1989), 'Philosophy and Painting in the Age of Their Experimentation: Contribution to an Idea of Postmodernity', trans.

M.Brewer and D.Brewer, in A. Benjamin (ed), *The Lyotard Reader*, Basill Blackwell, Oxford.

Macfie, A.L. (1958), Review of Knight, F.H., 'On the History and Method of Economics', *Economic Journal*, Dec, pp. 780-6.

Macgregor, D.H. (1906), *Industrial Combination*, George Bell, London.

Machiavelli, N. (1513), *The Prince*. trans. H.C. Mansfield Jr, University of Chicago Press, Chicago.

MacIver, R.M. (1942), *Social Causation,* Ginn and Company, Boston.

Machup, F. (1935), 'Professor Knight and the Period of Production', *Journal of Political Economy*, vol. 43, Oct.

Mansfield, E. (1974), *Monopoly Power and Economic Performance - The Problem of Industrial Concentration*, W.W. Norwich and Company Inc, New York.

____ (1979), *Microeconomics: Theory and Applications*, W.W.Norton and Coy, New York.

Marshall, A. (1890), 'Some Aspects of Competition', in A.C. Pigou (ed), *Memorials of Alfred Marshall*, Macmillan, London.

____ (1919), *Industry and Trade,* Macmillan, London.

____ (1926), *Official Papers by Alfred Marshall,* J.M. Keynes (ed), Macmillan, London.

____ (1961), *Principles of Economics,* Variorum Edition, Macmillan, London.

Marshall, A. and Paley, M. (1881), *The Economics of Industry*, McMillan, London.

Marx, K. (1867), *Capital,* Lawrence and Wishart, London.

Mason, E.S. (1937), 'Monopoly in Law and Economics', in American Economics Association, *Readings in the Social Control of Industry*, Blakiston, Philadelphia.

____ (1939), 'Price and Production Policies of Large-Scale Enterprise', in *Economic Concentration and the Monopoly Problem*, Harvard University Press, Cambridge.

____ (1951), 'Schumpeter on Monopoly and the Large Firm', in S.E. Harris (ed), *Schumpeter Social Scientist*, Harvard University Press, Cambridge.

____ (1982), 'The Harvard Department of Economics from the Beginning to World War II', *The Quarterly Journal of Economics,* vol. 3, pp. 383-433.

Maxwell, J.A. (1958), 'Alfred Marshall and the Competitive Firm', *The Economic Journal,* vol. 68, Dec.

____ (1958b), 'Some Marshallian Concepts, Especially the Representative Firm', *Journal of Political Economy,* Dec.

McCloskey, D.N. (1983), 'The Rhetoric of Economics', *Journal of Economic Literature,* vol. 21, Jun.

McKinney, J. (1977), 'Frank H. Knight on Uncertainty and Rational Action', *Southern Economic Journal,* vol. 43, no.4, Apr, pp. 1438-52.

Mill, J.S. (1909), *Principles of Political Economy*, W.J. Ashley and Miller, H.L. Jr. (eds), Longman Green, London.

____ (1962), 'On The Chicago School of Economics', *Journal of Political Economy,* Feb, pp. 64-7.

Minford, P. and Peel, D. (1983), *Rational Expectations and the New Macroeconomics*, Martin Robertson, Oxford.

Montesquieu, Baron de (Charles Secondat) (1949), *The Spirit of the Laws*, G. Truc (ed), Collection des Classiques Garnier, Paris.

Myint, H. (1948), *Theories of Welfare Economics*, Longmans Green and Co, London.

Myrdal, G. (1957), *Economic Theory and Underdeveloped Regions,* University Paperbacks, London.

Nash, S.J. (1996), 'Uncertainty and Welfare: Knight's Expansion of Welfare Economics', *Paper Presented at the HETSA Conference, University of NSW*, Sydney, Aug.

____ (1997), 'Chamberlin and Knight: Uniform and Heterogeneous Uncertainty', *Paper Presented at the 27th Conference of Economists*, University of Tasmania, Hobart, Sep.

Neitzsche, F. (1910), *The Complete Works of Friedrich Nietzsche,* O. Levy (ed), T.N. Foulis, London.

Nichol, A.J. (1934), 'Robinson's Economics of Imperfect Competition', *Journal of Political Economy,* Apr, pp. 257-9.

Odriscoll, G.P, (ed) (1979), *Adam Smith and Modern Political Economy*, The Iowa State University Press, Iowa.

Paine, T. (1942), *The Basic Writings of Thomas Paine*, Wiley, New York.

Pangle, T.L. (1973), *Montesquieu's Philosophy of Liberalism: A commentary on The Spirit of the Laws*, University of Chicago Press, Chicago.

____ (1990), *The Spirit of Modern Republicanism: The Moral Vision of the American Founders and the Philosophy of John Locke*, University of Chicago Press, Chicago.

____ (1992), *The Ennobling of Democracy: The Challenge of the Postmodern Age*, University of Chicago Press, Chicago.

Pareto, V. (1910), 'Walras', *Economic Journal,* vol. 20.
____ (1971), *Manual of Political Economy*, trans. A. S. Schwier, Augus M. Kelly.
Parsons, T. (1931), 'Wants and Activities in Marshall', *Quarterly Journal of Economics*.
Patinkin, D. (1973a), 'Frank Knight as Teacher', *American Economic Review,* vol. 63, pp. 787-807.
____ (1973b), 'In Search of the Wheel of Wealth: On the Origins of Frank Knight's Circular Flow Diagram', *American Economic Review,* Dec, pp. 1037-46.
____ (1981), *Essays on and in the Chicago Tradition*, Durham.
Pigou, A.C. (1912), *Wealth and Welfare*, Macmillan, London.
____ (1922), 'Empty Economic Boxes: A Reply', *Economic Journal* vol. 32, Dec.
____ (1924), 'Comment on D.H. Robertson's Those Empty Economic Boxes', *Economic Journal,* vol. 34, Mar.
____ (1927), 'The Laws of Diminishing and Increasing Cost', *Economic Journal,* vol. 27, Jun.
____ (1928), 'An Analysis of Supply', *Economic Journal,* vol. 38, Jun.
____ (1932), *The Economics of Welfare,* Macmillan, London.
____ (1935), *The Economics of Stationary States,* Macmillan, London.
____ (1938), *Socialism Versus Capitalism,* Macmillan, London.
Plattner, M.F. (1990), *Confronting the Constitution: The Challenge to Locke, Montestquieu, Jefferson and the Federalists from Utilitarianism, Historicism, Marxism, Freudianism, Pragmatism and Existentialism*, The American Enterprise Institute, Washington.
Raines, J.P, and Jung, C.R. (1988), 'Monopolies as Mechanical Defects', *HES Bulletin*, vol. 10, no.2, Fall, pp. 135-43.
Reder, M. (1982), 'Chicago Economies: Permanence and Change', *Journal of Economic Literature*, vol. 20, no.1, Mar, pp. 1-38.
Reinwald, T.P. (1973), 'The Genesis of Chamberlinian Monopolistic Competition Theory: Addendum - Comment', *History of Political Economy,* vol. 17, pp. 400-2.
Rima, H.R. (1991a), 'Introduction', in H.R. Rima (ed), *The Joan Robinson Legacy*, M.E.Sharpe, New York.
____ (1991b), Robinson and the Other Half of the Keynesian Revolution, in H.R. Rima (ed), *The Joan Robinson Legacy*, M.E.Sharpe, New York.

Robinson, E.A.G. (1931), *The Structure of Competitive Industry,* Nisbett and Co, London.

____ (1941), *Monopoly*, Nisbett and Co. Ltd, London.

____ (1950), 'The Pricing of Manufactured Products', *The Economic Journal*, Dec.

Robinson, J. (1933a), *The Economics of Imperfect Competition*, Macmillan, London.

____ (1933b), 'The Economics of Imperfect Competition', *Quarterly Journal of Economics,* vol. XLV, pp. 442-70.

____ (1934), 'What Is Perfect competition?', *Quarterly Journal of Economics,* vol. XLIX, pp. 104-20.

____ (1953), 'Imperfect Competition Revisited', *The Economic Journal,* vol. LXIII, pp. 579-93.

____ (1960), *Collected Economic Papers,* Basil Blackwell, Oxford.

____ (1974), 'History versus Equilibrium', in *Thames Papers in Economics*, Thames Polytechnic, London.

Rodgers, D. T. (1982), 'In Search of Progressivism', *Review of American History*, Dec, p. 10.

Rorty, R. (1979), *Philosophy and the Mirror of Nature,* Princeton University Press, Princeton.

____ (1984), 'The Historiography of Philosophy: Four Genres', in R. Rorty, J.B. Schneewind, and Q. Skinner (eds), *Philosophy in History: Essays in the Historiography of Philosophy*, Cambridge University Press, Cambridge.

Ross, D. (1979), 'The Development of the Social Sciences', in A. Oleson, and J. Voss (eds), *The Organisation of Knowledge in Modern America: 1860-1920*, John Hopkins University Press, Baltimore.

Rostow, E.V. (1963), 'The Ethics of Competition Revisited', *California Management Review*, Spring.

Rotwein, E. (1983), 'Jacob Viner and the Chicago Tradition', *History of Political Economy,* vol. 15, pp. 265-80.

Samuelson, P.A. (1967), 'The Monopolistic Revolution', in R.E. Kuenne (ed), *Monopolistic Competition Theory*: *Studies in Impact*, John Wiley, New York.

Santiago, V.W. (1980), 'Is F. Knight the Victor in the Controversy Between the Two Cambridge?', *History of Political Economy,* vol. 12, p. 1.

Schultz, T.W. (1973), 'Frank Knight as Colleague', *Journal of Political Economy,* pp. 516-7.

Schumpeter, J.A. (1928), 'The Instability of Capitalism', *Economic Journal,* vol. 38, pp. 361-86.

____ (1934), Review of Robinson J., 'Robinson's Economics of Imperfect Competition', *Journal of Political Economy,* Apr, pp. 249-57.

____ (1937), 'Allyn Young', in J.Seligman and A.Johnson (eds), *Encyclopaedia of the Social Sciences,* Macmillan, New York.

____ (1939), *Business Cycles*, Macmillan, New York.

____ (1941), 'Alfred Marshall's Principles: A Semi-Centennial Appraisal', *American Economic Review,* vol. 31, p. 2.

____ (1950), *'Capitalism and the Process of Creative Destruction',* E. Mansfield (ed).

____ (1954a), *Capitalism, Socialism and Democracy*, George Allen & Unwin, London.

____ (1954b), *History of Economic Analysis*, George Allen and Unwin, London.

____ (1956), *Ten Great Economist: From Marx to Keynes*, George Allen and Unwin, London.

Schweitzer, A. (1975), 'Frank Knight's Social Economics', in *History of Political Economy,* vol. 7, no. 3, pp.279-92.

Schwendinger, H. and Schwendinger, J.R. (1974), *The Sociologists of the Chair: A Radical Analysis of the Formative Years of North American Sociology 1883-1922,* Basic Books, New York.

Scraffa, P. (1926), 'The Laws of Return Under Competitive Conditions', *Economic Journal,* vol. 36, pp. 535-50.

____ (1930), 'Increasing Returns and the Representative Firm: A Criticism', *Economic Journal,* Mar, p. 40.

Seligman, E.R.A, and Johnson, A. (1937), *Encyclopaedia of the Social Sciences,* Macmillan, New York.

Shackle, G.L.S. (1958), Review of Knight, F.H., 'On the History and Method of Economics', *Economica*, Feb, pp. 65-6.

____ (1967), *The Years of High Theory,* Cambridge University Press, Cambridge.

Shils, E (1981), 'Some Academics, Mainly in Chicago', *American Scholar,* pp. 179-96.

Shove, G.F. (1942), 'The Place of Marshall's Principles in The Development of Economic Theory', *The Economic Journal*, Dec, p. 42.

Simons, H. (1948), *Economic Policy for a Free Society,* University of Chicago Press, Chicago.

Skinner, A.S. (1982), 'E.H. Chamberlin: The Origins and Development of Monopolistic Competition', *The Journal of Economic Studies,* vol. 9, no.1, pp. 52-67.

Skinner, Q. (1969), 'Meaning and Understanding in the History of Ideas', *History and Theory,* vol. 8, pp. 3-53.

____ (1979), Introduction to *An Inquiry into the Nature and Causes of the Wealth of Nations* by A. Smith, in *The Works and Correspondence of Adam Smith,* Penguin, London.

Smith, A. (1937), *An Inquiry into the Nature and Causes of the Wealth of Nations,* Modern Library, New York.

Smith, D. (1988), *The Chicago School: A Liberal Critique of Capitalism,. Theoretical Traditions in the Social Sciences*, St. Martin's Press, New York.

Stigler, G. J. (1949), 'Monopolistic Competition in Retrospect', in *Five Lecture on Economic Problems*, Macmillan, New York.

____ (1957), 'Perfect Competition, Historically Contemplated', in G.J. Stigler (ed), *Essays in History of Economics*, University of Chicago Press, Chicago.

____ (1970), 'The Government of the Economy: a Dialogue on the Proper Economic Role of the State', in P. Samuelson (ed), *Readings in Economics*, Macmillan, New York.

____ (1973), 'Frank Knight as Teacher', *Journal of Political Economy,* pp. 518-20.

____ (1982), 'Textual Exegesis as a Scientific Problem', in *The Economist as Preacher and Other Essays*, University of Chicago Press, Chicago.

____ (1987), 'Frank Hyneman Knight', in J. Eatwell, M. Milgate, and P. Newman (eds), *The New Palgrave: A Dictionary of Economics,* Stockton Press, New York.

Stone, J. and Mennell, S. (1982), *On Democracy, Revolution, and Society,* University of Chicago Press, Chicago.

Strauss, L. (1952), *Persecution and the Art of Writing,* University of Chicago Press, Chicago.

Taine, H. (1976), *The Ancient Regime*, trans. J. Durrand, Henry Holt, New York.

Tarcov, N. (1984), *Locke's Education for Liberty*, University of Chicago Press, Chicago.

Tawney, R.H. (1922), *Religion and the Rise of Capitalism,* John Murray Press, London.

Taylor, O.H. (1957), 'Frank Knight's Perspective On the History and Method of Economics', *Review of Economics and Statistics*, Aug, pp. 342-5.

Temple-Smith, R. (1986), 'Aristotle as a Welfare Economist: A Comment', *History of Political Economy*, vol. 18, p. 3.

Triffin, R. (1940), *Monopolistic Competition And General Equilibrium Theory*, Harvard University Press, Cambridge.

Valentine, W. S. (1980), 'Is Frank Knight the Victor in the Controversy Between the Two Cambridges?', *History of Political Economy*, vol. 12, no.1, Spring, pp. 41-64.

Viner, J. (1941), 'Marshall's Economics, in Relation to the Man and to His Times', *American Economic Review,* vol. 31, p. 2.

____ (1958), *The Long View and the Short View,* The Free Press, Glencoe.

____ (1972), *The Role of Providence in the Social Order,* American Philosophical Society, Philadelphia.

Vining, R. (1950), 'Methodological Issues in Quantitative Economics: Variations Upon a Theme by F.H. Knight', *American Economic Review*, Jun, pp. 267-84.

Walker, D.A. (1984), 'Is Walras's Theory of General Equilibrium A Normative Scheme?', *History of Political Economy,* 16.

Walras, L. (1954), *Elements of Pure Economics*, trans. W. Jaffe, Irwin, Homewood.

Weber, M. (1968), *General Economic History*, trans. F.H. Knight (1950a), in S.N. Eisenstadt (ed), *On Charisma and Institution Building: Selected Papers,* University of Chicago Press, Chicago.

Whitaker, J.K. (1975), *The Early Economic Writings of Alfred Marshall: 1867-1890*, Macmillan, London.

Wick, W. (1973), 'Frank Knight, Philosopher At Large', *Journal of Political Economy,* pp. 513- 5.

Wicksell, K. (1925), 'Mathematical Economics', in *Selected Papers on Economic Theory*, Harvard University Press, Cambridge.

Williams, P.L. (1986), 'The Place of Industry and Trade, in the Analysis of Alfred Marshall', in K.Tucker and B.Fuller (eds), *Firms and Markets, Essays in Honour of Basil Yamey*, Croom Helm, London.

____ (1987), 'Perfect Competition as a Policy Norm: Economists and Antitrust Policy in the 1930s', Paper prepared for the *Fourth H.E.T.S.A. Conference*, University of Newcastle.

____ (1989), 'The Attitudes of The Economics Professions in Britain and The United States To The Trust Movement, 1890-1914', *Working*

Paper No.21 Graduate School of Management, University of Melbourne, Melbourne.

____ (1990), 'Marshallian Applied Welfare Economics: The Decline and Fall', *Economic Appliquee*, vol. 1, pp. 231-45.

____ (Unpublished), 'John Bates Clark and Antitrust: A Leader of Progressive Economists', University of Melbourne - Graduate School of Management, Melbourne.

Young, A A. (1900), *The Comparative Accuracy of Different Forms of Quinquennial Age Groups*, Publications of the American Statistical Association, 7.

____ (1911), 'Some Limitations of the Value Concept', *Quarterly Journal of Economics,* vol. 25.

____ (1913), 'Pigou's Wealth and Welfare', *Quarterly Journal of Economics,* vol. 25.

____ (1915), 'The Sherman Act and the New Anti-trust Legislation', *Journal of Political Economy,* vol. 23.

____ (1919), 'The Economics of the Treaty', *New Republic*, vol. 21.

____ (1924), 'The Trend of Economics, as Seen By Some American Economists', *Quarterly Journal of Economics,* vol. 39, pp. 158-83.

____ (1925), 'Papers Relating to Political Economy', *American Economic Review,* vol. 15.

____ (1927a), *Economic Problems New and Old*, Houghton Mifflin Boston.

____ (1927b), 'Economics as a Field of Research', *Quarterly Journal of Economics,* Nov.

____ (1928), 'Increasing Returns and Economic Progress', *Economic Journal,* vol. 38.

____ (1931c), 'Relation of Utility Theory to Method in the Work of William Stanely Jevons and Others', in S. Rice (ed), *Methods in Social Science*, University of Chicago Press, Chicago, pp. 59-69.

Index

abnormal profit, 5, 7, 121, 122, 150, 152, 155, 156
- Chamberlin's analysis, 102
- conflict with Knight's SWF, 140
- credit markets, 138
- economic rent, 146
- exploitation of time lags, 103
- imperfectly competitive market, 114
- inflation of power imbalance, 111
- Knightian analysis, 140
- long-run, 5
- orthodox theory, 93, 94
- relationship with uncertainty, 133
- Robinson's analysis, 104
- transformation to normal profit, 117

access, 11, 16, 20, 24, 45, 46, 51, 63, 64, 65, 66, 67, 68, 75, 77, 84, 85, 86, 89, 92, 94, 101, 107, 110, 111, 113, 129, 130, 131, 133, 134, 137, 140, 142, 143, 144, 145, 154, 156, 157
- acquisition of, 137
- compensation for lack of, 165
- constraints and market power, 63
- credit access, 20
- crowding out, 164
- deficiency in, 11
- distribution of, 9
- distribution problem, 9
- economic rent, 146
- economies of scale, 111
- enjoyment by monopolist, 143
- exploitation without payment, 145
- increasing returns, 163
- investment in human capital, 17
- market knowledge, 7
- monopolisation of, 164
- orthodox analysis, 9
- overhead costs, 163
- prevention of equilibrium, 118
- problematic resource allocation, 163
- property rights associated with, 114
- uncertainty-control costs, 133

Albon, R., 173

Allen, W.A., 173, 175, 183, 184, 190, 203

American Economics Association, 4, 153, 173, 177, 182, 194, 199

Archibald, G.C., 173

Arrow, 63, 68, 173, 197

Bain, J.S., 117, 173

Bannister, R.C., 173

Barber, W.J., 173

Barone, E. (1935), 174

Barzel, Y., 151, 174

Baumol, W.J, Panzar, J.C, and Willing, R.D., 124

Berlin, I., 44, 47, 174

Bharadwaj, K., 119, 174

Blaug, M., 88, 99, 100, 119, 121, 174

Blitch, C.P., 26, 46, 69, 70, 89, 174

Bloom, A., 1, 90, 152, 174

Bohm-Bawerk, 90, 174

Bowley, A.W., 174

Bronfenbrenner, M., 174

Buchanan, J. M., 1, 127, 146, 151, 175

Buechner, M. N., 175

Burns, A.M., 175

Burstein, J. Inc., 175

Caldwell, B.J., 175

Carey, G.V., 175

Carver, T.N., 175

Chamberlin, E.H., 2, 6, 44, 74, 93, 94, 95, 96, 97, 98, 99, 100, 101,

102, 103, 104, 105, 106, 111, 113, 114, 115, 116, 117, 118, 119, 120, 121, 122, 123, 124, 125, 126, 127, 128, 129, 150, 152, 155, 158, 163, 173, 175, 181, 200, 204
Clapham, J.H., 175
Clark, J.B., 6, 49, 50, 51, 52, 54, 55, 56, 57, 58, 59, 62, 69, 78, 79, 80, 85, 86, 87, 91, 113, 120, 163, 176, 177
Clark, J.M., 22, 45, 51, 54, 78, 79, 80, 81, 82, 83, 84, 85, 86, 87, 88, 89, 91, 95, 120, 163, 177
Clemens, E.W., 176
Coase, R.H., 176
Coats, A.W., 176
compensation for lack of, 164
cost differentiation, 130
    based on relative access, 6
    intra-firm, 6
    Knightian analysis, 164
cost shelter
    access to market knowledge, 129
Cournot, A., 176
Crockett, J.A. Jr., 176

Davis, 177
demand, 5, 6, 37, 56, 61, 65, 68, 74, 77, 90, 91, 92, 99, 100, 104, 107, 109, 112, 121, 122, 125, 127, 128, 150
    horizontal demand curve, 140
    in orthodox analysis, 130
    small (marginal) firm, 138
Dewey, D., 54, 177, 182
Dorfman, J., 53, 69, 80, 83, 87, 88, 89, 91, 177

economic efficiency, 4, 9, 21, 22, 23, 30, 31, 32, 34, 37, 41, 42, 43, 45, 46, 48, 55, 141, 142, 143, 145
    alleged 'philosophical' discourse, 2
    distribution assumption, 28
    distributional consequences, 129
    economic rent, 7
    framework for discussion, 30
    idealsing assumptions, 24
    Knight's SWF, 5, 8
    maximisation of welfare, 162
    relation to the SWF, 41
    social injustice, 29
    unstable competitive structure, 29
economic freedom, 8, 9, 15, 18, 29, 30, 31, 32, 33, 34, 35, 36, 39, 40, 41, 42, 43, 44, 45, 48, 83, 129, 141, 142, 143, 145
    alleged 'philosophical' discourse, 2
    conception of value, 37
    contrast to physical sciences, 14
    contrast with ideal feedom, 14
    dimensions of freedom, 15
    flexibilty of economic character, 42
    important part of social welfare, 161
    intra-firm, 145
    J.B. and J.M. Clark, 79, 83
    Knight's SWF, 5, 8
    Knight's novel conception, 3
    perfect equality as a problem, 39
    relation to economic character, 16, 18
    relation to economic power, 142
    relation to human capital, 3
    relation to SWF, 41
    relation to political freedom, 3
    relation to uncertainty, 3
    systematic denial of, 9
    two main contraints upon, 8
    Viner's conception, 39
economic power, 8, 9, 16, 17, 18, 19, 20, 26, 28, 29, 32, 33, 34, 35, 36, 37, 38, 39, 40, 41, 42, 43, 44, 45, 48, 52, 65, 72, 73, 74, 75, 76, 77, 78, 79, 80, 82, 83, 85, 86, 89, 91, 132, 134, 137, 141, 142, 143, 145, 151
    alleged 'philosophical' discourse, 2
    barrier to entry, 11
    complexities underlying, 9
    cumulative growth, 19
    difficulty with distribution, 29
    disenfranchisement, 39

dynamic dimension, 17
incentive to efficient action, 40
increasing returns, 27
interaction with SWF, 42
inter-generational transmission, 17
J.B. Clark, 55
J.M. Clark, 79
Knight's SWF, 5, 8
modification of access, 9
optimal distribution as a mean, 33
optimal regulation is a mean, 40
problems with perfect balance, 38
problems with adequate diffusion, 34
realtion to sociol conditioning, 16
relation to consumption patterns, 37
relation to economic progress, 36
relation to human capital, 75
relation with uncertainty, 51
Scumpeter's analysis, 76
static dimension, 16
substantive economic power, 11
Young analysis of concentration, 73
Young's concerns, 72
economics, 1, 2, 5, 6, 8, 10, 17, 22, 23, 26, 27, 29, 33, 41, 42, 43, 45, 49, 50, 51, 52, 53, 55, 58, 59, 60, 65, 68, 74, 83, 85, 86, 88, 89, 94, 96, 97, 129, 146
efficiency, 4, 7, 8, 9, 21, 22, 23, 26, 28, 29, 30, 31, 32, 33, 34, 35, 36, 37, 38, 41, 42, 43, 45, 46, 48, 52, 55, 74, 76, 83, 126, 127, 128, 129, 131, 140, 142, 143, 144, 145, 146, 148, 155, 156, 157
alleged 'philosophical' discourse, 2
distribution assumption, 28
distributional consequences, 129
economic rent, 7
idealising assumptions, 24
Knight's SWF, 5
relation to the SWF, 41
subordination to Knight's SWF, 8
unstable competitive structure, 29
Ekelund, R.B.Jr. and Herbert, R.F., 121
Emmett, R.B., 127, 151, 161, 177
entrepreneur, 56, 57, 60, 61, 62, 63, 78, 90
equilibrium, 4, 9, 26, 27, 28, 46, 49, 94, 95, 96, 97, 98, 102, 103, 104, 105, 106, 112, 114, 115, 116, 117, 119, 122, 125, 127, 150
error, 89, 108, 122, 125, 136

Feiwel, G.R., 119, 177
Fellner, W., 116, 117, 177, 195
Fetter, F.A., 54, 58, 178
Fisher, I.N., 50, 59, 63, 64, 65, 66, 67, 68, 85, 89, 163, 173, 176, 178, 187, 192
friction, 52, 57, 58, 80, 89, 103
Friedman, M., 46, 48, 178, 183, 190
Furner, M.O., 178

Galbraith, J.K., 152, 178
Gildin, H., 44, 178
Golffing, F., 178
Gonce, R. A., 178
Gordon, K., 123, 134, 150, 178, 179
Gordon, S., 123, 134, 150, 178, 179
Gower, E., 179
Graham, F.D., 179
Guillebaud, C.W., 179

Hahn, F.H., 179
Hammond, J.D., 8, 22, 33, 45, 127, 151, 179
Harris, S.E., 175, 179
Harrod, R.F., 93, 97, 119, 122, 150, 179
Hart, N., 26, 46, 89, 179
Hawley, F.B., 50, 59, 60, 61, 62, 63, 68, 85, 163, 179
Hawthorn, G., 179
Hayek, F., 174, 179, 190
Hegel, G.W.F., 44, 179, 198
Henry, J.F., 87, 174, 180, 188, 204
Herskovits, M.J., 180
Hildebrand, G.H., 53, 91, 180
Hollander, J.H., 53, 54, 58, 91, 180
Horsburgh, H.J.N., 180
Hoselitz, B.F., 180
Howey, R.S., 87, 180

human capital, 3, 9, 16, 17, 18, 19, 20, 27, 34, 38, 39, 41, 75, 76, 78, 90, 142
Hutchison, T.W., 180, 193

imperfect competition, 2, 3, 5, 6, 93, 94, 95, 97, 98, 101, 104, 106, 113, 115, 119, 122, 126, 129, 130, 133, 134, 136, 139, 142, 146, 150, 152, 157
insurance, 19, 24, 64, 66, 67, 89, 110, 138, 151

Jaffe, W., 180, 205
Jalladeau, J., 87, 180
Johnson, A.S., 69, 87, 180, 183, 203

Kahn, R.F., 180
Kaldor, N., 180, 192
Kasper, S.D., 181
Kay, J., 7, 181
Kern, W.S., 8, 33, 42, 181
Keynes, J.M., 181, 191, 199, 203
Kirzner, I.M., 181
Knight, F.H., 1, 2, 3, 4, 5, 6, 7, 8, 9, 10, 11, 12, 13, 14, 15, 16, 17, 18, 19, 20, 21, 22, 23, 24, 25, 26, 27, 28, 29, 30, 31, 33, 34, 35, 36, 37, 38, 39, 40, 41, 42, 43, 44, 45, 46, 47, 48, 49, 50, 51, 52, 55, 56, 57, 58, 59, 60, 61, 62, 63, 64, 65, 67, 68, 69, 70, 71, 72, 73, 74, 75, 76, 77, 78, 79, 81, 82, 83, 84, 85, 86, 87, 88, 89, 90, 91, 92, 93, 94, 95, 97, 98, 100, 101, 106, 107, 108, 109, 110, 111, 112, 113, 114, 115, 116, 117, 118, 119, 120, 123, 124, 125, 126, 127, 129, 130, 131, 132, 133, 134, 135, 136, 137, 138, 140, 141, 142, 145, 146, 147, 150, 151, 152, 153, 154, 155, 156, 157, 158, 159, 160, 161, 162, 163, 164, 165, 173, 174, 175, 177, 178, 179, 180, 181, 182, 185, 191, 192, 198, 199, 200, 201, 202, 203, 204, 205
knowledge, 3, 7, 12, 17, 18, 24, 42, 45, 52, 57, 58, 62, 63, 68, 82, 86, 87, 90, 94, 95, 100, 101, 102, 103, 104, 107, 111, 112, 114, 118, 123, 125, 126, 129, 130, 131, 133, 134, 136, 137, 138, 140, 141, 142, 143, 144, 145, 146, 152, 154, 156, 157
Kolb, D., 44, 198
Koutsoyiannis, A., 198

Lachmann, L.M., 198
Lawson, T., 198
Leigh, A.H., 198
Lerner, A.P., 198
Letiche, J.M., 91, 198
Levine, A.L., 119, 198
Levitt, T., 198
Loasby, B.J., 119, 198
LRAC, 93, 104, 122, 126, 127, 150
Lyons, G. M., 198
Lyotard, J.F., 198

Macgregor, D.H., 199
Machiavelli, N., 162, 199
Machup, F., 199
MacIver, R.M., 199
Mansfield, E., 2, 75, 136, 199, 203
market share, 7, 17, 64, 65, 68, 74, 77, 83, 85, 89, 94, 114, 133, 136, 141, 143, 145, 146, 154, 155, 156
Marshall, A., 6, 21, 26, 27, 173, 174, 179, 198, 199, 201, 203, 205
Marx, K., 199, 203
Mason, E.S., 75, 181, 199
Maxwell, J.A.., 199
McCloskey, D.N., 200
McKinney, J., 200
Mill, J.S., 200
Minford, P. and Peel, D., 124
monopoly, 2, 4, 9, 25, 29, 36, 50, 51, 56, 73, 74, 75, 76, 78, 79, 84,

86, 90, 96, 98, 100, 102, 121, 129, 131, 147, 151, 152
Montesquieu, Baron de (Charles Secondat), 150, 153, 160, 200
Myint, H., 1, 2, 200
Myrdal, G., 200

Nash, S.J., 200
Neitzsche, F., 200
Nichol, A.J., 200

Odriscoll, G.P,, 200
opportunities, 3, 9, 16, 18, 19, 20, 27, 37, 39, 51, 58, 79, 89, 92
overhead costs, 51, 78, 79, 80, 81, 82, 83, 84, 85, 86, 92

Paine, T., 200
Pangle, T.L., 153, 200
Pareto, V., 42, 157, 201
Parsons, T., 193, 201
Patinkin, D., 49, 52, 55, 87, 88, 134, 150, 151, 152, 165, 201
perfect competition, 9, 24, 28, 35, 37, 78, 83, 84, 85, 93, 95, 96, 97, 98, 100, 102, 104, 106, 112, 118, 121, 127, 128, 142, 152
philosophy, 1, 4, 34, 53, 54, 131
Pigou, A.C., 24, 26, 27, 97, 174, 201, 206
Plattner, M.F., 201
preferential access, 130, 131, 137, 140, 141, 142, 143, 144, 146, 156, 157
premium, 61, 62, 110, 138
product differentiation, 5, 6, 93, 98, 100, 101, 117, 121, 128, 130, 133, 152
profit, 5, 7, 19, 50, 52, 54, 56, 57, 58, 59, 60, 62, 63, 64, 68, 69, 71, 77, 81, 82, 89, 91, 94, 96, 98, 102, 103, 104, 105, 106, 107, 111, 112, 113, 117, 121, 122, 123, 127, 128, 130, 133, 138, 140, 144, 145, 146, 150, 151, 155, 156

Reder, M., 201
Reinwald, T.P., 95, 201
Rima, H.R., 119, 174, 175, 198, 201
risk, 1, 2, 19, 24, 50, 58, 59, 60, 61, 62, 63, 64, 66, 67, 68, 69, 71, 79, 85, 86, 89, 106, 107, 108, 110, 123, 124, 133, 136, 138, 145
Robinson, J., 6, 93, 94, 95, 97, 101, 103, 104, 106, 111, 117, 119, 120, 122, 126, 127, 128, 129, 131, 150, 163, 174, 175, 177, 198, 200, 201, 202
Rodgers, D. T., 202
Rorty, R., 202
Ross, D., 202
Rostow, E.V., 202
Rotwein, E., 48, 89, 202

Samuelson, P.A., 72, 90, 202, 204
Santiago, V.W., 202
Schultz, T.W., 161, 202
Schumpeter, J.A., 51, 65, 73, 74, 75, 76, 77, 90, 120, 174, 175, 179, 196, 199, 203
Schweitzer, A., 22, 33, 45, 134, 203
Scraffa, P., 203
Shackle, G.L.S., 203
shelter, 77, 129, 145, 152
Shils, E., 87, 150, 203
Shove, G.F., 203
Simons, H., 156, 174, 203
Skinner, A.S., 95, 202, 204
Skinner, Q., 95, 202, 204
Smith, A., 26, 70, 186, 200, 204, 205
social philosophy, 1, 4, 34, 153, 159
  involvement in economics, 4
  misrepresentation of Knight, 1, 2, 4, 159
  of utilitarianism, 34
Stigler, G. J., 1, 4, 52, 87, 121, 127, 131, 134, 150, 152, 154, 161, 178, 182, 183, 190, 204
Stone, J. and Mennell, S., 164

Strauss, L., 135, 136, 204
supply, 5, 7, 27, 56, 66, 68, 74, 77, 80, 92, 96, 100, 104, 125, 127, 136, 138, 155
SWF (Social Welfare Function), 2, 7, 42, 43

Taine, H., 160, 204
Tarcov, N., 3, 204
Tawney, R.H., 192, 196, 204
Taylor, O.H., 189, 205
Triffin, R., 205

UCC (Uncertainty Control Costs), 157
uncertainty, 9, 16, 17, 18, 19, 20, 24, 27, 29, 36, 39, 45, 50, 51, 56, 57, 58, 59, 60, 62, 63, 64, 65, 66, 67, 68, 69, 71, 72, 77, 78, 82, 84, 85, 86, 90, 94, 95, 96, 97, 100, 101, 102, 103, 106, 107, 108, 109, 110, 111, 112, 113, 114, 115, 116, 117, 119, 120, 122, 123, 124, 125, 130, 131, 133, 136, 138, 140, 142, 143, 144, 145, 146, 151, 152, 154, 155, 156, 157
- abnormal profit, 5
- Chamberlin and Robinson, 94
- Chamberlin's obfuscation, 118
- contingent on market power, 63
- creation of opportunities, 3
- cumulative tendencies, 21
- differential access to uncertainty, 9
- exclusion by orthodox theory, 24
- extremes of distribution, 36
- Fisher's analysis, 60
- heterogeneous, 109
- hinderance economic character, 162
- J.M. Clark, 79
- Knightian definition, 107
- linkage to profit, 6
- Marshall's obfuscation, 6
- methodological difficulties, 2
- parallel with Machiavelli, 162
- preferential access and cost, 137
- relation to credit, 20
- relation to profit, 64
- relation to Young's analysis, 70
- risk-uncertainty distinction, 1, 107
- time lags in response, 105
- transforms orthodox theory, 161
- uncertainty-control costs, 5
- uniform uncertainty, 96
- vehicle of acquisitiveness, 18

Valentine, W. S., 205
Viner, J., 39, 42, 48, 78, 89, 131, 162, 183, 202, 205
Vining, R., 205

Walker, D.A., 205
Walras, L., 180, 201, 205
Weber, M., 14, 22, 45, 48, 134, 152, 184, 185, 195, 205
welfare, 1, 2, 3, 4, 5, 6, 10, 31, 33, 42, 43, 46, 146
Whitaker, J.K., 205
Wick, W., 151, 205
Wicksell, K., 205
Williams, P.L., 78, 87, 91, 205

Young, A A., 26, 27, 35, 43, 46, 50, 69, 70, 71, 72, 73, 74, 75, 76, 77, 86, 89, 90, 95, 153, 163, 164, 174, 203, 206